WORLDVIEW
of the
CHRISTIAN FAITH

STANDING FOR GOD'S TRUTH

Joseph Charles Beach

Copyright © 2022 Joseph Charles Beach.

All rights reserved. No part of this book may be used or reproduced by any means, graphic, electronic, or mechanical, including photocopying, recording, taping or by any information storage retrieval system without the written permission of the author except in the case of brief quotations embodied in critical articles and reviews.

WestBow Press books may be ordered through booksellers or by contacting:

WestBow Press
A Division of Thomas Nelson & Zondervan
1663 Liberty Drive
Bloomington, IN 47403
www.westbowpress.com
844-714-3454

Because of the dynamic nature of the Internet, any web addresses or links contained in this book may have changed since publication and may no longer be valid. The views expressed in this work are solely those of the author and do not necessarily reflect the views of the publisher, and the publisher hereby disclaims any responsibility for them.

Any people depicted in stock imagery provided by Getty Images are models, and such images are being used for illustrative purposes only. Certain stock imagery © Getty Images.

Scripture quotations taken from the (NASB®) New American Standard Bible®, Copyright © 1960, 1971, 1977, 1995, 2020 by The Lockman Foundation. Used by permission. All rights reserved. www.lockman.org

Scripture quotations marked (NLT) are taken from the Holy Bible, New Living Translation, copyright ©1996, 2004, 2015 by Tyndale House Foundation. Used by permission of Tyndale House Publishers, a Division of Tyndale House Ministries, Carol Stream, Illinois 60188. All rights reserved.

Scripture taken from the New King James Version® Copyright © 1982 by Thomas Nelson. Used by permission. All rights reserved.

ISBN: 978-1-6642-7747-2 (sc)
ISBN: 978-1-6642-7748-9 (hc)
ISBN: 978-1-6642-7749-6 (e)

Library of Congress Control Number: 2022916456

Print information available on the last page.

WestBow Press rev. date: 10/26/2022

Contents

Preface ix
Introduction xix

Section 1: The Bible, God, and Humanity

Chapter 1   The Bible. 1
Chapter 2   God. 13
Chapter 3   Humanity 48

Section 2: Worldviews and Beliefs

Chapter 4   Worldviews 61
Chapter 5   Humanism .64
Chapter 6   Atheism 67
Chapter 7   Agnosticism. 69
Chapter 8   Moral Relativism 70
Chapter 9   Naturalism 73
Chapter 10   Pantheism .75
Chapter 11   Other Worldviews 78
Chapter 12   The Christian Worldview 81
Chapter 13   The Meaning of Life 89
Chapter 14   What is Truth? 91

Section 3: Morality and Values

Chapter 15   Morality .95
Chapter 16   Christian Morality 99
Chapter 17   Homosexuality 102

Chapter 18	Marriage	109
Chapter 19	Family Values	113
Chapter 20	Sexual Gender Identity	118
Chapter 21	The Sanctity of Human Life	123
Chapter 22	Values	128
Chapter 23	Ethics	129
Chapter 24	Liberalism	131
Chapter 25	Socialism	137
Chapter 26	Censorship and the Cancel Culture	144
Chapter 27	Liberalism in the Christian Church	149

Section 4: Science and Religion

Chapter 28	Astronomy	159
Chapter 29	Cosmology	164
Chapter 30	Evolution	169
Chapter 31	DNA	177
Chapter 32	Archeology	181
Chapter 33	Geology	187
Chapter 34	Creationism	193

Section 5: Salvation

Chapter 35	The Narrow Path	203
Chapter 36	Hell	208
Chapter 37	The Plan of Salvation	213
Chapter 38	How Did Jesus' Death Pay Our Penalty?	217
Chapter 39	How to Receive Jesus Christ?	220
Chapter 40	Having a Relationship with Jesus Christ	222
Chapter 41	Being Born Again	225
Chapter 42	Mercy and Grace	227
Chapter 43	Can a Christian Lose Salvation?	229
Chapter 44	Faith	235
Chapter 45	Heaven	240

Section 6: America and the Church

Chapter 46	Is America Abandoning the Church?	247
Chapter 47	Is America a Christian Nation?	251
Chapter 48	Was America Founded as a Christian Nation?	256

Chapter 49   Does it Matter if America is a Christian Nation?. . . . 262
Chapter 50   What is a Real Christian?. 266
Chapter 51   Turning to God. 269
Chapter 52   The Challenge 277

Conclusion 281
Acknowledgments. 287
Reference Notes 291

Preface

After witnessing many of the unfolding events of 2020, it became apparent to me that our country was undergoing a drastic change in direction. As I watched the news on television, the news networks were reporting many stories that were alarming to the values that I have had for many years. For me, it seemed as if everything was going out of control. First, there was Covid, then the not so peaceful ... peaceful demonstrations, followed by the election, and many other events in the news. The news agencies were offering many differing viewpoints and opinions, showing the huge divisiveness happening in this country, cries of large-scale racism, and so on. It was difficult to determine what and who to believe. It seemed as if my entire value system was under attack and no longer valued or accepted. I know there have been many times in the past when certain events flared up and caused a rift in society, but this time it seemed more drastic. Especially witnessing the great divide in our country, which was very upsetting. When did we as Americans start to exhibit such hate for one another? Had things gone too far this time? Would we ever return to normalcy? As a Christian believing in Biblical values, I had a real sense that culture and society values were changing rapidly, and I wasn't optimistic that things were changing in the right direction.

I had always believed our country was formed on Christian values, and all the laws and traditions of our country were founded within these values. It has always been clear that not everyone shared my point of view, and everyone certainly has the right to their values and viewpoints.

However, the very fabric of America was under assault. From people tearing down monuments of America's founders, from people occupying cities and chanting for a change to Marxism, from widespread looting to defunding the police, from cries of widespread racism, to cancel culture, mass media and social media blocking free speech, and on and on, there was a change all around us.

I began to wonder what was behind all these changes, and why society seemed to be moving away from the traditional values I had grown up believing in. Why was everything changing so rapidly? Was I just out of touch? Because of my Christian beliefs, I had always believed in treating everyone fairly, and that everyone is equal, but now I was being taught that because I was a white American male, I was now a racist. I was to blame for all the ills of the world. Social rules were changing in this country and I had better be in step with these changes. Are we as Americans losing our right to free speech? Are we losing the right to have and make our own opinion? Are we losing the right to believe in our values and beliefs? I had always been taught that all people and their beliefs could be different, but we were all to be treated as equals and respect each other's points of view.

We used to hear society teach about tolerance and everyone getting along. Today, this no longer appears to be the case. Society's message, whether society realizes it or not, is no longer about tolerance, but about one belief system and one set of values that everyone should agree with and comply with, if not you are to be shunned, criticized, silenced, re-educated, or canceled. This new attitude of society is no longer about tolerance but intolerance. To society, the idea is more important than the person. A person could be replaced or canceled if they don't agree with the ideas of those in charge in our society. It now seems as if society is redefining the principles of right and wrong, meaning we, who are in power, are right, and you, who disagree with us, are wrong. Don't agree with society and you are canceled, period. What society doesn't realize is that everyone should have the right to have their own opinions, ideas, and beliefs. Am I wrong? Isn't this the very definition of inclusion, that we are all different individuals that have the right, in this country, to freely express ourselves without fear of retribution? That is if society still believes in democracy, but I have strong doubts about this anymore. It's clear that socialism and Marxism are on the rise in this country and democracy may soon be a thing of the past.

Society has lost the concept of including everyone, even though this is the very message they teach. Now the focus is all about power, and whoever has the power, can dictate their influence on everyone else. If you disagree with those who hold the power then you become their enemy, and you are subject to being silenced. There is no place for the enemy in the eyes of society. There is no longer any tolerance for being out of step with the views and beliefs of those who hold the power.

But what about truth? This is another subject that I have witnessed today that appears to be changing rapidly. The very definition of truth in our society has become clouded and controversial.

Everyone has their truth or truth is what you make it out to be for yourself. It appears people today have no value for the learned experience of others. They believe something is not true unless they experience it for themselves.

The society also believes there is nothing to be learned from history or the past. Even though we used to believe that history taught us valuable lessons, and we learned that if we don't pay attention to mistakes made in the past, then we would be subject to repeating those mistakes in the future. Today society has little regard for the past or the lessons learned in the past.

The view of society today seems to be that people in the past were uneducated and unenlightened, their knowledge is outdated, and there is no way their experience would have any relevance in today's modern culture.

With this viewpoint, we are doomed to repeat all the mistakes from the past. If you look at history, you can see the causes of the decline of all the great and powerful nations of the past. When you look at America today you may see that America is already making many of the same mistakes as these nations in the past. If we want to be smart about it, we would try to eliminate these same mistakes and make whatever corrections are needed to not repeat these same mistakes. However, we continue to ignore all these valuable lessons, and blindly march down the same road as these past nations.

If we must continue learning repeatedly what we should have learned in the past, then how on earth will we ever advance? We will be continually stuck in this circle of relearning everything from scratch, without having enough time to move forward and better society. Today we are witnessing this happening in full force. Not only are we failing to advance as a society, I believe we are declining as a society.

What about truth? Society seems to have little regard and respect for the concept of truth. By that, I mean how everyone distorts the truth or just tells outright lies to promote their agenda. The opinion seems to be if it's for the greater good, whatever that may be, then it's justified to tell lies and distort the truth. You can't watch the news on American television without watching some news reporter spinning a story to make it fit their agenda. The facts don't matter, the truth doesn't matter, the only thing that matters are that the story is slanted so that it teaches the reporter's point of view, or the network's point of view, in their attempt to control what the public should believe. News is no longer news; it is now a springboard for persuading public opinion to believe in a particular point of view. Truth has no value anymore, and it testifies to how badly the morals of society have gone astray.

This viewpoint also accounts for the reasons why social media wants to be in the business of controlling and blocking free speech. If the truth differs from their point of view, then social media wants to block it and hide the truth. If you post a value or point of view that is contrary to that platform's point of view, then the post is taken down immediately so no one will see it. Social media networks do not want anyone persuaded by a viewpoint that is different from theirs, so initially, they will suppress the post. If this happens more than once, you get canceled. Your account gets closed and you are no longer allowed to post your opinion on their social media platform.

But is this right? Are we no longer allowed to speak our opinions freely? Apparently Not! Just think about it, we are losing our freedom of free speech, and very few people seemed to be alarmed. As a society, we are in danger of losing the freedoms this country has enjoyed for over 240 years. So then, what's next. What rights will we lose next? How about the second amendment? It's just around the corner. The government will now use gun violence and so-called white supremacy threats as an excuse for abolishing the rights of citizens to bear arms. If the government achieves this there will be no turning back. Our long-lived democracy will be over. The government will have full power to impose any restrictions on the public it chooses.

Views of society are rapidly changing. But how would these changes in society impact me as a Christian, and how would it impact other Christians? Christians would not be immune from the changes in society, and this caused me to wonder how strong society's influence is over what Christians believe in, their moral values, and how we view

God and the Bible. As I thought about this, I soon began to realize that society has had a strong influence over Christian values for many years. The first question I wanted to look at was, what values are Christian children learning in society today? With the schools no longer teaching anything about God, children only learn the values of the society. Sure, these children may learn about God in Church and Sunday school, spending four to five hours at most in a Church setting, compared to thirty to forty hours a week in a school setting. They are going to hear and learn more teachings at a school than they will from Church, Sunday school, or even from home. This will have a great impact on any child.

After going to public school, many Christian students start to develop doubts about their faith. They are bombarded by many different cultures, viewpoints, and teachings that greatly differ from what they know from Church. Then when they move on to college, they enter a realm that does not teach anything about God, strongly rejects God, and boldly proclaims that God is a myth. By this time many Christians have completely lost their faith, or have abandoned Christianity and the Church. These Christians have now come to believe many false teachings about God, the Bible, and the Christian faith.

This is what caught me off guard the most during all the events of 2020. Many self-professed Christians were in lockstep with the views of society, even though these views are completely different than the views presented in the Bible. There are many Christians who express completely different views on society, the world, faith, social behavior, morals, and so on, views that were quite different than my own.

This took me somewhat by surprise. I had always assumed that Christians would have the same beliefs, the same moral values, would believe the words from the Bible and all stand together with one common faith. But in talking with many different people, Christians, and non-Christians alike, it became apparent that many Christians were supporting many of these new values of society instead of believing in the Godly values taught in the Bible. If we're Christians, shouldn't we all believe in the same thing, have the same values, and see the Bible in the same way?

But again, the first thing I had to remember is that all people are influenced by society and by the views of society. Just like I mentioned earlier, going to public school and college can have a very powerful impact on anyone, even a Christian. The generation growing up in this country after 1964, is the first generation in America that hasn't been taught anything about God in the public schools. So naturally, people growing up in public schools after 1964, would certainly have a wide range of values and beliefs to pick and choose from and take for their very own. Values and beliefs no longer included any teachings of God or the Bible.

But why would a Christian ignore what is written in the Bible and reject it, and choose instead to believe in what is taught in society? Are society's views and teachings more important than God's views and teachings? How would a Christian be influenced to believe in the values of society more strongly than the values of the Bible, especially when these values differ from one another?

I can certainly understand people who are not Christians having completely different values and beliefs, but for Christians to have different values and beliefs was very puzzling. I even began to doubt myself. Was I reading and understanding the Bible incorrectly? Or is the Bible out of date and do I need to keep up with the times and reevaluate my views and values?

Then, I decided to investigate my Christian faith and see if I could discover the truth about Christianity. I wanted to know why there are so many different beliefs among people who call themselves Christians? Why would one Christian believe in one point of view, but another Christian believe in the complete opposite point of view?

So then, what exactly should a Christian believe in? What should a real Christian look like? How should a Christian act, and what should a Christian believe? Perhaps some of my beliefs and values had been corrupted by what I have learned by being a member of society. After all, I didn't grow up in Church and I went to public school, so it's possible that I could have some un-Biblical beliefs and values that are counter to God's teachings in the Bible. I decided to dig in and do some fresh research. I wanted to almost forget what I knew or thought I knew, clean the slate, and start over. Maybe my perceptions had gone awry and I needed a new viewpoint. I wanted to be like a child learning about God for the very first time.

I started looking into the basics of Christianity, asking the questions, who is God, what is the Bible, and who am I? Is there room for different beliefs in the Christian faith? As I began looking into some of these issues it became apparent, as I said earlier, that all people, including

Christians, are framed by what goes on around them. It's hard to know who to trust and how to determine what is right and what is wrong. It became apparent that to truly discover what a Christian is, one would have to look at the other value systems of the world. After all, we can't help being impacted by all the things we hear around us from people of different faiths. After starting my research, I became very surprised that many so-called Christian websites posted things I couldn't believe. These were Christian websites that posted that Jesus never claimed to be God and that the Trinity was false. So, I had to dig deep into the Bible to see what it said about these ideas.

Another huge influence in today's culture is science. It's important to look at science and what science has to say and its impact on our beliefs. Science has a strong grip on society in this modern age, and few people would be able to survive today without all the modern marvels of science. So do science and religion have a connection, or any common ground, or is science and religion completely at odds with one another? We all are taught things about science as we go to school, and we learn about scientific advancements continually in the media. But what exactly are the real facts? Where does science get its point of view and how does science arrive at the conclusions that it does? Does science consider anything the Bible has to say or does science discredit what the Bible has to say, thusly starting with a completely different premise and set of assumptions? Is there any way to arrive at the facts, or do the preconceptions and assumptions drive the direction of how the facts are interpreted? After all, we all have the same evidence and pieces of information, so shouldn't it point to the same conclusions?

Our preconceptions about what we believe in do impact the results we arrive at? In many regards' science is looking to make assessments about the past by looking at the information and evidence we possess in the present. The Bible also investigates the past and people reading the Bible may judge the past based on their understanding of what we know about living in the present.

There are many events written about in the Bible that we need to examine. The Bible teaches us valuable lessons but many people question whether these events happened. What are these events trying to teach us today? Are these events used only to teach us a moral or spiritual lesson? Do these events impact the way we look at the modern world? Are we not able to believe in these past events because we are influenced by what society says about them? It's important to know what society has to say about these events. How does society look at these events and what does society believe about these events? These events shape the Christian perspective, impact the way Christians look at the world, and they teach us many lessons on who God is and on our understanding of what God means to us in a personal way.

What is the most important thing that God wants to teach us and for us to know, and how does that impact the way we should live in society? If you are a nonbeliever who wants to know more about the meaning of life, I urge you to keep reading. You have absolutely nothing to lose except for the time you spend reading this. I just want to give you something to consider. If you are truly looking for the purpose and meaning in your life, you should be considering all options, even this one. You can choose to accept it or you can choose to reject it. This is totally up to you and you alone. I do not desire to force anything on you that you do not want. The Bible states that God's greatest desire is that no one should perish. God does not want anyone to be separated from Him, He chooses to have a relationship with every Human Being on this planet, past, present, and future, and that includes you. You may have been taught differently but God, by definition, is love. This doesn't mean that God is capable of love, it means that God is complete and total love. He loves you just as much as He loves anyone else. He loves the non-Christian just as much as He loves a Christian. I don't deserve His love but I freely accept it. This may all sound too good to be true, but is it? An infinite and Holy God loves every one of us with total unconditional love.

As Christians, it is our mission to seek out those who are not close to God. We are instructed to share with them God's Word. We are to do this with respect, gentleness, and kindness. We must share with them our story and what we know, but we are never to try to force them into believing what we say or what we believe in. We are messengers, not Saviors. We plant the seed, but God makes it grow. Only God saves. Why must we reach out to nonbelievers? As I mentioned earlier because God desires that no one should perish. How would the world look upon us as Christians, if we had the cure for cancer but keep it a secret? The world would think evil of us if we kept it a secret, as they rightly should. We have the keys to eternal life and we must share it with all the people of the world. We cannot keep this a secret. All Christians have this responsibility.

I hope that all people come together in peace and love. We are all created by God, and that means we are all equal in His eyes. There should be no racism, hatred, prejudice, or intolerance. Every Human Being on this earth is valuable to God and therefore has value to us as well. People are what matter in the scheme of things, people are the most important creation in all the world, this includes every individual, not just some. All people are due love and respect. We all live on this earth, and we must all do everything in our power to help any person in need. Even though we may have different points of view, we must all unite in our common goals to help the helpless, feed the poor, and make the world a safer and better place.

It is not my intention to insult or criticize any group or individual. I know however, that you may read something written here that you don't believe, or something may even offend you. I may write something here that goes against something you passionately believe in. If so, I truly apologize in advance. If you disagree with what I have to say you certainly have the right to do so. Again, it is not my intent to force my beliefs on you. I am merely trying to speak the truth from a Godly and Biblical perspective as best I can. I know I am far from perfect. I am a flawed individual that can make mistakes and I am capable of hurting others because of my sinfulness. This is not my desire or intent. We are all individuals, and as such we will certainly have our differences. It is only my intent to share with you the things I have learned and discovered for myself, and then allow you to make up your mind. After all, maybe you have also asked yourself some of the very same questions I have mentioned here? My goal is for everyone to be reconciled with God, and that no one is condemned. Every Human Being that has ever lived on this earth is valuable to God. God has a plan for everyone and desires that everyone is in a close relationship with Him, not only in this temporary life here on earth but for all eternity. Our time here on earth is very short. We are all eternal beings that will exist after this life on earth is over and for all eternity. That's a long time. The question is where do you want to spend your eternity?

Introduction

Today Christianity is the world's largest religion, with over two billion people identifying themselves as Christians. But does proclaiming to be a Christian make you a Christian? What exactly does it take to be a Christian? Is a Christian simply a person born in a Christian family or a person you occasionally go to church with?

Many people call themselves Christians. Some people use the word, Christian, to declare their birth heritage, some say they were born a Christian, some say they are a Christian because they are a good person, and some say they are a Christian because they attend church. Some even think Christian refers to a political viewpoint. For others, the term Christian is no more than a box to check off on an application or survey form.

The Bible first identified followers of Jesus Christ as Christians in (Acts 11:26), "and when he had found him, he brought him to Antioch. And for an entire year, they met with the church and taught considerable numbers of people, and the disciples were first called Christians in Antioch." The word Christian literally means, belonging to the party of Christ or simply a follower of Christ.

So then, what is a Christian? When a Jewish religious leader named Nicodemus came to talk with Jesus one night, he acknowledged that God was with Jesus because of all the miraculous signs Jesus performed. Jesus said to Nicodemus, "Truly, truly, I say to you, unless someone is born again, he cannot see the kingdom of God." (John 3:3).

To be a Christian, you must be born again, meaning that you make a conscious choice to turn from your sins, that you repent, and by faith believe that Jesus is the Son of God, who loved us, and paid the price of our sins on the cross, shed His blood, died, was buried, and was raised to life on the third day. CRU, Evangeline Vergo, *How to Know God, What is a Christian?*[1]

A true Christian, not only obeys the word of God but also puts their faith and trust in the person and the works of Jesus Christ. We place our faith in the fact that Jesus died on the cross as payment for our sins and was resurrected on the third day. The mark of a true Christian is love for others and obedience to God's Word. 1 John 2:4-10 says, "the one who says, I have come to know Him, and does not keep His commandments, is a liar, and the truth is not in him; The one who loves his brother and sister remains in the Light, and there is nothing in him to cause stumbling." A true Christian is indeed a child of God, a part of God's true family, and one who has been given new life in Jesus Christ.

Does this mean that Christians are perfect? Of course not. Christians are still hypocrites and sinners, just like everyone else. But remember, people don't go to hell because of their sin, they go to hell for their unbelief. The Bible says that good works do not make us acceptable to God. Simply being a good person or doing good things does not make us Christian. It's not about the good works, it's about faithful obedience to God and His word. If Christians have obedience and faith, then good works will also come.

Paul talks about the importance of love. One must love God and love their neighbor as themselves, love … even their enemies. Paul says in 1 Corinthians 13:13, "Three things will last forever faith, hope, and love and the greatest of these is love." Jesus replied to the question of what is the greatest commandment as follows in Matthew 22:37, Jesus replied, "you must love the Lord your God with all your heart, all your soul, and all your mind.' This is the first and greatest commandment. A second is equally important: 'Love your neighbor as yourself." The entire law and all the demands of the prophets are based on these two commandments. Jesus also said in Matthew 5:43–48, "You have heard that it was said, YOU SHALL LOVE YOUR NEIGHBOR and hate your enemy. But I say to you, love your enemies and pray for those who persecute you, so that you may prove yourselves to be sons of your Father who is in Heaven."

The core beliefs of Christianity are summarized in 1 Corinthians 15:1–4, "Now I make known to you, brothers and sisters, the gospel which I preached to you, which you also received, in which you also stand, by which you also are saved if you hold firmly to the word which I preached to you unless you believed in vain. For I handed down to you as of first importance what I also received, that Christ died for our sins according to the Scriptures, and that He was buried, and that He was raised on the third day according to the Scriptures."

Is this what you believe about Christianity? Do you consider yourself to be a real Christian? Being a Christian is not just what you do, but what you think and how you think. Christianity is a worldview. The Bible is the first source of what God says to us and we must truly follow the teachings we receive from the Bible to be true Christians.

If you are a Christian and disagree with anything you have read so far, I urge you to continue reading and think about your stance. Ask yourself why you believe the things you believe? Have you heard something different about Christianity from people you know, or from a Church you attend? Perhaps you've heard something different from your Pastor or Priest. If you have, I urge you to dig into the Word, the Holy Bible. This is where truth begins. We should always test everything we hear and compare it to the Word of God. Remember, no human is perfect. Not even your priest or pastor. Only God is perfect. If the Word of God tells you something different than what you hear or believe, you may need to rethink your beliefs. God's Word is the source of truth. The Bible is the source you should always trust. If you trust something or someone more than the Bible, then it's time to question why! We all get caught up in believing things that we hear and assume we are hearing the truth. It's easy to be deceived and believe what is false. People may have good intentions, but everyone is capable of speaking mistruths. It's not intentional, but it does happen. Think about the source and determine for yourself who or what you will trust. The only true unmistakable source of truth is God's word and the Bible.

Chose to follow the Word of God, and make God's Word your number one priority. When in direct contradiction to God's Word a true believer must choose to walk away from anything they may believe that is contrary to God's revelation in the Holy Bible.

I often hear that some Christians look at Christianity as a set of values and beliefs, and like a smorgasbord, they just pick and choose which of these values and beliefs to follow, and then just ignore the rest. Unfortunately, that doesn't work. As a true Christian believer, you must follow and believe in all Biblical values. If you don't believe in all of them, then how can you believe in any of them? The Bible is either all true, or all false. God has given us complete truth, not partial truth. If you are a smorgasbord Christian, I implore you to rethink this approach. If you truly disagree with anything written in the Bible, you need to make it a priority to determine why this is the case. Again, society pulls us in all directions, and we can all be influenced by this, but we must remember that the Bible is the source of truth, not the values and beliefs of society.

Once you answer the question, Am I truly a Christian, then you have the personal responsibility to ask yourself, what does this mean to me? Have I rejected or accepted God's Word, and am I following all of God's commands as I should?

If you've accepted God's gift of salvation, how has your life changed? Do you have the marks of a follower of Jesus Christ? Is your life characterized by love for others and obedience to God's Word? Whoever claims to live in Him must live as Jesus did.

A true Christian is a person who repents. This means to feel pain, sorrow, or regret for something they have done or left undone. It means changing your mind and determining to change your actions. It means to experience such sorrow for sin as it produces an adjustment to one's life, be grieved over one's past life, and seek forgiveness. As stated in Acts 2:38, "Repent, and each of you be baptized in the name of Jesus Christ for the forgiveness of your sins; and you will receive the gift of the Holy Spirit."

The Bible speaks extensively about the subsequent lifestyle of believers in what it calls fruit of the spirit. For example, we read about the fruit of the Spirit: "But the fruit of the Spirit is love, joy, peace, long-suffering, kindness, goodness, faithfulness, gentleness, and self-control. Against such, there is no law. And those who are Christ's have crucified the flesh with its passions and desires" (Galatians 5:22–24). This wholesome fruit stands in contrast to the unfruitful works of darkness: "Therefore, be imitators of God as dear children. And walk in love, as Christ also has loved us and given Himself for us, an offering, and a sacrifice to God for a sweet-smelling aroma. But fornication and all uncleanness or covetousness let it not even be named among you, as is fitting for saints; neither filthiness, nor foolish talking, nor coarse jesting, which are not fitting rather giving of thanks. For this you know, that no fornicator, unclean person, nor covetous man, who is an idolater, has any inheritance in the kingdom of Christ and God. Let no one deceive you with empty words, for because of these things the wrath of God comes upon the sons of disobedience. Therefore, do not be partakers with them. For you were once darkness, but now you are light in the Lord. Walk as children of light (for the fruit of the Spirit is in all goodness, righteousness, and truth), finding out what is acceptable to the Lord. And have no fellowship with the unfruitful works of darkness, but rather expose them. For it is shameful even to speak of those things which are done by them in secret." (Ephesians 5:1–12). All About Religion, *"What is a Christian?"* [2]

Walking in the fruit of the Spirit is often a telltale sign that people are living out their Christian lives as a tribute to the Lord who redeemed them from sin and death. Identifying true Godly believers can be difficult. The book of 1st John speaks extensively about how to identify those unbelievers. A true Christian believer must not love the world. Christians must love one another.

Christians should also know that the world will probably not accept them, and the world will probably even hate them. Christians should be in the truth. Christians must know and listen to God and know that God is love. Christians must confess that Jesus is God and we know that the Son of God has come, and has given us understanding so that we may know Him who is true. If someone continues to live evil lives even though they claim to follow Christ, that person cannot be a true Christian. Only in believing in the name of His Son Jesus Christ, and loving others, just as He commanded us can you be a true Christian. Christianity.com, Jack Graham, *"What is a Christian?"* [3]

Those who belong to God practice righteousness. Those who do not practice righteousness do not belong to God. When a person is truly reconciled to God, when a person is truly converted, when a son is truly regenerated and born again, then when all that occurs, when there is new birth and regeneration, and redemption and conversion, a real transformation of that person takes place.

"If any man is in Christ, he is a new creation" (2 Corinthians 5:17). We used to be the slaves of sin and now we are the slaves of righteousness. This marks a true Christian. Romans 3:10 says; "There is none righteous, no not even one." Only through Jesus does a Christian obtain righteousness. Then righteousness is now the truest expression of the Christian believer's inner person. We are manifestly righteous, we who are truly regenerated.

We have just touched the surface of what we know a Christian is like. As we continue, we will look in more depth at the Bible to gain insight into its validity and teachings, look at God to learn who He truly is, and finally at Humanity to understand our importance and relationship with God.

SECTION 1
The Bible, God, and Humanity

CHAPTER 1

The Bible

In all of history, the Bible is probably the most unique book ever written. It's unique because it has forty authors, and these authors took about 1,500 to 2,000 years to write it. Also, the Bible is not just one book but sixty-six books. Each book of the Bible was written and developed completely independently from one another. John Adams, the second president of the United States, is rumored to have said; "I have examined all religions, and the result is that the Bible is the best book in the world." JOHN ADAMS, ALLEGED QUOTE [1]

The word *Bible* comes from the Latin and Greek words meaning "the books". It can also have the meaning of scroll. By the second century B.C., Jewish groups began calling the books of the Hebrew Bible, or the Old Testament, "the scriptures," and they referred to them as holy, and Christians now commonly call the Old and New Testaments of the Christian Bible, "the Holy Bible" or "the Holy Scriptures."

The Bible has some books that concentrate on the law, some on history, some on poetry, some on prophecy, and some on biographies. Some of the books are letters, which are also called epistles. The Christian Bible has two main sections. The first section is called the Old Testament, and the second section is called the New Testament. The Old Testament was written by Jewish authors. The first author Moses, was credited with writing the first five books of the Old Testament, which is called the Torah (meaning "law," "instruction," or "teaching") or the Pentateuch ("five books"). The first book, Genesis, tells the story of creation, the fall, the flood, the dispersal of people on the earth, and

God's building of a nation through Abraham. God promised to use Israel to bless the whole world through the lineage of Abraham. The Pentateuch, together with the book of Joshua, is the history of the Jews becoming a nation and possessing the Promised Land. These books make up the first part of the Old Testament.

The Old Testament then has a second part called the Nevi'im, meaning; "the Prophets." This section continues the story of Israel in the Promised Land, describing "the establishment of the monarchy and presenting the messages of the prophets to the people. Once Israel was established as a nation, God raised a family within that nation through whom the blessing would come: the family of David- (Psalm 89:3–4). Then, from the family of David was promised one Man who would bring the promised blessing.

The third and final part of the Old Testament is called the Ketuvim, meaning "the writings," or Hagiographa. This section contains the psalms, proverbs, and narrative histories. The writings include speculation on the place of evil and death in the scheme of things (Job and Ecclesiastes), along with some poetical works, and some additional historical books. These three sections were written mostly in Hebrew, with some parts in Aramaic.

These books mark the completion of the Hebrew Bible. Greek-speaking Jews in Alexandria and elsewhere in the Jewish movement considered additional scriptures. These additional texts were included in a translation of the Hebrew Bible into Koine Greek known as the Septuagint (meaning "the work of the seventy"), which began as a translation of the Torah. The Septuagint contained all the books of the Hebrew Bible. This Hebrew Bible is what is included in the Old Testament of the Christian Bible. Not only is the Old Testament the story of the Jews as a nation, but it is also the preview of a needed Savior. From the Jews, God brought Jesus into the world.

From this point begins the New Testament of the Christian Bible. During the rise of Christianity in the first century A.D., new scriptures were written. These scriptures were written in Greek about the life and teachings of Jesus Christ, who Christians believed was the Messiah prophesied in the books of the Old Testament and the Hebrew Bible. Two collections of these new scriptures – the Pauline epistles and the Gospels – were accepted as canon by the end of the second century A.D. Between A.D. 385 and 405, the early Christian church translated its canon into Vulgar Latin (the common Latin spoken by ordinary people). This translation known as the Vulgate, included in its Old Testament the books that were in the Septuagint. The Vulgate introduced stability to the Bible, but also began the East-West schism between Latin-speaking Western Christianity (led by the Roman Catholic Church) and multilingual Eastern Christianity (led by the Eastern Orthodox Church).

The New Testament begins with four books, called the Gospels. The four gospels, Matthew, Mark, Luke, and John, deal with the life, the person, and the teachings of Jesus, as He was remembered by the Christian community. Like the Old Testament, the New Testament is a collection of several books. The book of Acts begins the story of Christianity from the Resurrection of Jesus to the time of the death of Paul. Next are many letters written by various leaders of the early Christian church. Lastly, the Book of Revelation is the writing of prophecy. The New Testament developed over time, after the death, burial, resurrection, and ascension of Jesus Christ.

Christians believe that Jesus is more than just a historical figure; and that He is more than a mere human. He is God in the flesh, and His coming was the most important event in the history of the world. God Himself became a human to give us a clear, understandable picture of who He is, and what God is like. Jesus is God in human form.

Jesus is the central character of the entire Bible. The Old Testament predicts His coming, and the New Testament describes His arrival in the world and His work to bring salvation to our sinful world.

God created humanity and placed them in a perfect environment; however, humanity rebelled against God and fell from what God intended them to be. God placed the world under a curse because of sin but immediately set in motion a plan to restore humanity and all creation to its original glory.

As part of His plan of redemption, God called Abraham out of Babylonia into Canaan (about 2,000 B.C.). God promised Abraham, his son Isaac, and his grandson Jacob, also called Israel, that He would bless the world through a future descendant of theirs. Israel's family emigrated from Canaan to Egypt, where they grew to be a nation. About 1,400 B.C., God led Israel's descendants out of Egypt under the direction of Moses and gave them the Promised Land, Canaan, as their own. Through Moses, God gave the people of Israel the Law and made a covenant (testament) with them. If they would remain faithful to God and not follow the idolatry of the surrounding nations, then they would prosper. If they forsook God and followed idols, then God would destroy their nation. About four hundred years later, during the reigns of David and his son Solomon, Israel was solidified into a great and powerful kingdom. God promised David and Solomon that a descendant of theirs would rule as an everlasting king. After Solomon's reign, the nation of Israel was divided. The ten tribes to the north were called Israel, and they lasted about two hundred years before God judged them for their idolatry. Assyria took Israel captive about 721 B.C. The two tribes in the south were called Judah, and they lasted a little longer, but eventually they, too, turned from God. Babylon took them captive about 587 B.C. After about seventy years of captivity, God brought a remnant of the captives back into their land. Jerusalem, the capital, was rebuilt about 444 B.C., and Israel once again established a national identity. About four hundred years later Jesus Christ was born in Bethlehem. Jesus was the descendant promised to Abraham and David, the One to fulfill God's plan to redeem humanity and restore creation. Jesus faithfully completed His work but was sentenced to death by the Romans because the Jewish religious leaders claimed He was a false teacher claiming to be God. Jesus died for our sin and rose from the dead. The death of Christ is the basis for a new covenant (testament) with the world. All who have faith in Jesus will be saved from sin and live eternally.

After His resurrection, Jesus appeared to His followers for forty days. He commanded them not to leave Jerusalem, to wait for what the Father had promised, and to receive power and be filled with the Holy Spirit. God's promise, as spoken by the prophet in the Old Testament, was to "pour out My Spirit on all humankind" (Joel 2:28). This event of receiving the gift of the Holy Spirit is the event referred to as Pentecost. After receiving the gift of the Holy Spirit, the disciples responded to Jesus's instructions to spread the good news everywhere of His life and His power to save. Jesus's disciples went in every direction spreading the news of Jesus and salvation. They traveled through Asia Minor, Greece, and all the Roman Empire. The Bible closes with a prediction of Jesus's return to judge the unbelieving world and free creation from the curse.

All the books of the entire Bible flow without wavering in their message and teachings. This unity is because, ultimately, it has one Author, God Himself. The human authors wrote exactly what God wanted them to write, and the result was the perfect and Holy Word of

God, (Psalm 12:6). The Bible is regarded by Christians as divinely inspired. The Bible has done more to shape literature, history, entertainment, and culture than any book ever written. Its influence on world history is unparalleled and shows no signs of abating. With estimated total sales of over five billion copies, it is widely considered to be the best-selling book of all time. It sells approximately one hundred million copies annually.

How Society Views the Bible

Society looks at the Bible in many ways. Some view the Bible as a good book to learn some valuable lessons from, while others view the Bible as a series of unbelievable fairy tales not to be taken seriously. The truth is, most people in society don't give much thought to the Bible and place little importance on the Bible and its teachings. Many in society believe the Bible is old and outdated, merely a collection of stories from the past that have little or no meaning in today's modern world. Society will tell us that the Bible is not true. Because they choose not to believe in God, they refuse to take seriously something written so long ago that they haven't witnessed for themselves. They say the Bible is not reliable and it contains many errors. Isn't this exactly what you would expect from people who don't believe in God in the first place?

Even Christians have varying viewpoints on the interpretation of the Bible. So then, what is society supposed to believe about the Bible? If they don't believe in the reliability of the Bible, can we blame them? It becomes clear that the Bible is viewed in many ways, it can be interpreted in many ways, and just because you call yourself a Christian, it doesn't mean that we all see the Bible in the same light.

Even though many in our society do not believe in the Bible, awareness of the Bible is very high. Here are some interesting facts about the Bible from Barna Research: Barna Research, *What Do Americans Really Think About the Bible?* [2]

- 88% of Americans own a Bible. Despite such a high number, that's declined since 1993, when 92% of Americans owned a Bible.
- On average, American Bible owners have three and a half Bibles in their homes, and 24% of Bible owners have six or more.

- 79% of Mosaics (people aged eighteen to twenty-eight) own a Bible, compared with 95% of Elders (who are aged sixty-five plus).
- 59% who have no faith or who identify as atheists own a Bible.
- 40% of Mosaics say they are interested in the Bible's wisdom on dealing with illness and death, compared to 28% of adults.
- 35% of Mosaics are interested in the Bible's perspective on dating and relationships.
- 42% of Mosaics want to know what Scripture says about parenting.
- 47% of adults said the Bible contains everything a person needs to live a meaningful life.
- 39% of Americans believe that the Bible, the Koran, and the Book of Mormon are all different expressions of the same spiritual truths.
- 25% of Americans believe the Bible to be inspired but contains errors.
- 23% of Americans are antagonistic to the Bible.
- 17% of Americans never or rarely read the Bible.

Culture has certainly changed over the years and is far different now than it was in the time that the Bible was written. Our understanding of scripture is influenced by our cultural background and circumstances. Since culture has changed so much over the years, do we need to look at the Bible differently as we read it? In today's culture, we often focus more on ourselves. Every person has a distinct worldview, which influences their approach to the Bible. As believers, the goal is to read the Bible for what it says, not what we want it to say.

More people today than ever before are denying the truth of both God and the Bible. Society views truth as so much different today than it did in the past. Today it's all about my truth, meaning whatever is true for me is my truth and whatever is true for you is your truth.

The modern world hates authority and focuses on self-worth, which causes individuals to become more sinful and self-centered and turn away from the teachings of the Bible.

Changing culture is unavoidable. Even though culture has changed and will continue to change, there is always a way to read and understand the teachings in the Bible. As believers, we can still read and get everything we need out of the Bible no matter what the culture believes. As believers, we can still read and understand the Bible correctly despite the changing values of our culture.

How Christians View the Bible

The Bible should be the Christian guide on how to live, what to believe, and how we should conduct ourselves. The Bible gives us our moral laws and obligations. Sometimes these rules are hard to follow. As Christians, we must do all we can to follow what the Bible says, even though it can be very difficult. Even Christians, don't like following rules or being told how to act. The Bible teaches all aspects of life: how we should live, why we exist, what happens when we die, and what our meaning and purpose in life are. But as Christians, what should we believe about the Bible?

First, Christians should believe that the Bible is God's inspired source for revelation. Christians believe that God gave us a collection of writings that were inspired by God. For Christians, the Bible is the authoritative, written testimony to the highest source of revelation, Jesus Christ. The Bible is Inspired by God – The Apostle Paul, explains why the scriptures are trustworthy. "All Scripture is God-breathed and is useful for teaching, rebuking, correcting, and training in righteousness, so that the servant of God may be thoroughly equipped for every good work" (2 Timothy 3:16–17). God-breathed is the literal translation of inspired. Much more than a feeling that motivates an artist's creativity, inspiration is God working through the writer He chose to record authoritative truth. Even though the Bible is inspired we know that the Bible is written by people. Peter, described how words breathed by God can be delivered through humans. Above all, you must understand that no prophecy of Scripture came about by the prophet's interpretation of things. For prophecy never had its origin in the human will, but prophets, though human, spoke from God as they were carried along by the Holy Spirit. It seems God delights in using humans as instruments for His most important work.

Second, Christians should believe that the Bible is reliable. The Bible has undergone rigorous scrutiny for centuries from skeptics and believers alike, from documentary evidence cross-referencing other historically credible sources to extensive archeological verification. The more scrutiny it undergoes, the more trustworthy it has been proven to be. Christian theologians attribute such a high degree of reliability to how the Bible came into existence. Consider these points:

The Bible is remarkably consistent, despite having been written by more than forty different writers over 1,500 to 2,000 years. God's moral laws are consistent and are the same from the Old Testament to the New Testament. The Bible is consistent with the fall and humanities rebellion against God through God's plan of Salvation, never changing throughout all of scripture. It is consistent throughout the pages of Scripture. We would expect this consistency if the Bible claims to be God's revelation.

The Bible is also most authentic compared to all ancient literature in terms of the number of ancient manuscripts found and the short amount of time between when they were first written and the oldest surviving manuscripts. This eliminates any possibility of alteration from the original texts. The Bible has been accurately communicated throughout the ages, far more so than any other ancient document. Few people would doubt that Plato wrote the works identified to him, yet the Bible is far more authenticated than Plato's writings. The Bible has also been accurately translated from the past to the present.

Third, the Bible is the Ultimate Guide. The best way to understand why the Bible is such an influential book is to experience it for yourself. King David wrote; "Your words are a lamp for my feet, a light on my path" in Psalm 119:105. Christians in every generation have relied upon the Bible for …

- instruction: Knowing right from wrong, truth from error,
- inspiration: Amazing, true stories of God's work in the world,
- and insight: Discovering where we came from, what's broken, and what God has done to fix it.

Today we have a very accurate representation of the original texts. We have copies of very old manuscripts and throughout history, these copies show that the Bible has been translated accurately. Despite many skeptical claims that the Bible has often been changed through the centuries, the evidence points to the truth and reliability of the Bible. The New Testament writings are incredibly accurate. There are minor differences in manuscripts, but none of these variant's impact or change any Christian beliefs or claims.

No one could argue that the Bible's authenticity is in doubt unless they are willing to doubt all other works of antiquity because they are far less substantiated than our Bible. Mark 13:31 says, "Heaven and earth will pass away, but my words will never pass away."

Another strong case for believing the truth of the Bible is this: If you were to set out to create a new religion and wrote a book about it, wouldn't you build the characters in that book to be almost superhuman? Well, just look at the characters in the Bible. Everyone was flawed. Adam sinned, Abram lied about his wife, claiming to the Egyptian King that she was his sister, Jacob deceived his father Isaac and brother Esau, Joseph was boastful to his brothers, Moses murdered a man, King David was adulterous and sent a man into battle so he would die. And on and on. Every single character in the Bible is flawed, none of them anywhere close to superhuman. The people in the Bible were far from perfect. If this story was just made-up, wouldn't you create better people? Look at Jesus' disciples. They all fled when Jesus was arrested and went into hiding. None of the disciples believed that Jesus was God until after the resurrection. Yet after the resurrection, they all came out of hiding to boast of Jesus and to spread the gospel. Would you do that if the resurrection was a lie? Of course not! Every disciple was put to death for spreading the gospel, except for John who was sentenced to exile. They were no longer fearful; they boldly shared their belief in Jesus Christ and died because of it. They all could have been spared if they would only admit that Jesus was not the Messiah. They would have lived by telling a lie, but they chose to die for telling the truth. They knew the truth because they were witnesses to the life of Jesus Christ and His resurrection. The change in the disciples is a huge reason to believe that the Bible is true. The disciples saw the resurrected Christ, and they willingly died for speaking about Him. They knew without a doubt, that Jesus is our Lord and Savior, and they died to teach this to all the people they encountered. Would you choose to die to protect a lie, when you could live by staying silent? Of course not! You couldn't make this up if you tried! The Bible uses imperfect people to deliver the message of God to the entire world. But still, we must look at the evidence of what is written in the Bible and discern that evidence as it relates to us today.

God used about forty people to write the Bible and His Spirit rested on each writer in such a way that allowed each author to write what God intended for them to write, using their own words, but the message from

God was accurately captured in their writing's. If the Bible were God's Word, we would expect it to be consistent and unified, and it is.

Many prophecies were made in the Old Testament that were later proven true. The remarkable evidence of fulfilled prophecy is just one case in point. Hundreds of Bible prophecies have been fulfilled, specifically and exactly, often long after the prophetic writer had passed away.

Daniel the prophet predicted in about 538 B.C. in Daniel 9:24–27, that Christ would come as Israel's promised Savior and Prince 483 years after the Persian emperor would give the Jews authority to rebuild Jerusalem, which was then in ruins. This was fulfilled, hundreds of years later. Daniel also describes the future course of history in the Middle East for five centuries in detail. He predicts the demise of the Babylonian Empire and the rise and fall of Alexander the Great. Daniel interprets Nebuchadnezzar's dream of a statue made of various materials and from the vision of ghostly handwriting on a wall at King Belshazzar's feast. These prophecies predicted that Babylon's empire would fall to the Persians, which would subsequently fall to the Greeks, themselves superseded by the Romans. As this was indeed the succession of power in that part of the world, many people take the fulfillment of Daniel's prophecy as proof of the accuracy of the Bible.

The prophet Isaiah lived in the eighth century B.C. and served as an adviser to multiple kings of Judah when the major world power was the Assyrian Empire. Isaiah predicts Assyria's failed siege of Jerusalem and warns of the threat of Assyria, with many of Judah's kings disregarding Isaiah's and God's advice. It isn't until the reign of Hezekiah, considered the first righteous king in a long time in Judah, that someone in charge listens to what Isaiah had to say. Isaiah, around 701 B.C., predicted the Assyrian king Sennacherib would come to Judah and capture many of its cities. Hezekiah would ask Isaiah for advice, and the prophet very helpfully told him to do nothing, because the siege would fail. And this turned out to be right. 180,000 Assyrian soldiers died right outside the walls of Jerusalem, and Sennacherib returned home. Only to soon be murdered by two of his sons. Isaiah correctly predicted the rise of the Babylonian Empire and Judah's fall to it, nearly a century later.

The prophet Jeremiah predicted Jerusalem's siege by the Babylonians roughly fifty years after Isaiah. Jeremiah warns the people of Judah that Babylon is coming as God's righteous punishment upon his unfaithful people. God's righteous punishment hit hard. The Babylonian king Nebuchadnezzar laid siege to the capital city of Jerusalem in 597 B.C., pillaged the great temple of Solomon, and took the King and many prominent citizens back to Babylon as exiles. Jeremiah warned the King to surrender to Babylon, but he revolted, and as punishment, the temple and the whole city of Jerusalem were destroyed in 587 B.C.

The prophet Ezekiel predicts the fall of Tyre and Egypt. He lived during the time of the Babylonian exile. His prophecies promise the end of the captivity and the restoration of Jerusalem and its temple. The middle chapters of his prophecies contain warnings of destruction against foreign nations. This isn't an uncommon theme in biblical prophecy. Jeremiah named many kingdoms of the world and predicting the demise and destruction of all these nations. Ezekiel's predictions against Egypt and the great city of Tyre show proof of the prophet's accuracy. Ezekiel foretold that Tyre would be swept away by enemies, and Egypt would be a desolate waste. Then Nebuchadnezzar's thirteen-year war against Tyre drove the Tyrian people off the mainland and onto an island, and the Muslim invasion of Egypt in the seventh century A.D. left Egypt relatively insignificant.

Many prophecies are made about Jesus the Messiah as well. Here are a few of the prophecies:

- It was predicted that Jesus would be born in Bethlehem and He was (Micah 5:2). God even used a census to bring His parents there to make sure it would happen.
- It was prophesied that the Messiah would be born of a virgin. (Isaiah 7:14)
- Jesus would ride into Jerusalem on a donkey. (Zechariah 9:9)
- Jesus would take our sins. (Isaiah 53:4–6)
- Jesus would be pierced. (Zechariah 12:10)
- Jesus would be a light for the nations of the world. (Isaiah 42:1–7)

We mentioned earlier that there are sixty-six different books included in the Bible. In the earliest centuries, there was little debate among Christians over which books belonged in the Bible.

The Christian community both in the days of Jesus and in the centuries following did not doubt there was a body of books that made up the records of the Old Testament. The New Testament contains hundreds of direct quotations or clear allusions to Old Testament passages by Jesus and the apostles, it is evident what the early Christians thought of the Hebrew Scriptures.

The conviction that there was a canon of old covenant books that could not be added to or subtracted from, doubtless led the early Christians to expect the same divine order for the story of Jesus, the record of the early church, and the letters of the apostles.

The earliest available list of New Testament books is known as the Muratorian Canon and is dated around AD 150. It includes the four Gospels, Acts, thirteen letters of Paul, Jude, two (perhaps all three) letters of John, and the Revelation of John. It claims that these were accepted by the universal church. By AD 240, Origen from Alexandria was using all our twenty-seven books of the New Testament as Scripture, and others referred to these twenty-seven books as the complete works of the New Testament. He believed them to be inspired by the Spirit. But it was not until AD 367 that Athanasius, also from Alexandria, provided us with an actual list of New Testament books identical to ours. Study and Obey, *What is the Bible?* [3]

God, by His Holy Spirit, has put His seal upon the New Testament. We are confident that the twenty-seven books of our New Testament are the only books that belong there. This divine intervention guards the process by which all the books, and no others, were accepted.

We can be sure the Bible we have today, is the sacred scripture that God intended for us to have. All sixty-six books of the Old Testament and the New Testament were put together as God designed them to be, the true Holy Bible, the book we can trust to teach us what we need to know about God, His people, His story, and His plan of salvation for all people. This Bible is worthy to be read and studied and regarded as God's true inspiration to all humanity.

The entire Bible claims it is written in truth. Every story, event, and prophecy in the Bible is true, if not, why would God tell us they are true? We can trust in and rely on the Bible as being accurate and reliable.

CHAPTER 2

God

Who, or what is God? According to the Merriam-Webster dictionary, the definition of God is: the perfect and all-powerful spirit or being that is worshipped especially by Christians, Jews, and Muslims as the one who created and rules the universe, or a spirit or being that has great power, strength, knowledge, etc., that can affect nature and the lives of people: and a spirit or beings worshipped in some religions. MERRIAM WEBSTER DICTIONARY, THE DEFINITION OF GOD.[1]

Is God a concrete thing like a chair or a human; or is God an abstract thing, like love or goodness? Is there something that all concepts of God have in common, some feature that all cultures attribute to God?

What properties would God have to possess? Is God a person, a spirit, or something different? The simplest explanation of a world that has physical laws is that they are brought about by a personal being. This gives us certain reasons to expect our existence in the world.

What kind of powers would God have? Would a God need to be all-powerful and all-knowing, two concepts not normally referable to any person? Would God be good or evil, must God be perfect, and if God does exist, how could a finite mind understand an infinite concept like God?

Around the world, there are many concepts of God. Each culture has defined God in one way or another. These definitions can have similar aspects but at the same time, God could be defined by these cultures in many ways. Today, the trend seems to be shifting to a belief that there is no God, or that we are gods.

How Society Views God

Today people in our society have many viewpoints and beliefs about God. Fewer people believe in God than ever before. Let's start with the group that doesn't believe that God even exists.

- Atheists believe that God was created by humans because human survival was important and as fear arose around them, they created God to protect them from ferocious beasts and natural calamities. Humans began to worship elements like the sun, fire, and water, out of a sense of extreme fear. Humans started praying, hoping some imaginary superior power could rescue and protect them. God is thusly accredited to the survival extinct needing a helping hand. This imaginary source of protection is the creation of the initial God concept, invented by the human mind. Out of fright and wonder, the idea of a creator and controller of the universe was born, who was believed to be the ultimate protector. This view is very prevalent in our society today. This concept of a supernatural being spread. God's existence grew with gradual mental modifications into differing opinions, evolving to create and produce philosophy.
- Agnostics, are people who claim they don't know if God exists are not. Some may be seeking God, or at least some proof that God exists, while other agnostics don't seek or care if God exists or not. Even though many people don't believe in God or don't know if God exists, many other people do believe in God, or at least believe in a higher power. These people have so many different opinions about God that it is hard to keep track of them all. Other than Christianity there are many other religions around the world. Not all these beliefs will be covered, but below you will see many of the popular religious systems around the world.
- Aristotelianism - In his Metaphysics, Aristotle discusses the meaning of; being as being. Aristotle holds that being, primarily refers to the unmoved movers, and assigned one of these to each movement in the heavens. Aristotle's definition of God attributes perfection to this being, and, as a perfect being, it can only contemplate upon perfection and not on imperfection;

otherwise, perfection would not be one of his attributes. God, according to Aristotle, is in a state of stasis untouched by change and imperfection.
- Hermeticism - In the ancient Greek philosophical Hermetica, the ultimate reality is called by many names, such as God, Lord, Father, Mind (Nous), the Creator, the All, the One, etc. However, peculiar to the Hermetic view of divinity is that it is both the all (Greek: to pan) and the creator of the all: all created things preexist in God, and God is the nature of the cosmos. Yet the things themselves and the cosmos were all created by God. Thus, God creates itself, and is both transcendent (as the creator of the cosmos) and immanent (as the created cosmos).
- Bahá'í Faith - The Bahá'í Faith believes in a single, imperishable God, the creator of all things, including all the creatures and forces in the universe. In Baha'i belief, God is beyond space and time but is also described as a personal God, unknowable, inaccessible, the source of all Revelation, eternal, omniscient, omnipresent, and almighty. Though inaccessible directly, God is nevertheless seen as conscious of creation, possessing a mind, will, and purpose. Baha'is believe that God expresses this will always and, in many ways, including Manifestations, a series of divine messengers or educators.
- Jainism - Jainism does not support belief in a creator deity. According to Jain doctrine, the universe, and its constituent's soul, matter, space, time, and principles of motion have always existed. All the constituents and actions are governed by universal natural laws. It is not possible to create matter out of nothing and hence the total of matter in the universe remains the same (like the law of conservation of mass). The Jain text claims that the universe consists of Jiva (life force or souls) and Ajiva (lifeless objects). Similarly, the soul of each living being is unique and uncreated and has existed since beginningless time.
- Buddhism - The nonadherence to the notion of a supreme God or a prime mover is seen as a key distinction between Buddhism and other religious views. In Buddhism, the sole aim of the spiritual practice is the complete alleviation of distress (dukkha) in samsara, called nirvana. The Buddha neither denies nor accepts a creator by endorsing any views on creation and states

that questions on the origin of the world are worthless. Some teachers instruct students beginning Buddhist meditation that the notion of divinity is not incompatible with Buddhism, but dogmatic beliefs in a supreme personal creator are considered a hindrance to the attainment of nirvana. Despite this apparent non-theism, Buddhists consider veneration of the Noble Ones very important although the two main schools of Buddhism differ mildly in their reverential attitudes. While Theravada Buddhists view the Buddha as a Human Being who attained nirvana or arahanthood through human efforts, Mahayana Buddhists consider him an embodiment of the cosmic dharmakaya (a notion of transcendent divinity), who was born for the benefit of others and not merely a Human Being. Some Mahayana Buddhists worship their chief Bodhisattva, Avalokiteshvara, and hope to embody him. Buddhists accept the existence of beings known as devas in higher realms.

- Hinduism - In Hinduism, the concept of God is complex and depends on the tradition. The concept spans conceptions from absolute monism to henotheism, monotheism, and polytheism. In the Vedic period, the monotheistic god concept culminated in the semi-abstract, semi-personified form of creative soul dwelling in all gods such as Vishvakarman, Purusha, and Prajapati. In most Vaishnavism traditions, he is Vishnu, and the text identifies this being as Krishna, sometimes referred to as Svayam Bhagavan. The term Isvara - from the root is, to have extraordinary power. Some traditional Sankhya systems contrast Purusha (divine, or souls) to Prakriti (nature or energy), however the term for sovereign god, Ishvara is mentioned six times in the Atharva Veda, and is central to many traditions. As per the Advaita Vedanta school of Hindu philosophy, the notion of Brahman (the highest Universal Principle) is akin to that of God; except that unlike most other philosophies, Advaita likens Brahman to atman (the true Self of an individual). For Sindhi Hindus, who are deeply influenced by Sikhism, God is seen as the omnipotent cultivation of all Hindu gods and goddesses.

- Brahman - Brahman is the eternal, unchanging, infinite, immanent, and transcendent reality which is the divine ground of all matter, energy, time, space, being, and everything beyond in this

Universe. The nature of Brahman is described as transpersonal, personal, and impersonal by different philosophical schools. The word Brahman is derived from the verb brh (Sanskrit: to grow) and connotes greatness and infinity. Brahman is talked of at two levels (apara and para). He is the fountainhead of all concepts but he cannot be conceived. He is the universal conceiver, universal concept, and all the means of concept.

- Rosicrucian - The Western Wisdom Teachings present the conception of The Absolute (Unmanifested and unlimited, Boundless Being or Root of Existence, beyond the whole universe and comprehension) from who proceeds the Supreme Being at the dawn of manifestation: The One, the Great Architect of the Universe. From the threefold Supreme Being proceed the seven Great Logoi who contain within themselves all the great hierarchies that differentiate more and more as they diffuse through the six lower Cosmic Planes. These great beings are also threefold in manifestation, like the Supreme Being their three aspects are Will, Wisdom, and activity.

- Unitarian Universalism - Concepts about deity are diverse among us. Some have no belief in any gods (atheism); others believe in many gods (polytheism). Some believe the question of the existence of any god is most likely unattainable or unknowable (agnosticism). Some believe God is a metaphor for a transcendent reality. Some believe in a female god (goddess), a passive god (Deism), an Abrahamic god, or a god manifested in nature or the universe (pantheism). Many reject the idea of deities and instead speak of the spirit of life that binds all life on earth. Many people support each person's search for truth and meaning in concepts of spirituality. Historically, Unitarianism and universalism were denominations within Christianity. Unitarianism referred to a belief about the nature of Jesus Christ that affirmed God as a singular entity and rejected the doctrine of the Trinity. Universalism referred to a theological belief that all persons will be reconciled to God because of divine love and mercy (Universal Salvation).

- Mormonism - In the Mormonism represented by most Mormon communities, including The Church of Jesus Christ of Latter-day Saints, God means Elohim (the Father), whereas Godhead means a council of three distinct entities; Elohim, Jehovah (the Son, or Jesus), and the Holy Spirit. The Father and Son have perfected, material bodies, while the Holy Spirit is a spirit and does not have a body. This conception differs from the traditional Christian Trinity; in Mormonism, the three persons are physically separate beings or personages, but indistinguishable in will and purpose. As such, the term Godhead differs from how it is used in traditional Christianity. The Mormon concept of God has expanded since the faith's founding in the late 1820s.

- Islam - Islam's most fundamental concept is a strict monotheism called tawḥīd. God is described in the Surat al-Ikhlas as: Say: He is God, the One; God, the Eternal, the Absolute; He begot no one, nor is He begotten; Nor is there to Him equivalent anyone. Muslims deny the Christian doctrine of the Trinity and the divinity of Jesus, comparing it to polytheism. In Islam, God is beyond all comprehension or equal and does not resemble any of his creations in any way. Thus, Muslims are not iconodules and are not expected to visualize God. The message of God is carried by angels to 124,000 messengers starting with Adam and concluding with Mohammad. God is described and referred to in the Quran by certain names or attributes, the most common being Al- Rahman, meaning Most Compassionate and Al-Rahim, meaning Most Merciful. Muslims believe that the creation of everything in the universe is brought into being by God's sheer command; Be and so it is.

- Sikhism - The term for God in Sikhism is Waheguru. Guru Nanak describes God as Nirankar (from the Sanskrit nirākārā, meaning formless), Akal (meaning eternal), and alakh (from the Sanskrit alakśya, meaning invisible or unobserved). Sikhism's principal scripture, the Guru Granth Sahib, starts with the figure one, signifying the unity of God. Nanak's interpretation of God is that of a single, personal, and transcendental creator with whom the devotee must develop a most intimate faith and relationship to achieve salvation. Sikhism advocates the belief in one God who is omnipresent (Sarav vi'āpak), whose qualities are infinite, and who is without gender.

- Scientology - Scientology is a set of beliefs and practices invented by American author L. Ron Hubbard. It has been variously defined as a cult, a business, or a new religious movement. In the United States there were about 25,000 followers (in 2008), around 2,300 followers in England (2011), and about 1,700 each in both Canada (2011) and Australia (2016). Hubbard initially developed a set of ideas that he called Dianetics, which he represented as a form of therapy. This he promoted through various publications, as well as through the Hubbard Dianetic Research Foundation that he established in 1950. The foundation soon entered bankruptcy, and Hubbard lost the rights to his book Dianetics: The Modern Science of Mental Health in 1952. He recharacterized the subject as a religion and renamed it Scientology, retaining the terminology, doctrines, and the practice of auditing. Within a year, he regained the rights to Dianetics and retained both subjects under the umbrella of the Church of Scientology. Scientology followers believe that a human is an immortal, spiritual being (Thetan) that is resident in a physical body.

- Satanism - Anton LaVey, founder of the Church of Satan, espoused the view that God is a creation of humanity, rather than humanity being a creation of God. In his book, The Satanic Bible, the Satanist's view of God is described as the Satanist's true self—a projection of his or her personality, not an external deity. Satan is used as a representation of personal liberty and individualism. LaVey discusses this extensively in The Book of Lucifer, explaining that the gods worshipped by other religions are also projections of humanities true self. He argues that human's unwillingness to accept his ego has caused him to externalize these gods to avoid the feeling of total narcissism that would accompany self-worship.

- New Age Spirituality - New Age thinking is so diverse for everyone that it is not possible to make any general statement about the religion of the New Age that could not be challenged by someone pointing out significant exceptions to the rule. Nevertheless, a few common features dominate so much of New Age spirituality that they need to be highlighted as key characteristics of the mainstream of the movement. Pantheism, for example, is the common belief of many, but not all, in the New Age movement. This, of course, is the view that God is everything and everything is God. Thus, the universe itself and all of nature constitute the true God, so there is no valid distinction between the Creator and creation. Other New Agers would hold instead to panentheism, the belief that God is in everything and everything is in God. The difference here is that pantheists retain some notion of a kind of divine transcendence so that God is thought to be someone or something like an impersonal force bigger than the universe. Either way, the New Age concept of deity is rooted in monism, not biblical monotheism. The individual and the universe are ultimately the same. All beings, God included, are ultimately one with the universe.

- The Universe - Today's pop culture has moved away from even saying the word God. You can watch just about any network television show today in America, and when one of the characters on the show gets to the point you think they are about to say the word God, you end up hearing the term; the universe, instead. You will hear terms like; the universe has judged you. Not so long ago, one would've been hard-pressed to encounter such a quote anywhere outside of a course on Eastern religions, at least in North America. Such lines spoken on television or in movies go past the viewer with hardly a notice. Actors (and the characters they portray) routinely praise the universe for their good fortune or express fear that the universe will pay them back for their bad choices. In a relatively short time, then, the universe has become the Hollywood stand-in for God. Replacing God with the universe has become a standard practice in popular culture, showing up in movies, TV shows, interviews, and social media posts. Almost any type of story that requires mention of a higher power will routinely invoke the universe as that power. This occurs so often that it almost escapes notice, largely because it's a belief shared by many in the wider culture. Even professing Christians will at times speak of the universe rewarding or punishing them, or else teaching them a lesson.

As we can well see, there are many religious beliefs and opinions about God, and we have only scratched the surface. With all these options, it's almost no wonder so many people in our society are confused. Many of these religious beliefs, are hostile toward one another and Christianity. Christian believers are faced with the challenge to be even more vocal to spread the good news of God to others so that others can be saved. These increasing antichristian culture attacks in America should be a warning that the chasm is widening between what is Christian and what is not. Will Christians decide to stand back and do nothing about these attacks, or will they stand up for the truth?

Some non-believers are accusing Christian parents who teach their children about creation or hell of committing child abuse. They go on to say that homeschooled children of such Christian parents should be taken away from their parents. This belief is becoming prevalent in society. Christians are being looked on as the enemy in America. Christians are being called child abusers, intolerant, and judgmental. Even simply talking about the Christian faith is being looked at as hate speech by many in our society. Christians are now being seen as the moral outlaws of society.

The move away from God has caused many in society to look down on Christians, and many in society have turned their faith away from religion and are now focused on science. Believe in the Science, is the new battle cry of the American culture. Many in society view Christianity as an outdated backward religion and they look at Christians as backward and unintelligent. They believe that science has trumped the Bible, and proven the Bible to be a fairy tale while proving that God does not exist.

Have we as Christians, failed to accurately represent the true values of hope, faith, and love that Christianity represents? It is important that we truly know God, and who He is, to be better able to defend our faith, and communicate what we believe about God to an unbelieving world.

How Christians View God

God has no beginning and has no end. God has always existed and there has never been a time when God did not exist. You often hear the question: who, or what created God? The simplest answer is no one did. God has existed before time and for all time. The Bible begins: In the beginning God. There is no attempt to prove the existence of God or imply in any way that God had a beginning. God is outside time and space. He is eternal. God also knows all things, God is all present, and God is all-powerful. Christians claim that God created everything, the Heavens, the earth, the universe, and all life. God rules over all things that have been created including humanity. There are some specific things the Bible tells us about God, His traits, and His character including the following:

1. <u>God Is Infinite, Eternal, Self-existing, Without Origin</u> – God, unlike everything else, had no beginning and has no end. God is infinite, the Self-existent One. God created time, matter, and space. God has no beginning since He is beyond time and space. God does not need a cause. God is an eternal Being who has always existed even though it might be difficult to comprehend. The Bible says, "and He is before all things, and in Him, all things hold together" (Colossians 1:17). Great is our Lord, and abundant in power; his understanding is beyond measure (Psalm 147:5). The fact that God is self-existent - that He was not created but has always existed and will exist forever - is perhaps one of the hardest attributes of God for anyone to understand. The root of the name, Jehovah, means self-existing, one who never came into being, and one who always will be. When Moses asked God, "Who shall I tell Pharaoh has sent me?" God said, "I AM THAT I AM." Scripture states that God is from "everlasting to everlasting" (Psalms 41:13). Christ describes himself by saying, "I am the Alpha and Omega, the beginning, and the end, the first and the last" (Revelation 22:13). God existed from eternity past and will exist for all eternity.

2. <u>God Never Changes</u> – "I, the LORD, do not change; therefore you, the sons of Jacob, have not come to an end." (Malachi 3:6). God does not change. Who He is never changes! His attributes are the same from before the beginning of time into eternity. His character never changes – He never gets better or worse. He is perfect the way He is in the past, now, and, always. His plans do not change. His promises do not change. This ought to be a source of incredible joy for believers. God is dependable! His purposes are unfailing, his promises unassailable.

3. <u>God Has No Needs, He Is Self-Sufficient</u> – "For as the Father has life in himself, so He has granted the Son also to have life in himself" (John 5:26). God has never had any need for anything.

God is perfect and complete. The self-sufficiency of God means He possesses infinite wisdom, goodness, and power.

4. <u>God is Creator of All Things</u> – Our God is the creator of everything that exists, and He created all things for His pleasure. After the sixth day of creation, Moses records God's thoughts: "And God saw everything that He had made, and, behold, it was very good (Genesis 1:31)." And speaking of Christ as part of the Godhead, the apostle Paul writes in Colossians 1:16–17, "For by Him were all things created, that are in Heaven, and that are in earth, visible and invisible, whether they be thrones, or dominions, or principalities, or powers: all things were created by Him, and for Him: And He is before all things, and by Him, all things consist." John tells us in John 1:1–3, "In the beginning was the Word, and the Word was with God, and the Word was God. All things were made by Him, and without Him was not anything made that was made."

5. <u>God is All-Powerful - Omnipotent</u> – God has the power to do anything and everything! God has unlimited power (Omni = all; potent = powerful). God is able and powerful to do anything He wills without any effort on his part. It's important to note the anything He wills part of that statement because God cannot do anything contradictory or contrary to his nature. Hebrews 6:18 declares; God did this "so that by two unchangeable things in which it is impossible for God to lie, we who have taken refuge would have strong encouragement to hold firmly to the hope set before us." God can do anything He desires to do. Nothing can prevent God from doing what He wants to do.

6. <u>God Is All-Knowing - Omniscient</u> – God knows all things! God is omniscient, which means He knows everything. God is aware of every moment of every day. He knows our way and is with us always. God knows all that can be known. And this He knows instantly and with a fullness of perfection that includes every possible item of knowledge concerning everything that exists or could have existed anywhere in the universe at any time.

7. <u>God Is All Present - Omnipresent</u> – God is always present in all places! Where can I go from Your Spirit? Or where can I flee from Your presence? If I ascend to Heaven, you are there; If I make my bed in Sheol, behold, you are there. If I take the wings

of the dawn, If I dwell in the remotest part of the sea, even there Your hand will lead me, and your right hand will lay hold of me (Psalm 139:7–10). "Am I a God who is near, declares the LORD, and not a God far off? Can a person hide themself in hiding places so that I do not see him?" declares the LORD. "Do I not fill the heavens and the earth? declares the LORD." (Jeremiah 23:23–24). It is important to understand that for God to be in a place is not the same way we are in a place. God's being is completely different from any physical matter. God exists on a dimension we have no access to, that we cannot perceive with our human senses. Nevertheless, He is with us, the fullness of his presence is all around us.

8. <u>God Is Perfect and Has All Knowledge</u> – God is infinitely wise, consistently wise, perfectly wise. "Oh, the depth of the riches both wisdom and knowledge of God! How unsearchable are His judgments and unfathomable His ways!" (Romans 11:33). Wisdom is more than just head knowledge and intelligence. Even the wisest human on earth would never come close to being as wise as God.

9. <u>God Is Faithful, Unchangeable, and Forever True</u> – God remains faithful, for He cannot deny himself! "Know therefore that the LORD your God is God; He is the faithful God, keeping his covenant of love to a thousand generations of those who love Him and keep His commands" (Deuteronomy 7:9). "If we are faithless, He remains faithful— for He cannot deny himself" (2 Timothy 2:13). God's faithfulness cannot be understood apart from his immutability, the fact that He never changes. The fact that He is unchanging means He can be faithful. God is always faithful and true. His Word of Promise is sure. He may be safely relied upon. No one ever trusted Him in vain. We find this precious truth expressed almost everywhere in the Scriptures, for His people need to know that faithfulness is an essential part of the Divine character.

10. <u>God Is Always Good</u> – By His nature, God is inclined to bestow blessedness and He takes holy pleasure in the happiness of His people. O, taste and see that the Lord is good (Psalm 34:8). The goodness of God set Him to be kind and full of goodwill. He is tenderhearted toward all human beings. Christians find it easier

to affirm the goodness of God when things are going well. When life takes a nosedive, though, that's when we begin to question God's goodness. When the Psalmist writes, Taste and see that the LORD is good; How blessed is the man who takes refuge in Him! (Psalm 34:8) In this psalm, the psalmist affirms his experience of God's goodness from a place of suffering.

11. <u>God Is Always Just</u> – God always does what is right and good for all humans. God is always fair! "His work is perfect, for all His ways are just; a God of faithfulness and without injustice, Righteous and just is He." (Deuteronomy 32:4). Likewise, although this is hard for many to accept, his sentencing of evil, unrepentant sinners to hell are also right and good. A natural question that arises from this is, how then can a just God justify the unjust (as each of us is without Christ!)? We find the answer through the Christian doctrine of justification and redemption. Through the work of Christ in atonement, justice is not violated but satisfied when God spares a sinner. His mercy does not forbid Him to exercise his justice, nor does his justice forbid Him to exercise his mercy. He is both fully merciful and fully just.

12. <u>God Is Merciful and Compassionate</u> – God is inexhaustibly, and actively compassionate. God shows mercy repeatedly throughout the entire Bible. God displays extravagant compassion on His people. It does not depend on the person who wills or the human who runs, but on God who has mercy. God's mercy is inseparable from his justness. He is infinitely, unchangeably, unfailingly merciful – forgiving, lovingly kind toward us. His mercy is also undeserved by us. All true mercy must be, if we deserved it, it wouldn't be mercy. Without the mercy of God, we would have no hope of Heaven. Because of our disobedient hearts, we deserve death. But because of mercy, we don't get what we deserve.

13. <u>God Is Gracious</u> – Because grace is a part of who God is and not just an action He bestows, it means we can trust that grace is eternal. "The LORD is gracious and merciful; Slow to anger and great in loving-kindness" (Psalm 145:8). If mercy is not getting what we do deserve (damnation), grace is getting what we don't deserve (eternal life). Mercy is God's goodness confronting human misery and guilt. Grace is God's ultimate goodness bestowed to sinful humans. God gives humans forgiveness

through His grace and wipes away our debt. God's grace is something we do not earn.

14. <u>God Is Love and Loves Us Unconditionally</u> – The love of God is eternal, sovereign, unchanging, and infinite. Beloved, let us love one another, for love is from God, and whoever loves has been born of God and knows God. Anyone who does not love does not know God, because God is love. As with all attributes, we can only begin to comprehend God's love considering his other attributes. God has allowed His heart to be emotionally connected to humans. God wants our love and will not be satisfied till He gets it. God's love is active and His love is personal. He doesn't just love humanity; He loves human beings. He loves you and me. And his love for us knows no beginning and no end.

15. <u>God Is Holy</u> – God never sins and God is incapable of sin because sin goes against God's nature. "Holy, Holy, Holy, is the Lord Almighty" (Revelation 4:8). The angels proclaim God's holiness: And one cried unto another, and said, "Holy, holy, holy, is the LORD of hosts: the whole earth is full of His glory" (Isaiah 6:3). The word holy means sacred, set apart, revered, or Devine. And yet none of those words is adequate to describe the awesome holiness of our God. Holiness may be the most difficult of God's attributes for us to understand. The word holiness refers to His separateness, His otherness, and the fact that He is unlike any other being. It indicates His complete and infinite perfection. Holiness is the attribute of God that binds all the others together. God being holy means He is endlessly, always perfect.

16. <u>God Is Glorious</u> – God's radiance and beauty emanate from all that He is and all that He does. "His radiance is like the sunlight; He has rays flashing from His hand, and the hiding of His might is there." (Habakkuk 3:4). God's glory is infinite and His greatness displays perfection. God's character and His worth and attributes, all His perfections and greatness reveal His ultimate glory. When we think of the glory of the Lord, we often image a brilliant light, as scripture often describes the glory of God in terms of a light that shines brighter than anything we could experience on earth. Isaiah 43:7 says that "man was created by God for his glory." Our whole existence and purpose are to glorify Him as we are created in His image and do the good work, He has prepared for us to do.

I hope reading all these characteristics and attributes of God has given you a more positive viewpoint and opinion of God and who He truly is. We have all heard so many negative things about God from unbelievers, who are angry at God for one reason or another. Perhaps they have lost someone very dear to them or they have undergone immense hardship and suffering. Perhaps even they have been hurt or victimized by someone calling themselves a Christian. Evil and hardship do exist in the world but it is not because of God. God gave His creation, man and women, the gift of free will. We were not created like robots unable to make our own decisions and choices. Satan and humanity rebelled against God and opened the floodgates to evil and suffering. However, we know that this time is only temporary. One day we will be freed from this curse and will live out all eternity without any pain or suffering. Revelation 21:4–5 states, "and He will wipe away every tear from their eyes and, and there will no longer be any death; there will no longer be any mourning, or crying, or pain; the first things have passed away. And He who sits on the throne said, Behold, I am making all things new."

God is far greater than we could ever imagine. God is the very definition of perfection. This should give us reason to put our full trust and hope in Him. In God, we cannot go wrong! God invites every person on this earth into His community. All we must do is say YES!

Is God Real?

After reading the previous section, it may sound as if God is too good to be true? Sometimes we may even ask ourselves is God real? We can't physically see God or hear God or touch God, so what evidence would we need to know that God does exist? Even though we have the Bible, does that prove the existence of God?

We can recognize God's handiwork, all His creation. The entire universe contains the stars, the sun, the moon, and all the creatures living on the earth. We know that things didn't just come into existence by themselves? After all, how did the first speck of dust just appear and show up out of nowhere? If there is no God, why would anything exist in the first place? The answer is it wouldn't. Things just don't appear out of nowhere and create themselves by themselves. Humans are not able to create themselves, so how would a speak of dust, without any intelligence whatsoever, create itself? Yet humans cannot? We know that God exists because we can see the design in nature. We can recognize that design needs an intelligent designer. We see human-made objects all around us planes, cars, computers, trains, refrigerators, stereos, houses, and so on. We recognize these objects to be human-made, not self-made. They didn't just come into existence all by themselves or by some random accident. We know they had a designer. We can see God's design throughout the entire universe, from the stars, planets, animals, people, tiny cells, atoms, molecules, and DNA within our human bodies. Design is everywhere. It would never enter our minds that metal, left to itself, would eventually form into engines, jets, skyscrapers, wheels, and automobiles. God is Real, *Is God Real?* [2]

This design argument is often associated with William Paley, an Anglican clergyman who wrote on this topic in the late eighteenth century. He is remembered for his example of the watch and the watchmaker. In discussing the watch, he concluded that the watch must have had a maker who formed it for its intended purpose. Paley thus believed that design in living things implies a Designer. William Paley, *The Watch and the Watchmaker, From Natural Theology, Or Evidences of the Existence and Attributes of the Deity Collected from the Appearance of Nature.* 1802, PP. 1-6. [3]

As we conduct research in the fields of fundamental biologicals, we see ever-increasing levels of design and complexity in almost everything we examine. Even the late Isaac Asimov, a self-proclaimed atheist commented about "the human brain being the most complex and orderly arrangement of matter in the universe." (Kwize, Isaac Asimov, *The human brain, quotes).* [4] It is much more complex than the most complicated computer ever built. Wouldn't it be logical to assume that if human's highly intelligent brain designed the computer, then the human brain was also the product of a higher design? Even scientists who reject the concept of a Creator God agree that all living things exhibit evidence of design. Living things are just too complex and organized to have come into existence by chance.

- The design implies a designer. To a Christian, the design we see all around us is consistent with the Bible's explanation: "In the beginning, God created the heavens and the earth" (Genesis 1:1). We can therefore conclude that the huge amount of information

in living things must have come from a super-intelligent being and designer. This could only be the work of an all-knowing, all-intelligent, and all-powerful God.
- God Is the foundation for science and reason. Why is there logic and order in the universe? How are humans able to think logically if we were just created by random circumstances? There are laws of science and logic that have been applied to all creation by a supreme designer. This supreme designer is the creator God! Logic and the ability to reason are required to prove things to be true or false. God must exist for reasoning to be possible. Without God, we couldn't prove anything at all. The existence of God is the precondition for knowledge and rationality. This is called the transcendental argument for God. Think about it: why is logical reasoning possible? There are laws of logic that we use when we reason. For example, there is the law of non-contradiction, which states that you can't have "A" and "not-A" at the same time and in the same relationship. We all know that this is true. But why is it true, and how do we know it?
- God is self-consistent. He is non-contradictory, and so this law follows from God's nature. Logical reasoning is possible because God is logical. But if the universe were merely a random process or a chance accident, then why should logical reasoning be possible? If my brain is merely the product of mutations (guided only by natural selection) and random chemical processes, then why should I be able to reason, think, or determine if anything is true? The secular, evolutionary worldview cannot account for the existence of logical reasoning.

Only a biblical worldview can account for the existence of science and the study of the natural world. Science depends on the fact that the universe obeys orderly laws which do not arbitrarily change. If the universe were merely an accident, why would it obey any logical, orderly laws?

This can be explained in the Bible, there is order because a logical Creator upholds the universe logically and consistently. God does not change; so, He consistently sustains the universe.

Describing God with words is impossible. However, God does make himself known in many ways and He reveals Himself in His Word and

His creation. So, who is God? We can see in the Bible that God is known by many names. These names help us to get a better understanding of who God truly is. Each of the many names of God helps describe a different aspect and characteristic of who God is and what makes Him unique. Below is a small sampling of some of the names God is known by in the Bible:

- I Am that I Am: The name that God gives himself and answered to Moses when he asked.
- I Am: Jesus also used this name for Himself, implying to the Jewish Religious leaders that He is God.
- The Alpha and the Omega: who is and who was and who is to come, the Almighty (Revelation 1:8).
- Yahweh (YHWH): Comes from a verb that means to exist, be.
- Elohim: The plural form of EL, meaning strong one.
- Adonai: Like Elohim, this too is a plural of majesty. The singular form means master, owner.
- Father (Abba): God becomes our personal Father.
- El Shaddai: God Almighty.
- El Shaddai Rohi: God Almighty, the mighty One of Jacob.
- El Elyon: The Highest God.
- El Chuwl: The God who gave birth.
- El Deah: God of knowledge.
- El Olam: The Everlasting God.
- El Gibhor: Mighty God– the name describing the Messiah, Christ Jesus.
- Attiyq Youm: The Ancient of Days.
- Yahweh Jireh (Yireh): The Lord will provide.
- Yahweh Rapha: The Lord Who Heals
- Yahweh Nissi: The Lord is my Banner.
- Yahweh M'Kaddesh: The Lord Who Sanctifies, Makes Holy
- Yahweh Elohim: LORD God
- Yahweh Rohi: The Lord Our Shepherd
- Yahweh Tsidkenu: The Lord Our Righteousness
- Yahweh Shalom: The Lord is Peace.
- Yahweh Sabbaoth: The Lord of Hosts.
- Yahweh Maccaddeshcem: The Lord your Sanctifier.
- Yahweh Ghmolah: The God of Recompense

- Yahweh Ro'i: The Lord my Shepherd.
- Yahweh Tsidkenu: The Lord our Righteousness.
- Yahweh Shammah: The Lord is there.
- Yahweh Elohim Israel: The Lord, the God of Israel.

The God of the Bible is not merely one of many gods from which we may pick and choose to worship nor is He to be put on par with other supposed deities. There is only one true God. God is the omnipotent Creator and Redeemer of humanity. Truly we worship a great God, the Mighty God, the Everlasting Father, and a great King above all gods.

The Trinity, Three in One

God is three in one. God exists as a Trinity, one God in three persons, God the Father, God the Son (Jesus), and God the Holy Spirit.

- <u>The Father Is God</u>: As history unfolded, God progressively revealed more about himself. It eventually became clear that while there is only one God, He has all the attributes of a deity such as being everywhere, all-knowing), all-powerful, holy, and eternal.
- <u>The Son Is God</u>: Jesus is also explicitly called God in Scripture (Titus 2:13). And He, too, has all the attributes of deity including being everywhere present, all-knowing, all-powerful, holy, and eternal.
- <u>The Holy Spirit Is God</u>: The Holy Spirit is also recognized as God (Acts 5:3–4). He, too, has all the attributes of deity including being everywhere present, all-knowing, all-powerful, holy, and eternal.

The resurrected Jesus instructed the disciples, "Go therefore and make disciples of all the nations, baptizing them in the name of the Father and of the Son and the Holy Spirit" (Matthew 28:19). The word name is singular in Greek, thereby indicating God's oneness. However, the definite articles in front of Father, Son, and Holy Spirit (in the original Greek) indicate they are distinct personalities, even though there is just one God.

These distinct personalities relate to each other. They know each other, love each other, and speak to each other. The Holy Spirit descended upon Jesus at His baptism, is called another comforter, was sent by the Father and Jesus, and seeks to glorify Jesus.

God the Father

Who is God the Father? Psalm 68:5 declares that "God is the Father of the fatherless and protector of widows, is God in his holy dwelling. God wants to display His abundant love to all His children and has adopted us into His family." Let's consider some of the following truths about God the Father:

- God the Father, the first person of the Trinity instructs and places all things according to His purpose and grace (1 Corinthians 8:6).
- God the Father, is the Creator of all things (Ephesians 3:9).
- God the Father is Father to all people (Ephesians 4:6), but Spiritual Father only to believers, those who acknowledge Jesus Christ as Lord and Savior. (2 Corinthians 6:18).
- God the Father, maintains, guides, and governs all creatures and events (1 Chronicles 29:11).
- God the Father is the only omnipotent and absolute ruler in the universe, He is sovereign in creation, providence, and redemption (Psalm 103:19).
- God the Father, has pronounced for His glory all things that come to pass (Ephesians 1:11).
- God the Father, in His sovereignty is neither author nor originator of sin (Habakkuk 1:13), nor does He reduce the accountability of moral, intelligent creatures (1 Peter 1:17).
- God the Father has graciously chosen those He would have as His own (Ephesians 1:4–6).
- God the Father saves from sin all those who come to Jesus, and He becomes Father to them (Hebrews 12:5–9).
- God the Father, is the only God (Isaiah 43:10).
- God the Father, is Holy (1 Peter 1:15).
- God the Father is just or righteous (Psalm 19:9).
- God the Father is Love (1 John 4:8).

- God the Father is Truth (Romans 3:4).
- God the Father is infinite and eternal and has always been and will forever be. (Genesis 21:33).
- God the Father is immutable and does not change (Malachi 3:6).

Again, Christians believe there is one God who exists in three Persons. This mystery of the faith cannot be fully understood by the human mind but is a key doctrine of Christianity. While the word Trinity does not appear in the Bible, several events include the simultaneous appearance of Father, Son, and Holy Spirit, such as the baptism of Jesus by John the Baptist.

Jesus urged us to think of God as our loving Father and went a step further by calling Him Abba, an Aramaic word roughly translated as Daddy, to show us how intimate our relationship with Him is. Abba is always followed by the word Father in Scripture, and the phrase is found in three passages.

Jesus addresses His Father as Abba, Father in His prayer in Gethsemane. Abba, Father is mentioned about the Spirit's work of adoption that makes us God's children and heirs with Christ. Again, in the context of adoption, the Spirit in our heart's cries out, Abba, Father. Together, the terms Abba and Father doubly emphasize the fatherhood of God. In two different languages, we are assured of God's care for His children.

When Jesus taught His disciples to pray, He began with the words Our Father. The holy and righteous God, who created and sustains all things, who is all-powerful, all-knowing, and ever-present, not only allows us but encourages us to call Him Father.

Because of our relationship with our Abba, Father, He no longer deals with us as enemies; instead, we can approach Him with boldness and in full assurance of faith. "The Spirit Himself testifies with our spirit that we are children of God, and if we are children, we are also heirs, heirs of God and fellow heirs with Christ, if indeed we suffer with *Him* so that we may also be glorified with *Him*." (Romans 8:16–17).

Becoming a child of God is the highest and most humbling of honors. Because of it, we have a new relationship with God and a new standing before Him. Being an adopted child of God is the source of our hope, the security of our future, and the motivation to live a life worthy of the calling you have received. Being children of the King of Kings and Lord of Lords calls us to a higher standard, a different way of life, and, in the future, an inheritance that can never perish, spoil or fade. What amazing grace that God would love us so much to call us His children. God the Father is the Supreme Being, Creator, and Sustainer, deserving of human worship and obedience. In the First Commandment, God warns us not to put anyone or anything above Him.

Jesus Christ the Son

Jesus Christ is God incarnate, which means, God in the flesh. Jesus is the second person of the Trinity, our creator, the resurrected Savior, and Redeemer, and the only means of salvation. Jesus is the Christ or Messiah (Anointed One) of Israel. He was born as God in the flesh, lived among humans, and taught a new covenant in the Jewish tradition. He was crucified by Roman authorities around A.D. 30. After He died, Jesus was buried and rose on the third day to prove his power over death. His life, ministry, miracles, death, and resurrection point to his mission: Jesus Christ is both God and the Savior of the world.

- Jesus' life, death, burial, resurrection, and ascension are confirmed in the biblical documents in the first four books of the New Testament: Matthew, Mark, Luke, and John.
- Jesus was miraculously conceived without sexual union when the Holy Spirit overshadowed his mother, Mary. He was born in the line of some of the most well-known people in the Old Testament including the women Tamar, Rahab, Uriah's wife, and of course Mary. When God established one of His earliest covenants, it was with a man named Abram. God promised Abram that he would be the father of a great nation. Abram gave birth to Isaac, then Isaac gave birth to Jacob, Jacob then had twelve sons, who became the twelve tribes of Israel. Later this line would continue to King David, then eventually to Jesus.
- Jesus of Nazareth was a Jewish teacher in the first century A.D. He was raised as an observant Jew, had brothers and sisters, and was trained to work as a carpenter. Around the age of thirty, He was baptized by the prophet John the Baptist and began ministering as an itinerant rabbi, a Jewish teacher. He called

disciples to himself and taught the crowds who gathered around Him. His followers eventually proclaimed Him to be the Christ, or anointed one. Christ (Messiah: Hebrew) was a royal and divine title in Jewish theology.

- The historical evidence for Jesus of Nazareth is both long-established and widespread. Within a few decades of his lifetime, He is mentioned by Jewish and Roman historians, as well as by dozens of Christian writings. Compare that with, for example, King Arthur, who supposedly lived around A.D. 500. The major historical source for events of that time does not even mention Arthur, and he is first referred to three hundred or four hundred years after he is supposed to have lived. The evidence for Jesus is not limited to later folklore, as are accounts of King Arthur.

The primary source material for Jesus' life is the four Gospels: Matthew, Mark, Luke, and John. These biographies each provide a different perspective on the life and ministry of Jesus. The first three Gospels, known as the Synoptics, are arranged in somewhat chronological order. The Gospel of John is arranged more topically with a heavy interest in theological themes.

In addition, every other New Testament manuscript (except 3 John) mentions Jesus by name. These documents often explore the teaching of the apostles and the early church. However, there are some mentions of events in Jesus' life, especially his death, burial, and resurrection.

Many non-biblical sources, *Evidence for Jesus Outside of the Bible – 1"*,[5] mention Jesus as well. These ancient documents further bolster the historicity of the biblical sources.

- Flavius Josephus (AD 37–101) was a Jew who did not proclaim to be a Christian but did have this to say about Jesus, "About this time there lived Jesus, a wise man if indeed one ought to call (him) a human. For He performed surprising deeds and was a teacher of such people as accept the truth gladly. He won over many Jews and many Greeks. He was the Messiah. And when, upon the accusation of the principal people among us, Pilate had condemned (Him) to a cross, those who had first come to love (him) did not cease. He appeared to them spending a third day restored to life, for the prophets of God had foretold these things and a thousand other marvels about (him). And the tribe of the Christians, so-called after (him), has still to this day not disappeared." P. L. Maier, ed./trans., *Josephus –The Essential Works* (Grand Rapids: Kregel Publications, 1994). [6]

- Thallus (AD 52) - Thallus is perhaps the earliest secular writer to mention Jesus and he is so ancient his writings do not even exist anymore. But Julius Africanus, writing around AD 221 does quote Thallus. He wrote: *"In the third book of his history Thallus calls this darkness an eclipse of the sun — wrongly in my opinion."* Julius Africanus, *In Georgius Syncellus, Chron*. [7]
- Cornelius Tacitus (AD 56–120) – Wrote "Christus, the founder of the name, was Put to death by Pontius Pilate, procurator of Judea in the reign Of Tiberius." Cornelius Tacitus, *The Annals*. [8]
- Mara-Serapion (AD 70) – Wrote a letter that refers to the unjust treatment of "three wise men": the murder of Socrates, the burning of Pythagoras, and the execution of "the wise king" of the Jews (Jesus). The letter is preserved in a 6th- or 7th-century manuscript (*BL Add*. 14658) held by the British Library.[9]
- Phlegon (AD 80–140) - Wrote a chronicle of history around AD 140. In this history, Phlegon also mentions the darkness surrounding the crucifixion of Jesus to explain it. Julius Africanus, *"Africanus, Chronography"* 18:1. [10]
- Pliny the Younger (AD 61–113) – "The also sang … a hymn to Christ, as to a God. This worship involved worship of Jesus Christ." Cale Clarke, *"Ancient Evidence for Jesus: Pliny the Younger."* [11]
- C. Suetonius Tranquillus (AD 69–140) – "As the Jews were making constant disturbances at the instigation of Chrestus, He expelled them from Rome." C. Suetonius Tranquillus, *"Lives of the Twelve Caesars" (The Heritage Press – 1965 Reprint)*. [12]
- Lucian of Samosata (AD 115–200) – "The Christians, you know, worship a human to this day the distinguished personage who introduced their novel rites, and was crucified on that account." Lucian of Samosata, *"The Passing of Peregrinus"* 11, 13. [13]
- Celsus (AD 175) - Celsus accuses [Jesus] of having "invented his birth from a virgin," and upbraids Him with being "born in a certain Jewish village, of a poor woman of the country." Jewish Talmud (AD 400–700) - The rabbis boast of responsibility for

Jesus' Crucifixion, "hanged," even though the Romans were inclined toward acquittal of Jesus (Sanhedrin 43a). James Bishop, *"Greek Philosopher Celsus on the Historical Jesus."* [14]
- Toledat Yeshu (AD 1000) - The Book of the Generations/History/Life of Jesus, often abbreviated as Toledat Yeshu, is an early Jewish text taken to be an alternative biography of Jesus. Sefer Toledot Yeshu, *"The Book of the Generations/History/Life of Jesus,"* 1874. [15]

Jesus taught many subjects and performed many miracles. His true passion was revealing the love that God has for humanity. He also taught about the kingdom of God, repentance, non-hypocritical faith, forgiveness, discipleship, prayer, marriage, divorce, eternal judgment, money, Heaven, hell, and eternal life for those who believed. His favorite method of teaching was through parables which are short stories designed to impart a spiritual lesson. Some of the miracles He performed include:

- Turned water into wine (John 2:1–11)
- Healed a paralytic (Mark 2:1–12)
- Healed a withered hand (Mark 3:1–3)
- Calmed a storm (Mark 4:35–41)
- Healed a servant from afar (Luke 7:1–10)
- Revived a dead human (Luke 7:11–17)
- Healed a man with leprosy (Matthew 8:2–4)
- Healed a bleeding woman (Luke 8:43–48)
- Healed a man born blind (John 9:1–12)
- Fed the multitude (Matthew 14:13–21)
- Walked on water (Matthew 14:22–33)
- Cast out demons (Matthew 17:14–21)
- Healed a man with a severed ear (Luke 22:50–51)
- Resurrected himself (Mark 16:1–7)

Is Jesus Really God? We turn to the Scriptures to show who Jesus truly is. Jesus has the names of God: names that can only be used by God. For example:

Jesus is Yahweh. Yahweh is a very common Hebrew name for God in the Old Testament, occurring over 5,300 times. It is translated LORD (all capitals) in many English translations of the Bible. Moses asked God by what name He should be called. God replied to him, "I AM WHO I AM. Thus, you shall say to the children of Israel, I AM has sent me to you" (Exodus 3:14). Yahweh is a shortened form of I AM WHO I AM. The name conveys the idea of eternal self-existence. Jesus implicitly ascribed this divine name to himself during a confrontation He had with a group of hostile Jews. He said, "I say to you, before Abraham was, I AM" (John 8:58).

- Jesus is Elohim. Elohim is a Hebrew name that is used by God 2,570 times in the Old Testament. The name means strong one, and its plural ending (in Hebrew) indicates fullness of power. Elohim is portrayed in the Old Testament as the powerful and sovereign governor of the universe, ruling over the affairs of humanity. Jesus is recognized as both Yahweh and Elohim in the prophecy in (Isaiah 40:3): "Clear the way for the Lord in the wilderness; Make straight in the desert a highway for our God."
- Jesus is Theos. The New Testament Greek word for God, Theos, corresponds parallel to the Old Testament Hebrew term Elohim. A well-known example of Christ being addressed as God (Theos) is found in the story of doubting Thomas. In this passage, Thomas witnesses the resurrected Christ and worshipfully responds: My Lord and my God [Theos]. Jesus is called Theos throughout the rest of the New Testament. For example, when a jailer asked Paul and Silas how to be saved, they responded: "Believe in the Lord Jesus, and you will be saved, you and your household" (Acts 16:31).
- Jesus possesses attributes that belong only to God. Jesus is eternal. (John 1:1) affirms: "In the beginning was the Word, and the Word was with God, and the Word was God." The word was in this verse is an imperfect tense, indicating continuous, ongoing existence. When the time-space universe came into being, Christ already existed.
- Jesus is self-existing: As the creator of all things, Christ himself must be uncreated.
- Jesus is everywhere present: Christ promised His disciples, "where two or three are gathered together in My name, I am there in the midst of them" (Matthew 18:20).

- Jesus is all-knowing: Jesus knew where the fish were in the water, and He knew just which fish contained the coin. He knew the future specific details that would be encountered, and knew from a distance that Lazarus had died.
- Jesus is all-powerful: Christ created the entire universe and sustains the universe by His power. During His earthly ministry, He exercised power over nature, physical, demonic spirits, and even death.
- Jesus is sovereign: Christ presently sits "at the right hand of God the Father, angels and authorities and powers having been made subject to Him" (1 Peter 3:22). When Christ comes again in glory, "And on His robe and on His thigh, He has a name written: KING OF KINGS, AND LORD OF LORDS." (Revelation 19:16).
- Jesus is sinless: Jesus challenged Jewish leaders: "Which of you convicts Me of sin?" (John 8:46). The apostle Paul referred to Jesus as Him who knew no sin (2 Corinthians 5:21). Jesus is one who loved righteousness and hated lawlessness and was without sin.
- Jesus Possesses the Authority of God: Jesus always spoke in His divine authority. He never said, thus saith the Lord as did the prophets; He always said, Verily, verily, I say unto you. He never retracted anything He said, never guessed or spoke with uncertainty, never made revisions, never contradicted himself, and never apologized for what He said.
- Jesus Performs the Works of God. Jesus' deity is also proved by His miracles. His miracles are often called signs in the New Testament. Signs always signify something in this case, that Jesus is the divine Messiah.
- Jesus Is Worshiped as God: Jesus was worshiped on many occasions in the New Testament. He accepted worship from Thomas, the angels, some wise men, a leper, a ruler, a blind man, an anonymous woman, Mary Magdalene, and the disciples. Scripture is emphatic that only God can be worshiped.

A comparison of the Old and New Testaments provides testimony to Jesus's identity as God. For example, a study of the Old Testament indicates that it is only God who saves. In (Isaiah 43:11), God asserts: "I, even I, am the Lord, and besides Me, there is no savior." This verse indicates that: a claim to be Savior is a claim to deity, and there is only one Savior the Lord God. It is highly revealing of Christ's divine nature that the New Testament refers to Jesus as our great God and Savior.

Many theologians believe that appearances of the angel of the Lord (or, more literally, angel of Yahweh) in Old Testament times were preincarnate appearances of Jesus Christ. (The word preincarnate means before becoming a Human Being.) There are pieces of evidence for this view:

- The angel of Yahweh appeared to Moses in the burning bush and claimed to be God
- The angel of Yahweh was sent into the world by Yahweh, just as Jesus was sent into the world in New Testament times by the Father.
- The angel of Yahweh prayed to Yahweh on behalf of the people of God, just as Jesus prays to the Father for the people of God today.
- The angel of Yahweh and Jesus engaged in amazingly similar ministries such as delivering the enslaved and comforting the downcast.
- It was the Angel of Yahweh who spoke from Heaven to Abraham when Abraham was about to sacrifice Isaac and stopped him from proceeding.

Genesis 18:3 says how Christ, along with two of His angels, visited Abraham. He is called the LORD. Whenever the word LORD appears in scripture with all caps, this identifies God's name Jehovah or Yahweh. As this chapter ends, two of the humans begin a journey to Sodom while Jesus remains behind to tell Abraham that Sodom will be destroyed. Upon learning of Sodom's upcoming destruction, Abraham intercedes on their behalf to Christ.

Genesis 32:24 says how Jacob wrestled with a being. This being was Jesus Christ. Since Jacob held his own against the Son of God in the wrestling match, he was granted a blessing. His name was changed to Israel. Israel means the who prevails with God or he will rule as God (rules). Jacob had prevailed with God by wrestling with Him in the person of Christ. Jacob realized who he wrestled with by naming the place Peniel, meaning the face of God, knowing he had seen Him and lived.

Joshua speaks of how Christ appeared to Joshua. God's servant was near Jericho when he saw a man with a sword drawn. Immediately Joshua asks in Joshua 5:13:15 "Are you for us or for our enemies? He said, no; rather I have come now *as* captain of the army of the LORD. And Joshua fell on his face to the ground, and bowed down." This man did not stop Joshua from worshiping Him as any other servant of the Lord would do. The Lord responded by telling Joshua "Remove your sandals from your feet, for the place where you are standing is holy."

Yes, Jesus is God the Son. Jesus must be viewed as God because He has the names, attributes, and authority of God; He does the works of God and He is worshiped as God. There is no doubt to Christians that Jesus is truly God, and fulfilled many supernatural miracles while on earth.

On multiple occasions, Jesus' divinity is taught directly in Scripture. The prophet Isaiah affirmed the divinity of the Messiah seven hundred+ years before He was born. The Bible clearly teaches Jesus' divinity. The most dramatic affirmation of Jesus' divinity is from (John 1:1) in which John stated that Jesus was God at the beginning of creation: "In the beginning was the Word, and the Word was with God, and the Word was God."

Jesus Christ, though sinless, suffered death and God the Father's just wrath against sinners on behalf of humankind for their sin. He died to satisfy the righteous demands of the holiness and justice of God, his Father. Jesus was the perfect sacrifice. He died on a cross, but on the third day, He rose again, conquering death, so that all who truly believe in Him, repent of their sin, and trust in Him, will be saved.

What the Bible says About Jesus:

- Jesus Christ is God (John 1:1).
- Jesus was born of a virgin (Luke 1:26–35).
- Jesus Christ became a human (Philippians 2:1–11).
- Jesus is fully God and fully human (Colossians 2:9).
- Jesus Christ is perfect and sinless (1 Peter 2:22).
- Jesus is the only way to God the Father (John 14:6).

The Bible says Jesus Christ is God, was born of a virgin, became a human, is fully God and fully human, is perfect and sinless, and is the only way to God the Father. Jesus clearly had a mission on this earth. The Bible also says that Jesus came to earth for many reasons including,

- to Do the Will of the Father. (Hebrews 10:7),
- to Save Sinners. (1 Timothy 1:15),
- to Bring Light to a Dark World. (John 12:46),
- to Bear Witness to the Truth. (John 18:37),
- to Destroy the Devil and His Works. (1 John 3:8),
- to Give Eternal Life. (John 6:51),
- to Receive Worship. (Matthew 2:1–2),
- to Bring Great Joy. (Luke 2:10),
- to Demonstrate True Humility. (Philippians 2:5–8),
- to Preach the Gospel. (Luke 4:18–19),
- to Bring Judgment. (John 9:39–41),
- to Give His Life a Ransom for Many. (Titus 2:13–14),
- to Fulfill the Law and Prophets. (Matthew 5:17),
- to Reveal God's Love for Sinners. (John 3:16),
- to Call Sinners to Repentance. (Mark 2:17),
- to Die. (John 12:24–27),
- to Seek and Save the Lost. (Luke 19:5),
- to Serve. (Mark 10:45),
- to Bring Peace. (Ephesians 2:14–18),
- to Bring a Sword. (Matthew 10:34),
- to Bind Up Broken Hearts. (Isaiah 61:1–3),
- to Give Us the Spirit of Adoption. (Galatians 4:6),
- to Make Us Partakers of the Divine Nature. (2 Peter 1:4),
- to Reign as King. (Isaiah 9:6–7),
- to Restore Human Nature to Holiness. (Luke 1:35),
- to Be a Merciful and Faithful High Priest. (Hebrews 2:17–18),
- to Be the Second and Greater Adam. (Romans 5:14–15),
- to Satisfy Our Deepest Thirst. (John 4:13–14),
- to Be Loved by God's Children. (John 8:42),
- to Reveal God's Glory. (John 1:14).

Jesus came into the world for the betterment of humanity and the fight against sin and evil. We can be sure that Jesus' love for us is real and that everyone is important to Him. Jesus did not come to earth for His benefit but our benefit.

God the Son willingly gave His life to save sinners from an eternal hell. "For this reason, the Father loves Me, because I lay down My life so that I may take it back. No one has taken it away from Me, but I lay it down on My own. I have authority to lay it down, and I have authority to take it back. This commandment I received from My Father." (John 10:17–18)

Looking unto Jesus the author and finisher of our faith; "who for the joy that was set before Him endured the cross, despising the shame, and is set down at the right hand of the throne of God" (Hebrews 12:2).

When Christ rose again on the third day, He did not rise as a spirit with no physical body, but appeared to over five hundred people and ate and drank with his disciples. He even offered to let Thomas place his hands in the nail and spear wounds (John 20:27). He laid down his life and He took it up again just as He said He would. His Father also would not allow His Holy One to see corruption (decay) (Psalm 16:10), proving that Christ was fully God and fully human.

No matter which god you serve, in the end, "for this reason also God highly exalted Him and bestowed on Him the name which is above every name, so that at the name of Jesus every knee will bow, of those who are in Heaven and on earth and under the earth, and that every tongue will confess that Jesus Christ is Lord, to the glory of God the Father" (Philippians 2: 9–11). Wouldn't you rather do this now and live, than wait and perish?

The Holy Spirit

The Holy Spirit is the third person in the Trinity. When you become a Christian, the Holy Spirit lives in you. Before Jesus was crucified, He said it is good that I go so that you can receive the comforter, which is the Holy Spirit. The Bible describes the Holy Spirit as the breath of God. Jesus said; "Peace be with you! As the Father has sent Me, I am sending you. And with that, He breathed on them and said; Receive the Holy Spirit" (John 20:21–22). The Holy Spirit is God's power in you. God sends out his spirit to any person to accomplish his will. (Psalm 104:30; 139:7) The Holy Spirit is the least understood member of the Godhead. In the Bible, the word spirit, is translated from the Hebrew word ru'ach and the Greek word pneu'ma. Most often, those words refer to God's active force or Holy Spirit. However, the Bible also uses those words in other ways:

- Breath – (Habakkuk 2:19).
- Wind – (Genesis 8:1).
- The vital, or animating, force in living creatures – (Job 34:14).
- A person's disposition or attitude – (Numbers 14:24).
- Spirit persons, including God and the angels – (1 Kings 22:21).

These meanings share the sense of something invisible to humans that produces visible effects. Since the Hebrew word for Spirit in the Old Testament means breath or wind, Jesus breathed on his apostles after his resurrection and said, "Receive the Holy Spirit" (John 20:22). He also commanded his followers to baptize people in the name of the Father, Son, and Holy Spirit. The Holy Spirit is hard to associate with for many, yet He dwells inside every true believer and is a constant companion in their walk of faith. The Holy Spirit is God. The Holy Spirit has thoughts and a will. Those who live to please the Spirit will harvest everlasting life from the Spirit. We please the Holy Spirit when we rely on Him. He gives us the strength to live in a way that's consistent with God's plan for us. The following characteristics describe the Holy Spirit:

- The Holy Spirit is a person with feelings and can become sad or angry, and people can insult Him and blaspheme against Him - And so, I tell you, "every kind of sin and slander can be forgiven, but the blasphemy against the Spirit will not be forgiven" (Matthew 12:31).
- The Holy Spirit has intentions, discretions, and shows willfulness and discretion. He loves, communicates, testifies, teaches, and prays -These are qualities that distinguish Him as a person. "You gave your good Spirit to instruct them. You did not withhold your manna from their mouths, and you gave them water for their thirst" (Nehemiah 9:20).
- The Holy Spirit helps us in our weakness, and He searches our hearts. He intercedes for God's people by the will of God.
- The Holy Spirit has a Mind - (Romans 8:27) "And He who searches our hearts knows the mind of the Spirit because the Spirit intercedes for the saints by God's will."

- The Holy Spirit has a Will - (1 Corinthians 12:11) "But the same Spirit works all these things, distributing to each one individually just as He wills."
- The Holy Spirit has Emotions and can Grieve - (Isaiah 63:10) "Yet they rebelled and grieved his Holy Spirit." So, He turned and became their enemy and He fought against them.
- The Holy Spirit Gives Joy - At that time Jesus, full of joy through the Holy Spirit, said, "I praise you, Father, Lord of Heaven and earth, because you have hidden these things from the wise and learned, and revealed them to little children. Yes, Father, for this was your good pleasure" (1 Thessalonians 1:6). You became imitators of us and the Lord; despite severe suffering, you welcomed the message with the joy given by the Holy Spirit.
- The Holy Spirit Teaches - (John 14:26) "But the Counselor, the Holy Spirit, whom the Father will send in my name, will teach you all things and will remind you of everything I have said to you."
- The Holy Spirit Testifies of Christ - (John 15:26) "When the Counselor comes, whom I will send to you from the Father, the Spirit of truth who goes out from the Father, He will testify about me."
- The Holy Spirit Convicts - (John 16:8) "When He comes, He will convict the world regarding sin, and righteousness, and judgment."
- The Holy Spirit Leads - (Romans 8:14) "Because those who are led by the Spirit of God are sons of God."
- The Holy Spirit Reveals Truth - (John 16:13) "But when He, the Spirit of truth, comes, He will guide you into all truth. He will not speak on his own; He will speak only what He hears, and He will tell you what is yet to come."
- The Holy Spirit Strengthens and Encourages - (Acts 9:31) "Then the church throughout Judea, Galilee, and Samaria enjoyed a time of peace. It was strengthened, and encouraged by the Holy Spirit, it grew in numbers, living in the fear of the Lord."
- The Holy Spirit Comforts - (John 14:16) "And I will ask the Father, and He will give you another Helper, so that He may be with you forever."
- The Holy Spirit Helps Us in our Weakness and Intercedes - (Romans 8:26) "In the same way, the Spirit helps us in our weakness.

We do not know what we ought to pray for, but the Spirit himself intercedes for us with groans that words cannot express."
- The Holy Spirit Searches the Deep Things of God - (1 Corinthians 2:11) "The Spirit searches all things, even the deep things of God. For who among humans knows the thoughts of a man except for the man's spirit within him? In the same way, no one knows the thoughts of God except the Spirit of God."
- The Holy Spirit Sanctifies - (Romans 15:16) "To be a minister of Christ Jesus to the Gentiles with the priestly duty of proclaiming the gospel of God so that the Gentiles might become an offering acceptable to God, sanctified by the Holy Spirit."
- The Holy Spirit Bears Witness and Testifies - (Romans 8:16) "The Spirit Himself testifies with our spirit that we are children of God." The Holy Spirit Forbids - (Acts 16:6–7) Paul and his companions "traveled throughout the region of Phrygia and Galatia, having been kept by the Holy Spirit from preaching the word in the province of Asia. When they came to the border of Mysia, they tried to enter Bithynia, but the Spirit of Jesus would not allow them to."
- The Holy Spirit was present during Jesus' life on earth - When the angel appeared to Mary, the mother of Jesus, he declared: "The Holy Spirit will come upon you, and the power of the Highest will overshadow you. Therefore, the holy one to be born will be called the Son of God" (Luke 1:35). Later, at the baptism of Jesus, the Holy Spirit was present and, on this occasion, could be seen in material form. "When Jesus was baptized, He went up immediately from the water. The heavens suddenly opened for Him, and He saw the Spirit of God descending like a dove and coming down on Him" (Matthew 3:16).
- The Holy Spirit works in the lives of believers - Jesus put a lot of emphasis on the Holy Spirit. He was the subject of intense prayer: "He is the Spirit of truth, whom the world cannot receive, because it does not see Him or know *Him; but* you know Him because He remains with you and will be in you." (John 14:17). The Holy Spirit was already real and He was about to come. At that time, the Spirit dwelled with the disciples, but they lacked having Him in them. The Holy Spirit is an important figure throughout the Bible. In Genesis 1:2, we find Him moving about

the surface of the waters, and we see in Revelation 22:17; "The Spirit and the bride say, Come. And let the one who hears say, Come. And let the one who is thirsty come; let the one who desires, take the water of life without cost." From beginning to end, the Holy Spirit has always been active and He comforts us, helps us, guides us, reminds us, teaches us, comes alongside us, counsels us, and intercedes and advocates for us.
- The Holy Spirit has the power to change lives - Acts clearly states how to recognize someone full of the Spirit: "You will be My witnesses" (Acts 1:8). Love is a distinguishing mark of the disciples while being a witness distinguishes those who are full of the Spirit.

In the same way that we receive Christ without doubting whether He will enter our lives or not, we should receive the Holy Spirit by faith and believe that He will respond to our requests. It is the Holy Spirit that brings conviction of sin. He shows the offense, reveals the foolishness of the sin, points out the consequences, convinces us of guilt, and leads the sinner to repentance. As we relate to the Holy Spirit we remember, that God is Spirit and the Holy Spirit is God.

CHAPTER 3

Humanity

God created human beings to be like Him. Unlike God who is perfect, humanity is flawed and sinful. God also said that it is not good for man to be alone, so He created a woman, so that man and woman could become one, and have a relationship with each other. It is also important that individual human beings have relationships with other people, and this is the very meaning of humanity. A group of individuals socializing with one another. Humanity, or being human, is what makes us different from other beings. As humans, we are socially interactive with one another and should treat each other with kindness and compassion. EssayBasics, *Definition of Humanity,* [1] Humanity is about the connection between individuals to strengthen one another within a society, so the society can become greater than the individual parts of the society. Humanity signifies human love and kindness towards each other. Wikipedia, *Humanity.* [2]

Today we are so occupied in this busy world with day-to-day life, we don't seem to have the time to show compassion towards someone in need. Technology was developed to save time for people, but now we are even more occupied because of smartphones, social media, and other technologies. Instead of having more time to socialize, we now have less time to physically interact with one another. Our physical presence with one another is being replaced by nonphysical interactions using smartphones and computers. This makes our relationships less personal. We begin to see people through the lens of technology and not as much through personal emotional relationships.

As a society, we also categorize people into different groups. We also divided people into different races. We have been taught there are many races of people, but is this true? Some believe in many races, but others believe that all humans are only one race. The point however is defined by the question; What does it mean to be human?

Humans are highly social beings and tend to live in social structures composed of many cooperating and competing groups, from families and networks to political states. Social interactions between humans have been established based on values, social norms, and rituals. The human desire to understand and influence our environment and to explain and manipulate our surroundings have motivated humanity's development of science, philosophy, religion, and other fields of knowledge.

The human mind is capable of introspection, private thought, imagination, and forming views on our existence. This has allowed great technological advancements and complex tool development possible through reason and the transmission of knowledge to future generations.

Humans want to know who we are, where we fit in society, and who we are as individuals. We all search for purpose and meaning in our lives. We seek and search and try to find ourselves. We look at many philosophies, political parties, clubs, and religions, and many of us have taken personality tests and other assessments to discover who we truly are. So now let's take a deeper look into what it means to be human.

How Society Views Humanity

Society generally believes humans evolved from other species of hominoids in Africa between 300,000 years ago to several million years ago. Early humans were hunter-gatherers, before settling in the Fertile Crescent and other parts of the Old World. This led to the formation of permanent human settlements and the domestication of animals. As populations became larger and denser, forms of governance developed within and between communities, and several civilizations rose and fell. Humans have continued to expand, with over 7.9 billion humans occupying almost all regions of the world in October 2021.

Society has many views about what makes us human and differing views about how valuable we as humans are. The topic of human existence has been pondered for thousands of years. Ancient Greek philosophers such as Socrates, Plato, and Aristotle all theorized about the nature of human existence as have countless philosophers since. With the discovery of fossils and scientific evidence, scientists have developed theories as well. While there may be no single conclusion, there is no doubt that humans are, unique. The very act of contemplating what makes us human is unique among all the animal species. Patheos, Paul Bane, *The Nature of Our Humanity and Being.* [3]

Society and science go on to teach that humans have much in common with other mammals on earth but are most like two other living primate species: the chimpanzee and bonobo, with whom we spent the most time on the phylogenetic tree. However, as much like the chimpanzee and bonobo as we are, the differences are vast.

Apart from the obvious intellectual capabilities that distinguish us as a species, humans have several unique physical, social, biological, and emotional traits. Although we can't know precisely what is in the minds of other animals, scientists do make inferences through studies of animal behavior that inform our understanding.

From a physical viewpoint, a human is a highly developed animal. Society clings to the concept and belief in evolution. So then if evolution is true, how does evolution define the value of human life? After all, how much value can there be for something that was created by accident, or mere chance, just a random act of chemical processes behaving in just the right sequence that caused life to spring up out of inanimate material? Just one random act followed by another random act and so on progressing life from simple to more complex life forms, then eventually we humans come into existence.

A debated issue is whether human beings are self-directed. Many have argued that people do not freely choose their actions, but are conditioned through external contingencies of reinforcement. They believe that human behavior is genetically determined. Some go so far as to say that we are nothing more than machines blindly programmed to preserve the selfish molecules known as genes.

Evolution gives no significant value to humanity. Human life has no real value. There can be no purpose for humans that were created by mere chance or random chemical and biological processes. Humans are only advanced animals, as far as evolution is concerned. Through creation by chance, there can never be a purpose or meaning for human life, because humans only exist because of a non-planned accident. With this viewpoint, how can society place any kind of value on Human Beings?

In society, the value of people is often summed up by two basic things. The ability to provide materially and financially to one's family or for society, and the ability to lead and direct one's family or society. Humanity is often divided between the haves and the have nots. Can you imagine how this could make you think that you don't quite measure up to the standard of who you need to be, or what you need to produce, to be of any use to society?

Are humans merely reduced to a set of expectations they never seem to be able to live up to? If I were to ask you how much a certain celebrity was worth, you would rightly assume that I would be asking how much money they have. Is this the value we place on Human Beings?

This is the world we live in, the world that far too often dehumanizes people by a set of expectations, by what we produce, instead of on who we are.

Human nature is naturally self-consumed. We strain our necks for approval and avidly practice comparison, lacking the outward perspective required to understand who we are. We question who we are - what our value is and what our purpose is. In society, we are assigned a value that ultimately defines us, for better or worse. Again, we are either in the haves or the have nots. It's not even up to us to decide, it is defined for us by our society. Socianz, Atif Yaseen, *Humanity by Human being.* [4]

Humans go after what they think will make them happy. Even when we achieve this thing that should make us happy, we often learn that it does not make us as happy as we expected. Then we try this repeatedly and continually expect a different result. If the definition of insanity is doing the same thing repeatedly and expecting a different result, then is not the entire human race insane?

Think about the history of our species. It is the story of great wrongs, wars, massacres, and the efforts of groups to dominate or enslave other groups, interwoven with the heroic efforts of some groups to advance ethical behavior. All these acts are essentially moral. Almost every decision we make has a moral component. The question that must be asked is, where do humans come up with their moral values? Are our moral values determined by those who are in power to influence others? Is it a combination of this and what we derive based on our feelings? It appears that we are greatly influenced by those in power. For the most part, those in power determine moral values for all those they subjugate. These moral values frame and shape human society and define and direct social action.

But where should we look for guidance? Should we rely on the values of other human beings? After all, if humans are merely just advanced animals, is this a good source to rely on? Is there perhaps another higher source we could learn from? Do humans have a higher value, a higher calling, and is there a purpose to our existence and any meaning to life itself? Life, Hope, and Truth, Ron Kelley, *What is Human Nature.* [5]

How God Views Humanity

God has a completely different view of humanity that is far different than the view of society. God said, let us make man in our image, after our likeness. And let them have dominion over the fish of the sea and the birds of the heavens and the livestock and all the earth and over every creeping thing that creeps on the earth.

The fact that humans are created by God in God's image is taught in the Bible. Man did not evolve but was thoughtfully designed and created by God. If one accepts the Bible as the Word of God in other matters, one must also accept the Bible when it indicates that God is the Creator and originator of all that has been created, including humanity. Below the Bible shows just a few of the ways that God views humanity:

Human Beings are created in the image of God. As God is triune, Father, Son, and Holy Spirit, Human Beings are also triune, Body, Soul, and Spirit. God, who spoke the world into existence, wants to communicate with us. Being made in His image explains our innate desire for something more than ourselves. We're built to seek and live life in communion with Him and are called to fulfill a unique purpose. His will for our lives reflects the loving Father that He is. The Lord God formed the man from the dust of the ground and breathed into his nostrils the breath of life, and the man became a living being. As man is discussed in Scripture, it becomes evident that in addition to material and immaterial, the immaterial part of man is considered under two major aspects of spirit and soul. When humans were created, they became living beings, humans became living souls. Several hundred times in both the Old and New Testaments humans are declared to possess a soul.

The Bible claims that Human Beings possess a spirit. In Hebrews 4:12 "the Word of God is said to penetrate human consciousness to the point that it penetrates even to dividing soul and spirit." In general, the word soul seems to refer to the psychological aspect of a human or his natural experience of life. The word spirit seems to refer to his God-consciousness and his ability to function in moral and spiritual realms. However, in the Bible, these terms are sometimes used to refer to the whole human, such as the words body or soul or spirit. For instance, in Romans 12:1, believers are urged to "offer their bodies as living sacrifices to God." In referring to a believer's body, Paul is referring to the whole person. Likewise, soul sometimes refers to the whole person, and sometimes spirit refers to the whole person. Isaiah 26:9 states, "my spirit within me seeks You diligently; for when the earth experiences Your judgments. The inhabitants of the world learn righteousness." This spirit in a human is not a separate being or life. It is our nonphysical element that God put into humanity to give them intellect greater than that of animals, but far less than that of God. The Bible speaks of another spirit the Holy Spirit which makes possible a relationship between humanity and God. "The Spirit Himself bears witness with our spirit that we are children of God" (Romans 8:16).

Human Beings were made with the capacity to interact with God, his Creator. Humans can receive in their mind and spirit God's Holy Spirit, which makes them a child of God. The result of that conversion is becoming a born child of God, composed of spirit, and living eternally as a member of the very family of God. "Not by might nor by power, but by My Spirit" (Zechariah 4:6). We are given the Holy Spirit and the Holy Spirit will guide us to truth, and help us obey, empowering us to do good works. Genesis 1:27 says that "the first Human Beings were made in God's image" and therefore created very intelligent. The early chapters of Genesis tell us that Adam and Eve were moral beings who could communicate with God and each other, rationalize, name things, and work. Their descendants were gardeners, musicians, builders, and metal workers. Man was made in the image of an intelligent, moral, and creative God. This means that Human Beings have the essential qualities of personality, which are intellect or mind, sensibility or feeling, and will, that is, the ability to make moral choices. These qualities do not exist in any creature other than humans, but they make it possible for us to have communion with God and to be morally responsible for our actions.

Other characteristics of human beings mentioned in the Bible include: mind, will, and conscience. While the body of a Christian is considered sinful, it, nevertheless, is referred to in Scripture as "the temple of the Holy Spirit" (1 Corinthians 6:19). The bodies of Christians should be kept under control and made to submit to the human mind.

Human Beings were created in greatness but soon rebelled against God. We had the potential for true greatness but we threw it away. We chose to abandon God's will and follow our own will. No one is righteous. In Romans 3:10–11 it is stated, "none is righteous, no not one; no one understands; no one seeks for God." The ultimate evil of human sin is the belittling of the glory of God by exchanging that glory for lesser things. There is a tremendous difference between what we were created to be and what we have become. But despite all our shortcomings, God has set us apart, through the works of Jesus Christ, our sins have been forgiven and we, who believe in Christ, will one day be restored to our past glory. The bodies of Christians, which now are corrupt and sinful, are going to be transformed, cleansed from sin, and made new like the resurrection body of Christ at the time of the resurrection. Though humans in their present humanity are sinful and come short of what God would have them to be and do, Christians can look forward to the time when their bodies will be made perfect in the presence of God. Paul describes the whole process of the transition of Christians from mortal human flesh to immortal spirit: "Now this I say, brethren, that flesh and blood cannot inherit the kingdom of God; nor does corruption inherit incorruption. Behold, I tell you a mystery: We shall not all sleep, but we shall all be changed in a moment, in the twinkling of an eye, at the last trumpet. For the trumpet will sound, and the dead will be raised incorruptible, and we shall be changed. For this corruptible must put on incorruption and this mortal must put on immortality" (1 Corinthians 15:50–53). We humans are not a finished product. Today as we live on earth, we are mortal and will eventually die. However, the scriptures tell us that our current condition is only temporary. We will be changed, our mortal bodies will one day change to immortal bodies. Our bodies will no longer decay or grow old. Our new bodies will last forever.

Human Beings are loved by God. "But God, being rich in mercy, because of His great love and with which He loved us, even when we were dead in our transgressions, made us alive together with Christ (by grace you have been saved)" (Ephesians 2:4–5). "Know therefore that the

LORD your God is God; He is the faithful God, keeping his covenant of love to a thousand generations of those who love Him and keep His commandments" (Deuteronomy 7:9). "But God demonstrates his love for us in this: While we were still sinners, Christ died for us" (Romans 5:8). "See what great love the Father has lavished on us, that we should be called children of God!" (1 John 3:1). And that is what we are! "I have been crucified with Christ and I no longer live, but Christ lives in me. The life I now live in the body, I live by faith in the Son of God, who loved me and gave himself for me" (Galatians 2:20). "We love because He first loved us" (1 John 4:19). In my great love, I gave my unique Son, that "all those who believe in Him will not perish but have everlasting life" (John 3:16). "But God demonstrates His own love toward us, in that while we were still sinners, Christ died for us." (Romans 5:8). Sin doesn't have the last word. Grace does (Romans 5:20). "The glory which You have given Me I also have given to them, so that they may be one, just as We are one; I in them and You in Me, that they may be perfected in unity, so that the world may know that You sent Me, and You loved them, just as You loved Me." (John 17:22–23).

Human Beings are valuable to God. God says, "I am the Creator and you are my creation. I breathed into your nostrils the breath of life. I created you in my image. My eyes saw your unformed substance" (Psalm 139:16). "I knit you together in your mother's womb" (Psalm 139:13). "I know the number of hairs on your head, and before a word is on your tongue, I know it" (Matthew 10:30). You are fearfully and wonderfully made (Psalm 139:14). For we are God's masterpiece. "He has created us anew in Christ Jesus, so we can do the good things He planned for us long ago" (Ephesians 2:10). "I have crowned you with glory and honor as the pinnacle and final act of the six days of creation" (Psalm 8:5).

Human Beings were created to live forever. "As you seek me and see more of my glory, I am transforming you into the image of my Son" (2 Corinthians 3:18). "One day you will be changed, in a moment, in the twinkling of an eye, at the last trumpet sound" (1 Corinthians 15:52). "When Jesus appears, you will be like Him, because you shall see Him as He is" (1 John 3:2). You will be delivered from your body of death through Jesus Christ, and your dwelling place will be with me. "And I will wipe away every tear from your eyes, and death shall be no more, neither shall there be mourning, nor crying, nor pain anymore" (Revelation 21:4). "You will drink from the spring of the water of life without payment, and

I will make for you a feast of rich food and well-aged wine" (Revelation 21:6). "You will enter my rest, inherit the kingdom I've prepared for you, and step into the fullness of joy and pleasures forevermore" (Hebrews 4:9–11). But most of all, "they will see His face, and His name *will be* on their foreheads." (Revelation 22:4).

Human Beings have a purpose. "Therefore, walk in a manner worthy of your calling" (Ephesians 4:1). "You are no longer darkness, but light in my Son. Walk as children of light" (Ephesians 5:8). "You are the light of the world, a city set on a hill. I have called you" (2 Peter 1:3). I have chosen you (Revelation 17:14). You are now a saint, a servant, a steward, and a soldier. You are a witness and a worker. Through Jesus you are victorious (1 Corinthians 15:57). You have a glorious future. You are a citizen of Heaven (Philippians 3:20). You are an ambassador for my Son (2 Corinthians 5:20). "But you are a chosen people, a royal priesthood, a holy nation, God's special possession, that you may declare the praises of Him who called you out of the darkness into his wonderful light" (1 Peter 2:9). "For I know the plans I have for you, declares the Lord, plans to prosper you and not to harm you, plans to give you hope and a future" (Jeremiah 29:11).

Human Beings are redeemed. Perhaps redeemed is the best way to describe how God sees us. Salvation is not a reward for the good things we have done, so none of us can boast about it. God says we are not the mistakes that threaten to define us but the biblical truth that proves our actual worth. We are created by Love to love as we walk with Love. We exist to make His name known. He desires to walk along beside us, blessing us, and filling our lives with more than we can ask for or imagine. Only by drawing close to Him, with a life prioritized to put Him first, will we see who we truly are.

Human Beings, like Jesus, are obedient to the Father's will and about His Father's business. Like Christ, the godly person will shun sin and follow righteousness. They will, in the power of the Spirit, seek to keep God's law and live in God's will. They will endeavor to accomplish God's will, whatever the cost. They will be a person of the Word, using Scripture to overcome temptation. They will be a person of prayer and a person of love and sacrifice. "Be on your guard; stand firm in the faith; be people of courage; be strong. Do everything in love" (1 Corinthians 16:13–14). According to these verses, a true human is vigilant against danger, faithful to the truth, brave in the face of opposition, persistent through trials, and, above all, loving.

Human Beings are far more valuable than anything else that God has created. We were created by God to provide God with pleasure. We are ultimately special to God. God loves us unconditionally, far more than you could ever imagine. Don't let the world define your value. Your value is defined by God and God alone. Who can put a value on you when the Most-High God made you? Will you choose to live God's version of your life? Have you taken advantage of God's grace and mercy to make your life right before God? Are you living life to the fullest? Every day we must choose to be a new creation in Christ. 2 Corinthians 5:17 says, "Therefore, if anyone is in Christ, the new creation has come: The old has gone, the new is here!"

This is the key to seeing and understanding the value we as Human Beings have, not just for Christians but for all the people in the world. We must see our value considering what Jesus did to save us! Let's remember how much value we have in God's eyes! And remember to be kind and loving to all the people in this world because of what Jesus has done for us, and the great worth He has placed on us all.

SECTION 2
Worldviews and Beliefs

CHAPTER 4

Worldviews

There are many ways in which we view our surroundings and the world around us. From these different worldviews, we form our values, perspectives, and philosophies on everything that exists and matters to us.

This worldview forms our opinions on how we judge people and ourselves, the world, the universe, our politics, religious beliefs, and almost every aspect of life that we choose to follow. It reflects how we would answer all the big questions of life, like human existence: essential questions about who we are, where we came from, why we're here, and where we're headed. From this worldview, we attain the meaning and purpose of life, the nature of the afterlife, and what counts as a good life. All About Worldview, *The Meaning of Life.*"[1] Few people think through these issues very deeply, except on rare occasions, but a person's worldview will lead us toward the questions and answers we accept or deny, and the decisions we make as to how we view the world and attain our values and opinions.

Worldviews impact what we see and how we see it. Depending on the color of the lenses, some things may be seen more easily, some things we see may be more distorted, and some things may not even be seen at all.

Worldviews also determine people's opinions on matters of morals, ethics, and politics. What a person thinks about abortion, euthanasia, same-sex relationships, environmental ethics, economic policy, public education, and so on will depend on this underlying worldview more than anything else.

As such, worldviews play a central role in all our lives. They shape what we believe and what we're willing to believe, how we interpret our experiences, and what we see happening around us. These worldviews even impact the way we act within society towards one another. Our thoughts and our actions are conditioned by the worldview we chose to accept.

Worldviews can operate at both the individual level and the collective societal level. Rarely will two people have the same worldview, but they may share the same basic type of worldview. Western civilization since around the fourth century has been dominated by a Christian worldview, even though there have been individuals and groups who have challenged it. But in the last couple of centuries, for reasons ranging from the technological to the theological, the Christian worldview has lost its dominance, and competing worldviews have become far more prominent. There are many worldviews in our society, so let us look at some of the most common. Ligonier, R.C. Sproul, *Christian Worldview*.[2]

Worldviews of Society

To understand our society, it is important to understand the different worldviews within our society. Our society has many different viewpoints and by looking at these worldviews, we can learn what influences our society into believing and following what it does. Even many Christians can fall into the trap of following these worldviews, even though they are vastly different than the teachings of God and the Bible. Society and Biblical beliefs may sometimes have many things in common, and at other times have viewpoints and beliefs that are extremely far apart. Often, what we all believe in results from receiving false information, misinformation, or just a lack of understanding. However, if you do see yourself as a Christian, and discover that you agree with one of the worldviews of society and not the Christian Biblical worldview, then perhaps this section will provide a chance to reevaluate what you believe. These ideas creep into our belief systems and we believe them because they sound rational or good-hearted, so we accept them without question. We all need the opportunity to take a step back and reevaluate our views and beliefs. To do this we need to understand these worldviews that are valued in the society we live in.

WHAT'S YOUR WORLDVIEW?

START HERE → **God exists**

- YES → **more than one God exists**
  - YES → **POLYTHEIST**
  - NO → **God exists independently of the world**
    - YES → **God is in everything in the world**
      - YES → **PANTHEIST**
      - NO → **the world is a part of God**
        - YES → **PANENTHEIST**
        - NO → **What is God's relationship to the world**
    - NO → **God is in everything in the world**
- DON'T KNOW → **AGNOSTIC**
- DON'T CARE → **APATHEIST**
- NO → **ATHEIST**

God is in control of the world now
- YES → **God is involved in the world**
  - YES → **THEIST** → **God can be known personally**
    - YES → **God made himself known in the world through the man Jesus Christ**
      - YES → **salvation is found only through faith in the death and resurrection of Jesus Christ**
        - YES → **CHRISTIAN THEIST**
        - NO → **How are you saved?**
      - NO → **How do you know God?**
    - NO → **meaning is found in experience**
      - YES → **EXISTENTIALIST**
  - NO → **DEIST**
- NO → **POLYTHEIST** / **DEIST**

meaning is found in the world
- YES → **meaning is found in humanity**
  - YES → **HUMANIST**
  - NO → **meaning is found in nature**
    - YES → **NATURALIST**
    - NO → **meaning is found by each individual**
      - YES → **RELATIVIST**
      - NO → **Where do you find meaning?**
- NO → **NIHILIST**

DON'T KNOW → **AGNOSTIC**

By Cameron Blair © 2010 FEVA Ministries Inc.

CHAPTER 5

Humanism

Humanism is a worldview that consists of many different ideas, values, and philosophies, that emphasize humanity as the focal point of thought and reason. Humanism focuses on human values and morality rather than a religious experience and humanity is more important than following any religion. The conviction of sharing and caring for other human beings is the stated priority of humanism. A true humanist does not believe in a particular religion and does not believe in God. American Humanist Association, Fred Edwords, *What Is Humanism?* [1]

The American Humanist Association defines Humanism on their website as; Humanism is a progressive philosophy of life that, without theism and other supernatural beliefs, affirms our ability and responsibility to lead ethical lives of personal fulfillment that aspire to the greater good of humanity.

Secular Humanism has two dimensions: (one) The critical negative dimension, the freethinking dimension of atheism, criticizing religion, the pseudoscientific, and paranormal; and (two) A philosophy of life, an ethic, political, and social framework for a better and more just world in which individuals can flourish and be happy.

Humanism shares some beliefs with Postmodernism and Marxism. In a Secular Humanist worldview:

- There is no God, no self-existing being. There is no revelation from God.

- There is no spirit. People are highly evolved animals but do not have immortal souls. There is no life after death.
- There is only this physical world; the here and now. Nature/matter is self-existing.
- Only things which can be proved through the scientific method are accepted as true. Science is in essence a god.
- Religion is viewed to be harmful, suppressing individual freedom, and is therefore aggressively opposed.
- Morals are based on human experience and needs, not on revelation from God. Morals are situational and not absolute.
- All forms of sexual expression between consenting adults are acceptable.
- Abortion for any cause and euthanasia is acceptable.
- Self-realization is the highest goal of each human.
- Humans are viewed as inherently perfectible.
- Religion is preventing people from fulfilling their full potential.

Secular Humanists claim that for the first time in human history, a significant percentage of the world's population no longer believes in God. This is especially true in developed nations, where some society's nonbelievers now outnumber believers. Over the past century, Secular Humanists have published six different declarations or manifestos (and numerous books and articles) which describe their human-centered and human-made religion/worldview.

- Humanist Manifesto I (1933)
- Humanist Manifesto II (1973)
- A Secular Humanist Declaration (1980)
- A Declaration of Interdependence (1988)
- Humanist Manifesto 2000
- Humanist Manifesto III (2003)

These declarations can easily be found on the internet. Secular humanism is fighting against biblical Christianity, and as they have stated, they have indeed made huge inroads into replacing Christian values in society. Whereas Christian thinking once dominated the public education system, today the Christian God, prayer, Bible study, and biblical creation have all been eliminated from our public education system. Yes, this is now the worldview that is being taught in all the public-school systems in the country. Students, even those from church homes, are being trained in a secular (anti-God) religion. They are being indoctrinated to believe that the universe and all that exists within it, can be explained without God.

If the Humanist view of the Bible is correct, millions of Bible believers and churchgoers are wasting their time, money, and energy. Humanity's condition could be greatly improved if those resources were used for solving the world's problems instead of worshiping a nonexistent God.

Humanists claim that they are not religious, but don't be deceived. They are very much religious, turning their worldview into something that should be worshipped. They have bought into the religion of humanism. Difference Between, Hasa, *Difference Between Humanism and Secularism*. [2]

Humanist organizations can also receive a tax-exempt status (the same as a Christian church in the United States and the United Kingdom), and they even have religious documents like the Humanist Manifesto. Surprisingly, this religion has free rein in state schools, museums, and media under the guise of neutrality, seeking to fool people into thinking it is not a religion. The truth is however that humanism is just another religion.

The Humanist's goal is to remove God from society at every level and to have all people believe that there is no God. If you are a Christian and not alarmed by this it is most tragic. Our goal as Christians is to save all humankind so they all may acquire eternal life. The humanist goal, if achieved, would destroy all humankind. And we are certainly as a society moving closer to this daily.

Humanists may reject the concept of God ruling over us but they do support the idea of some humans ruling over other humans. Someone must establish order, either God or Man. Would you prefer to be ruled by a just and loving God, or by imperfect and self-centered humans? Humanists claim they want what is best for humanity but, they are condemning all humanity into an eternal existence without God.

CHAPTER 6

Atheism

Atheism is the belief that God does not exist. Humanism is just another word society uses for Atheism. Humanism and Atheism are almost the same but there are a few differences.

Atheists are people that in effect reject all religions. An atheist is a person who does not believe in the existence of a god or a supreme being. Atheism claims that Christians must prove that God exists before they will consider believing in God. Would you base your entire eternal existence on the fact that we as humans have only limited access to this immense universe? Physically, we have only been on earth and the moon, nowhere else in the entire universe. Yet atheists have seen enough to feel comfortable believing that there is no God. That's just not logical. Atheism is built on emotional decisions, not on logic. This line of reasoning is flawed and made without scientific validity. Difference Between, Hasa, *Difference Between Humanism and Secularism.* [1]

Our educational system has for years not been allowed to mention God in the public classroom. This has been the law ever since 1962 in "Engel v. Vitale" a case against New York's Regents prayer, and 1963 when a case originated by a Philadelphia area man named Ed Schempp challenging mandatory Bible reading in Pennsylvania schools reached the Supreme Court. At the same time, Murray O'Hair was challenging a similar practice, the recitation of the Lord's Prayer in Maryland public schools. The Supreme Court consolidated the cases and in 1963 ruled eight to one that devotional Bible reading or other government-sponsored religious activities in public schools are unconstitutional. Since 1964 every child in America has grown up without learning Christian values in our public schools and has not been taught anything about God or the Bible. No wonder atheism is growing rapidly in this country. The values children have been taught and have learned are completely different than the Christian values the country had before the early 1960s. Today children grow up learning the values and beliefs of humans. Human's values, not God's moral values are now the general belief system for our society. The two are quite different and will determine the direction in which we are headed as a society.

CHAPTER 7

Agnosticism

Agnosticism is hardly a belief system because agnostics admit that they don't know if God exists are not. When the conversation turns to religion, many state their position with terms like skeptic, atheist, or agnostic.

The term agnostic is derived from two Greek words: a, meaning no, and gnosis, meaning knowledge. Often agnostics apply this lack of knowledge to the existence of God. In this case, an agnostic does not affirm or deny the existence of God. There are two basic forms of agnosticism. The weak form claims that God is not known. This view holds onto the possibility that God may be known. The strong form of agnosticism claims that God is unknowable. This form says God cannot be known by anyone.

The two most influential thinkers to advance the philosophy of agnosticism were David Hume (1711-1976) and Immanuel Kant (1724-1804). While Hume was technically a skeptic, his arguments inevitably lead to agnosticism.

An agnostic neither believes nor disbelieves in a god or religious doctrine. Agnostics assert that it is impossible for human beings to know anything about how the universe was created and whether divine beings exist. All About Philosophy, *Agnostic.* [1]

CHAPTER 8

Moral Relativism

Everything is relative, all values and morals are up to everyone to determine. There is no absolute truth, everyone determines what is true for them. Karma is another term we use to describe Moral Relativism. Since everyone is divine in the New Age, they need only get in touch with the universal god consciousness within to act morally. Every mindset and action are justified – with the notable exception of adhering to a worldview that believes in moral absolutes (such a view supposedly stunts a person's ethical progress).

The aspect of karma says that a person's actions in this life determine the person's destiny for the next life. Moral relativism is used to describe several philosophical positions concerned with the differences in moral judgments. An advocate of such ideas is often labeled simply as a relativist. Moral Relativism holds that people do disagree fundamentally about what is moral, with no judgment being expressed on the desirability of this. In such disagreements, nobody is objectively right or wrong but everyone ought to tolerate the behavior of others even when disagreements about the morality of things exist.

Moral relativism has been debated for thousands of years and arguments have been made in areas such as ancient Greece and historical India while discussions have continued to the present day. The concept has additionally attracted attention in diverse fields including art, religion, and science.

At the heart of Moral relativism, the view is that ethical standards, morality, and positions of right or wrong are culturally based and therefore subject to a person's individual choice. We can all decide what is right for ourselves. You decide what's right for you, and I'll decide what's right for me. Moral relativism says, it's true only if I believe it.

Moral relativism has steadily been accepted as one of the primary moral philosophies of modern society, a culture that was previously governed by a Judea Christian view of morality. While these Judea Christian standards continue to be the foundation for civil law, most people hold to the concept that right or wrong are not absolutes, but can be determined by everyone. Morals and ethics can be altered from one situation, person, or circumstance to the next. Essentially, moral relativism says that anything goes, because life is ultimately without meaning. Words like ought and should are rendered meaningless.

In describing her view on morality, the President of Planned Parenthood Federation of America once stated, " ... teaching morality doesn't mean imposing my moral values on others. It means sharing wisdom, giving reasons for believing as I do - and then trusting others to think and judge for themselves." Quoted from Stephen Law, *Relativism or Authoritarianism – you choose.*" [1] She claims to be morally neutral, yet her message is intended to influence the thinking of others ... an intention that is not, in fact, neutral.

Evidence that moral relativism is seen as more fair or neutral than a hardline stance on morality is seen in a 2002 column from Fox News analyst Bill O'Reilly, who asked, "Why is it wrong to be right?" In his article, O'Reilly cites recent Zogby poll findings regarding what is being taught in American universities. Studies indicate that 75% of American college professors currently teach that there is no such thing as right and wrong. Rather, they treat the questions of good and evil as relative to individual values and cultural diversity. The problem with this, according to O'Reilly, is that "they see the world not as it is, but as they want it to be." Moral Relativism, Bill O'Reilly, *Moral Relativism.* [2]

Anything you do is okay, because it ultimately doesn't matter. Moral relativism says anything goes ... but does it? After all we all have standards on how we want to be treated by others, and how we treat others! We all believe in some form of fairness. We are appealing to standard of behavior we expect the other person to know about. Where do you think that standard originates?

In his September 19, 1796 Farewell Address to the nation, George Washington stated: "Of all the dispositions and habits which lead to political prosperity, Religion and morality are indispensable supports. George Washington, *Farewell Address to the nation,* September 19, 1796. [3] In vain would that man claim the tribute of patriotism, who should labor to subvert these great pillars." William McGuffey, the author of *McGuffey's Readers, McGuffey's 5th Eclectic Reader* (1879), [4] which was the mainstay of America's public school system from 1836 till the 1920s, wrote: "Erase all thought and fear of God from a community, and selfishness and sensuality would absorb the whole man." Where do you think the world is heading today?

CHAPTER 9

Naturalism

Naturalism is another belief that supports the view that there is no God. Humans are just highly evolved animals and the universe is a closed physical system. Naturalism is the idea or belief that only natural laws and forces exist and that there are no supernatural or spiritual events that operate in the universe. Supporters of naturalism assert that natural laws are the only rules that govern the structure and behavior of the natural world and that the changing universe is at every stage a product of these laws. Wikipedia, *Naturalism*.[1]

As the name implies, this tendency consists essentially in looking upon nature as the one original and fundamental source of all that exists, and in attempting to explain everything in terms of nature. The limits of nature are also the limits of existing reality or at least the first cause. All events find their explanation within nature itself. The Spiritual Life, *Naturalism*.[2]

According to philosopher David Papineau, naturalism can be separated into an ontological sense and a methodological sense. David Papineau, *Naturalism: Ontological and Methodological philosophies.*[3] Ontological refers to ontology, the philosophical study of what exists. On an ontological level, philosophers often treat naturalism as equivalent to materialism. For example, philosopher Paul Kurtz argues in, The Spiritual Life, *Naturalism in Philosophy,*[4] that nature is best accounted for by reference to material principles. These principles include mass, energy, and other physical and chemical properties accepted by the scientific community. Further, this sense of naturalism holds that spirits, deities, and ghosts are not real and that there is no purpose in nature.

Some have argued that the success of naturalism in science meant that scientific methods should also be used in philosophy. According to this view, science and philosophy are not always distinct from one another but instead form a continuum. Naturalism is a philosophy that maintains that; nature encompasses all that exists throughout space and time; nature (the universe or cosmos) consists only of natural elements, that is, temporal physical substance mass and energy. Nonphysical or quasi-physical substances, such as information, ideas, values, logic, mathematics, intellect, and other emergent phenomena, either supervene upon the physical or can be reduced to a physical account; nature operates by the laws of physics and in principle, can be explained and understood by science and philosophy; the supernatural does not exist, only nature is real. Naturalism is therefore a metaphysical philosophy. As Carl Sagan succinctly put it in *RNS Religion News Service*, Kimberly Winston, "The Cosmos is all that is or ever was or ever will be." [5]

CHAPTER 10

Pantheism

God and the universe are one. We are all divine by nature. According to the World Pantheism website, pantheism.net, Pantheism focuses on saving the planet rather than saving souls. It respects the rights of humans, and of all living beings. It encourages you to make the most and best of your one life here. It values reason and the scientific method over adherence to ancient scriptures.

Pantheism is the view that God is identical to the cosmos, the view that there exists nothing which is outside of God, or else negatively the rejection of any view that considers God as distinct from the universe. Wikipedia, *Pantheism*. [1]

The term 'pantheism' is a modern one, first appearing in the writing of the Irish freethinker John Toland (1705) and constructed from the Greek roots pan (all) and Theos (God). Even though the name is new, the ideas are very old according to, World Pantheism, *Toland: father of modern pantheism*. [2]

Pantheism also believes that reality is identical to divinity, or that all things compose God. Pantheist belief does not recognize a distinct personal god but instead characterizes a broad range of doctrines differing between reality and divinity. Pantheistic concepts date back thousands of years, and pantheistic elements have been identified in various religious traditions. The term pantheism was coined by mathematician Joseph Raphson in 1697 and has since been used to describe the beliefs of a variety of people and organizations.

Pantheism was popularized in Western culture as a theology and philosophy based on the work of the 17th-century philosopher Baruch Spinoza his book *Ethics*. [3] A pantheistic stance was also taken in the 16th century by philosopher and cosmologist Giordano Bruno. Ideas resembling pantheism existed in South and East Asian religions before the 18th century (notably Sikhism, Hinduism, Sanamahism, Confucianism, and Taoism). These are the elements that make up the Pantheist statement:

- We revere and celebrate the Universe as the totality of being, past, present, and future. It is self-organizing, ever-evolving, and inexhaustibly diverse. Its overwhelming power, beauty, and mystery compel the deepest human reverence and wonder.
- All matter, energy, and life are an interconnected unity of which we are an inseparable part. We rejoice in our existence and seek to participate ever more deeply in this unity through knowledge, celebration, meditation, empathy, love, ethical action, and art.
- We are an integral part of Nature, which we should cherish, revere, and preserve in all its magnificent beauty and diversity. We should strive to live in harmony with Nature locally and globally. We acknowledge the inherent value of all life, human and nonhuman, and strive to treat all living beings with compassion and respect.
- All humans are equal centers of awareness of the Universe and nature, and all deserve a life of equal dignity and mutual respect. To this end, we support and work towards freedom, democracy, justice, and nondiscrimination, and a world community based on peace, sustainable ways of life, full respect for human rights, and an end to poverty.
- There is a single kind of substance, energy/matter, which is vibrant and infinitely creative in all its forms. Body and mind are indivisibly united.
- We see death as the return to the nature of our elements, and the end of our existence as individuals. The forms of afterlife available to humans are natural ones, in the natural world. Our actions, our ideas, and memories of us live on, according to what we do in our lives. Our genes live on in our families, and our elements are endlessly recycled in nature.

- We honor reality, and keep our minds open to the evidence of the senses and of science's unending quest for deeper understanding. These are our best means of coming to know the Universe, and on them, we base our aesthetic and religious feelings on reality.
- Every individual has direct access through perception, emotion, and meditation to ultimate reality, which is the Universe and Nature. There is no need for mediation by priests, gurus, or revealed scriptures.

CHAPTER 11

Other Worldviews

Other worldviews from, All About Worldview *"Worldview* [1] include:

- Non-naturalism: Because New Agers believe God is in everything, and everything is a part of God, they must conclude that everything, in essence, is spiritual. The things that we can see and feel are only a manifestation of spirit, and all matter will melt away when universal consciousness is achieved. This view leads the New Ager to believe all matter can be controlled by an enlightened mind, one that is in touch with the god within. Health, wealth, relationships, etc. are all perceived as the result of mind over matter. In essence, we are all gods.
- Postmodernism: there are no objective truths and moral standards; reality is ultimately a human social construction.
- Pluralism: the different world religions represent equally valid perspectives on the ultimate reality; there are many valid paths to salvation.
- Cosmic Evolution: The New Age worldview sees humanity as evolving from disharmony to harmony until evolution has guided people out of the material into becoming completely spiritual beings. Evolution is central to New Age doctrine because it ensures humanity's eventual progression to godhood.
- Higher Consciousness: Society and the environment, according to the New Age worldview, stifle our knowledge of the God

within. Thus, the aim of psychology should be to cause everyone to realize that they are fundamentally perfect and therefore should trust their intuitive urges. According to the New Age doctrine, a human's true self would never urge them to contribute in any way to disunity.
- Nontraditional Family, Church, and State: To explain the all-too-obvious evil done by humans, the New Ager resorts to blaming traditional society – especially the central principles of Western Civilization. Various New Age leaders blame different aspects: technology, male-dominant norms (including those of the traditional family), the free enterprise system, a central government, and dogmatic monotheistic religions. This results in a rebellion against all traditional values without examining their reason for existence.
- Self-Law: Individual autonomy means each person gets to decide what is right and act for themself. Any need for laws and legislation will quickly fade away as we grow closer to achieving God-consciousness. The unenlightened people who still believe humanity is inherently evil require laws, but once this outdated concept is exposed as a lie the world will function in complete harmony.
- Self-Government (New World Order): As with law, the need for politics and government only exists because some individuals refuse to get in touch with their true selves. The trend toward a one-world government is perceived by New Agers as a positive sign that we are evolving away from our need for government toward spiritual unity or finding the oneness with everything that is the real basis of all spirituality.
- Universal Enlightened Production: Traditional economic forms act as a hindrance to individual enlightenment because they emphasize only the material. This does not mean, however, that New Agers should not have possessions; rather, whatever is necessary for the happiness of New Agers will automatically flow toward them, if they stay true to the voice within. Mind over matter becomes a way of life; if you are in harmony with the spiritual realm, you can control the ebb and flow of material gain.
- Evolutionary Godhead: According to the New Age worldview, evolution is constantly moving humanity toward

God-consciousness. New Agers is assured by the scientific fact of evolution, that human and all reality are progressing toward unified enlightenment. The fittest already recognize this; the unfit are the Christians and other proponents of dogmatic worldviews (who act as a hindrance to evolutionary forces).

As you can see there are many worldviews to choose from, and there are many more not listed here. Each of these worldviews has profound implications for how people think about themselves, what behaviors they consider right or wrong, and how they orient their lives. Christians must recognize that many people will have different worldviews than ours, and we must be able to understand these worldviews and effectively communicate with the people who follow these worldviews. Christians need to understand the fundamental differences between these worldviews from the Christian worldview and make a well-reasoned case that the Christian worldview alone is true. Ligonier, R.C. Sproul, *Worldviews in Conflict.* [2]

CHAPTER 12

The Christian Worldview

If you're a Christian, the Christian or Biblical worldview is the worldview you agree with and choose to follow. Or at least it should be! If you're a Christian and follow one of the other worldviews we already mentioned, then perhaps reading this next section should persuade you to re-examine your viewpoint. After all, shouldn't a Christian believe in and follow the Christian worldview? The Christian worldview is far different than all of society's worldviews but does that make it any better, or is it rational or logical? A Christian worldview would include the concept of faith. However, many people have the impression that Christians live in two worlds, the world of faith and the world of reason. The world of faith is the realm that Christians live in on Sunday morning, or the world to which they refer when asked about spiritual or moral matters. However, Christians live in the world of reason throughout the rest of the week when dealing with practical, everyday matters. After all, do we need to believe in the Bible to put gasoline in the car, or to balance our checkbook?

The concept of faith versus reason is an extremely false idea that many people believe is the world Christians live in. It's entirely possible to live with both faith and reason, the two should not exclude the other. Faith is not the enemy of reason, nor is reason the enemy of faith. They can both co-exist incredibly well with one another. Biblical faith and reason work very well together in the Christian worldview. However, the problem seems to be that many people have a misunderstanding of faith. Faith is not a belief in unbelievable, unreasonable ideas, or a belief in something simply for the sake of believing it. Instead, faith is having confidence in something that we have not perceived with the senses. This is the biblical definition of faith, and follows from Hebrews 11:1 which says, "Faith shows the reality of what we hope for; it is the evidence of things we cannot see." Whenever we have confidence in something that we cannot see, hear, taste, smell, or touch, we are acting upon a type of faith. All people have faith, even if it is not saving faith in God. For example, people believe in laws of logic. When people use laws of logic, they have confidence in something they cannot observe with the senses; this is a type of faith.

When we have confidence that the universe will operate in the future as it has in the past, we are acting on faith. For example, we all presume that gravity will work the same next Friday as it does today. But no one has observed the future. So, we all believe in something that goes beyond sensory experience. From a Christian perspective, this is a very reasonable belief. God (who is beyond time) has promised us that He will uphold the universe in a consistent way. So, we have a good reason for our faith in the uniformity of nature. For the consistent Christian, reason, and faith go together.

It is appropriate and biblical to have a good reason for our faith. Indeed, God encourages us to reason (Isaiah 1:18). The apostle Paul reasoned with those in the synagogue and those in the marketplace (Acts 17:17). According to the Scriptures, the Christian faith is not a blind faith. It is a faith that is rationally defensible. It is logical and self-consistent. It can make sense of what we experience in the world. Moreover, the Christian has a moral obligation to think rationally. "We are to be imitators of God" (Ephesians 5:1), patterning our thinking after His revelation). Compelling Truth, *"Christian Worldview - What is it?* [1]

Some would challenge the rationality of the biblical worldview. Some say that the Christian worldview is illogical. After all, the Bible speaks of floating ax heads, the sun going backward, a universe created in six days, an earth that has pillars and corners, people walking on water, light before the sun, a talking serpent, a talking donkey, and a senior citizen taking two of every land animal on a big boat! The critic suggests that no rational person can believe in such things in our modern age of scientific enlightenment. He claims that to believe in such things would be illogical.

The Bible does make some extraordinary claims. But are such claims truly illogical? Do they violate any laws of logic? Some biblical criticisms involve a misuse of language: taking figures of speech like; pillars of the earth, as though these were literal when this is not the case. This is an error on the part of the critic, not an error in the text. Poetic sections of the Bible, such as the psalms, and figures of speech should be taken as such. To do otherwise is academically dishonest.

Most of the criticisms against the Bible's legitimacy turn out to be nothing more than a subjective opinion of what is possible. The critic arbitrarily asserts that the sun can't go backward in the sky, or for the solar system to be created in six days. But what is his evidence for this? He might argue that such things cannot happen based on known natural laws. With this, we agree. But who said that natural laws are the limit of what is possible? The biblical God is not bound by natural laws. Since the Bible is indeed correct about the nature of God, then there is no problem at all in God changing the rotation of the earth, or creating the solar system in six days. An infinitely powerful, all-knowing God can do anything that is rationally possible.

A worldview must come to grips with the three following questions:

- Where did we come from and why are we here?
- Why is there something wrong with the world?
- Can what be wrong with the world be fixed?

Different worldviews answer these three core questions very differently. Let's compare the Christian worldview with the naturalistic worldview on the three questions.

A naturalistic worldview would answer the three questions above as follows:

- We are the result of purposeless acts of nature.
- We are what is wrong with the world, as we do not respect nature.
- The world can be saved through environmentalism, conservation, and us coming to terms with our true nature.

The Christian worldview would answer the same questions in a completely different way:

- God created humanity in His image so we could have a meaningful relationship with Him and God put us on earth to rule over it.
- We sinned against God, subjecting ourselves and the world to the curse of evil, decay, and death (Romans 8:22).
- God became a human being and sacrificed Himself to pay the penalty for sin and to one day restore creation to a perfect state (2 Corinthians 5:21).

A Christian worldview should result in adherence to moral absolutes and belief in miracles, the value of human life, and the possibility of forgiveness and redemption. Our worldview affects how we spend money, how we treat our spouses and children, who we vote for, how we treat nature, and what we choose to do with our time. A true and complete Christian worldview is not something that can exist only at church on Sundays. There is no separating a Christian worldview from everyday life. Jesus, Himself is to be our worldview. Forming our worldview on His life and teachings is the only way to navigate through this world. That is what a Christian worldview is all about.

A well-developed worldview considers the existence of God (Person or force?), the origin of the universe (intelligent creation or accidental random creation?), human existence (where we came from and what we are?), the purpose of life (do we exist for a reason or by chance?), human morals (value absolute or relative?), the problem of evil (is evil real or merely a construct of the mind?), and the future (Heaven/hell or nothing?). A biblical worldview answers all these concerns.

Every worldview operates with some faith assumptions. Even atheists have faith, most of them believe the universe began with a spontaneous bang and that everything is the product of matter, motion, time, and chance. The Christian worldview operates by faith, and our faith is rooted in Scripture which provides insights into realities we could never know, except that God has spoken. By faith, we understand that the worlds were prepared by the word of God so that what is seen was not made from things which are visible. The final objective of a biblical worldview is love for God, love for others, and submission to the Lordship of Jesus Christ. This is the starting point of a Christian worldview? Ligonier, R. C. Sproul, *What is a Christian Worldview?*[2]

- God Does Exist: Hebrews 11:6 states, "and without faith, it is impossible to please Him, for whoever would draw near to God must believe that He exists and that He rewards those who seek Him." God does exist and He is the standard by which we measure everything else. A Biblical worldview teaches us: "that God created everything that exists and everything is held together by Him" (Colossians 1:17). We believe the Bible is God's divinely inspired Word, revealed to humanity (2 Timothy 3:16). We believe that the fullness of God came to earth and lived in the human body of Jesus Christ (Colossians 1:19). The Bible reveals God's character, what He has done in history, what He is doing now, and what He will do in the future. God exists as one God, in three persons, the Trinity, God the Father, God the Son, and God the Holy Spirit. "Be on your guard; stand firm in the faith; be people of courage; be strong. Do everything in love" (1 Corinthians 16:13–14). All three Persons are co-equal, co-infinite, co-eternal, and worthy of all praise and service. The three Persons of the Godhead are one in essence.
- God Created the Universe: God created the universe and it was very good. He created an open universe in which He continually operates in every detail, involving Himself in people's lives, directing history for His glory. The Lord assigns value and purpose to all His creation, whether rock or flower, wind, or rain, light or darkness, cat, or dog, etc. From the biblical perspective, everyone is part of God's creation, having design and purpose because God created everything to be what it is. "Life was perfect and not yet affected by the Curse— death, violence, disease, sickness, thorns, and fear had no part in the original creation. The character of a human is seen in the way they treat those under their care or at their mercy, even when they are animals. Humans have dominion over everything on earth" (Psalm 104:14).
- God Created Humankind in His Image: God also created humanity for a purpose, to have a relationship with Him and other people, and to exercise responsible dominion over His creation, caring for plants and animals. As God's unique creatures we find ourselves naturally bent toward art, music, literature, philosophy, science, mathematics, architecture,

sports, and other activities that enrich the soul and glorify the Lord. As Christians living in God's world and understanding what the Scriptures teach about His creation, we can enjoy the world around us and enjoy the creation as God intended.

- <u>God is the Standard for Right and Wrong</u>: God is the absolute standard for right and wrong, and He expects humanity to conform to that which He has revealed about Himself. God has spoken in the Bible, and what He says about humans and their actions is the final basis for correct thinking concerning morals and behavior.
- <u>Corruption: The Fall</u>: After God completed His perfect creation, He warned Adam that death would be the punishment for disobedience.
- <u>Evil Does Exist</u>: Evil exists in connection with the willful creatures who produce it. Evil first came into existence in the angelic realm when Lucifer rebelled against God. Adam and Eve introduced sin and evil into the human realm when they followed Satan and rebelled against God. Adam's sin ushered in death, sickness, and sorrow into the once perfect creation. God also pronounced a curse on the world and as a result, the world that we now live in is flawed. All humanity is corrupt in Adam, inclined toward sin, spiritually dead, and powerless to change their spiritually fallen condition. Because our Holy God must punish sin, He sacrificed animals to make coverings for Adam and Eve, and He sent the first couple from the garden, mercifully denying them access to the Tree of Life so that they would not live forever in their sinful state.
- <u>God is Involved with Humankind</u>: God is actively involved in the affairs of humanity. God has an agenda, a plan He formed before the creation of the world, and He is currently executing that plan according to His sovereign will and for His glory (Psalm 33:11). Within God's plan, He extends hope for the lost. God promised to one day send Someone who would take away the penalty for sin and death. God killed at least one animal in the Garden of Eden because of the sin of Adam;
- <u>Jesus Came to the Earth</u>: Jesus was born of a virgin (Isaiah 7:14), lived righteously according to the Mosaic Law (Galatians 4:4), and never sinned (Hebrews 4:15).

- <u>Jesus and the Cross</u>: Jesus died a substitutionary death on a cross (Mark 10:45), "was buried and rose to life on the third day" (1 Corinthians 15:3–4), "and ascended to Heaven where He is currently interceding for the saints" (Acts 1:10–11). While Adam disobeyed God's command not to eat the forbidden fruit, causing all humans to fall into sin, Jesus died on the cross to save humankind from sin. The first Adam brought death into the world through his disobedience; Jesus brought redemption into the world through His sacrifice. Adams's descendants had to sacrifice animals because of their sins, Jesus' sacrifice paid for their sins. Jesus bore God's wrath for our sin by dying in our place on the Cross (Isaiah 53:6). The Lamb of God was sacrificed once and for all (Hebrews 7:27) so that all those who believe in Him will be saved from the ultimate penalty for sin (eternal separation from God) and will live with Him forever. Jesus was not defeated by death. He rose three days after He was crucified, showing that He has power over all things, including death, the last enemy (1 Corinthians 15:26). Think of it: The Creator of the universe became part of His creation so that He might save His creation and His people from their sins! Jesus fulfilled more than fifty prophecies made about Him centuries before, showing He was the One promised over 4,000 years before by His Father.
- <u>Jesus Christ Will Return</u>: Jesus Christ will return to rule the earth (Revelation 19:11–16). There is a future hope for those who trust Christ as Savior and look forward to His return in which He suppresses all sinful rebellion and establishes His reign on the earth. This will be a time of righteousness and goodness for all those under Christ's rule. Ultimately, followers of Christ await with hope because Jesus Christ will one day restore all of Creation. "He will make a new Heaven and earth" (2 Peter 3:13), where old hostilities will be reconciled, old natures will be changed, and we will once again dwell in perfect harmony with each other and our Creator ... In this new place, there will be no death, crying, or pain. Those who have repented and believed in what Jesus did for them on the Cross can look forward to the consummation of God's kingdom, this new Heaven, and earth, knowing they will enjoy God forever in a wonderful place.

While Christianity is believed by faith, it is most definitely a reasonable and rational faith. It answers the questions of the mind and the heart. The Christian/Biblical worldview starts in Genesis 1:1, and ends with Revelation 22:21. It begins with, in the beginning, God, creates everything. It explains the cause of the universe, the purpose for humanity, and the mission of Jesus Christ to redeem those who are cut off from God for their sins (Isaiah 59:2). We see suffering as just a flash in time compared to the glorious eternity that's coming. We understand that whatever happens will be for our very best, regardless of what it feels like at the time. And it shows us how God can use evil for His good purposes. We need to look no further than the cross to see that. The Christian's desire is for all people to allow Christ to live in their hearts by faith, "and you will come to know and understand with us the height and the depth and the width and the length of the Love of Christ. The Reb, Katelyn Brown *A Biblical Worldview: What It Is and Why it Matters.*[3] It surpasses all human knowledge. We pray that you can be filled with the fullness of God." (Ephesians 3:18–19)

CHAPTER 13

The Meaning of Life

The Christian worldview offers purpose and meaning to life, not only in this realm but in the next. For Christians life is not temporary, it is eternal. There is hope that allows Christians to see with reason, that life can be purpose-driven, and life can have great meaning.

Christians believe in the existence of God, who created the universe. Our life's purpose, then, is aligned with God's purpose in creating the universe, and it is God that gives our lives meaning, purpose, and value. This is how and why we search for meaning beyond what is readily seen or understood. Our reason for emerging as something greater than ourselves— such as serving God's will and God's purpose.

The Bible reveals that humans are unique creatures designed for much more than just survival. Humans are creative, emotional, and spiritual beings, separate from the animal kingdom. We are designed to have deep relationships with others and with our Creator.

Humans have a unique ability to be creative in many areas. We have areas in the brain dedicated to the appreciation of beauty and creative thinking. Only humans have thousands of touch sensors on every finger. Only humans have a large part of the brain dedicated to controlling their hands with precision.

The precise abilities of the human hand are not what we would expect if we were descended from an apelike creature, but they are just what we would expect if we are made in God's image.

Humans have the unique ability to communicate thoughts and

emotions through language. Human speech and writing contain intricate sounds, sophisticated grammar, and thousands of words. Language enables humans to teach and learn, and develop relationships. Language requires many complex design features in the human body.

Scientists know that part of the brain is dedicated to emotional feelings, but science cannot explain where such feelings come from. Humans are capable of a vast range of emotions.

Humans also have a physical design that complements their emotional nature. This includes crying tears of emotion and communicating emotion by facial expressions. The human face has fifty facial muscles and the unique ability to make the order of 10,000 different facial expressions. Such characteristics cannot be explained by the idea of evolution.

Humans are also designed to derive pleasure in many subtle ways. We can appreciate beauty through sight, sound, smell, touch, and taste. Insofar as scientists have explored these subjects, only humans can stop to enjoy a sunset or appreciate a bird's song.

Finally, humans are uniquely capable of rational thought and self-awareness. We decide what course of action to take at every moment and in every area of life. In contrast, animals are predictably obedient to instinct. Apes do not worry about the meaning of life.

The ability to think and decide also means that humans are responsible beings. We are responsible for our actions and accountable to our Creator if we break His commands.

Throughout our culture, there seems to be an identity crisis. People do not know who they are. Daily, we are bombarded with lies. You are what you look like. You are what you buy. You're just an animal with a conscience. You are whatever you choose to be. You are nothing. No wonder people are confused.

What's behind this struggle for identity? It comes down to worldview. Because we are made in the image of God, God is the fixed reference point on which our design, purpose, and value are established. If we want to know who we are, we must start by looking up at Him, not around at others or within at ourselves. All About Worldview, *The Meaning of Life*.[1]

CHAPTER 14

What is Truth?

So how do we know what truth is? Jesus said to Thomas, "I am the way, and the truth, and the life. No one comes to the Father except through me" (John 14:6).

Many voices are speaking out in the news, on social media, and in our communities. We see that if we want the truth, we need the facts to confirm what is true and what is false. The Bible says that God's Word is truth. The truth is Jesus because the Bible states in John 1:14; "The Word became flesh and dwelt among us, and we beheld His glory, the glory as of the only begotten of the Father, full of grace and truth."

Yet, the disciples still struggled to believe that Jesus was the Son of God for a while. Even though you are a believer, the enemy will try to distort the truth in every way that he can. It is our job to stay in God's Word so that the enemy does not sway us from the truth. The Bible says to believers "and you will know the truth, and the truth will set you free." (John 8:32). Jesus spoke the truth, but many did not believe. It is disheartening that the world, society, and ourselves have been blinded from the real Truth.

Jesus speaks to the disciples about how He needs to go away so that the Holy Spirit, the Spirit of truth, comes to guide them into all truth. But now I go away to Him who sent Me, and none of you asks Me, where are You going? But because I have said these things to you, sorrow has filled your heart. Nevertheless, I tell you the truth. It is to your advantage that I go away; for if I do not go away, the Helper will not come to you; but if I depart, I will send Him to you. And when He has come, He will convict the world of sin, and righteousness, and of judgment: of sin, because they do not believe in Me; and regarding righteousness, because I go to My Father and you see Me no more; of judgment because the ruler of this world is judged. I still have many things to say to you, but you cannot bear them now. However, when He, the Spirit of truth, has come, He will guide you into all truth; for He will not speak on His authority, but whatever He hears He will speak; and He will tell you things to come. He will glorify Me, for He will take of what is Mine and declare it to you. All things that the Father has are Mine. Therefore, I said that He will take of Mine and declare it to you. Got Questions, *What is truth?*[1]

The Holy Spirit within us, as believers of Jesus Christ, guides us to what is true and what is false. We should hold close to the truth. The whole armor of God has been given to you so that the enemies' lies cannot keep your footing off of the truth. False truth is everywhere.

"God knitted me in my mother's womb" (Psalm 139). He created me for a purpose as well as all of you. "Every word of God is pure; He is a shield to those who take refuge in Him" (Proverbs 30:5).

John 14:17 states; *"the Helper is* the Spirit of truth, whom the world cannot receive, because it does not see Him or know *Him; but* you know Him because He remains with you and will be in you." Jesus promised the disciples another Helper, which is the Holy Spirit. The Holy Spirit speaks the truth. He has given you the truth because Jesus is the truth.

SECTION 3
Morality and Values

How does society determine and choose our human morals and values? Are they generated by random thoughts in our brains, or are they inspired and ingrained in us through an instinctive process? How do we know what's right and wrong? Some say that morality evolved as humans evolved and that humans eventually invented religion to build a system of moral behavior. Some even go so far as to suggest that apes possess the basic building blocks for morality. Does this mean that animals can be moral? There appears to be little evidence that this is true, so morality appears to be a strictly human trait.

Is it then that morality is something created by humans, or is it something humans eventually learn?

Do humans need someone to teach us morality? Do we need God to teach us morality?

Evolutionists generally believe the fact that humans have a sense of moral judgment and standards of moral behavior is taken as evidence that such morality is also a product of evolution. The question for the evolutionist is not whether evolution occurred but how to trace its steps. They never consider the possibility that an actual Creator created morality and life, and all that there is. They go on to say that the moral law is not imposed from above or derived from well-reasoned principles; rather it arises from ingrained values that have been there since the beginning of time.

Humans have a great tendency to personify animal behavior, interpreting animal actions in accord with our human thoughts. But animals are not human. Animals are not capable of abstract judgment and do not conceive the appropriateness of their actions. Neither do such moral mimicking animal behaviors prove anything about our moral origins. If we want to know why we have a conscience, a moral sense, then we need to dig deeper into the subject of morality to determine its true source. Answers in Genesis, Dr. Elizabeth Mitchell, *Where Did Morality Come From?*[1]

CHAPTER 15

Morality

All over the world, groups of people have come together in different societies, and each society has developed different cultures which encompass many different morals, ethics, and values. The problem of different morals and ethics raises some challenging questions. Are there universal principles of right and wrong? Are we born with a sense of morality or do we learn it? The implications of how we answer these questions will impact everything about how we live and find meaning and purpose in life.

Morality provides many benefits to human societies. They keep people safe and allow us to live in relative peace and harmony. They can provide a sense of direction, meaning, and purpose. And they often put us in accord with the natural world around us, providing rules and directions for how to treat the world and the other creatures with whom we live.

But morality can also drive us apart. Many of the most intense conflicts and wars have been caused by real or perceived moral differences. Even within a single culture, there can be conflict over moral principles. In America today we are certainly engaged in the ongoing battles that have been dubbed the culture wars. The culture wars are fought between conservatives and progressives on issues of abortion, women's rights, LGBTQ rights, free speech, political correctness, racial inequalities, global warming, and immigration, among many others. Over the past few years, the culture wars have become even more explosive, with protests and counter-protests often erupting into violence.

Amid these conflicts, there is a growing sense that we simply cannot talk or have a civil discussion anymore. We live in different worlds created by social media, news agencies, politicians, and others. One person's truths are another person's untruths. Is there any hope to find common ground?

Imagine the following dilemma: "A woman is dying and there is only one drug that can save her life. The druggist paid $200 for the materials and charges $2,000 for the drug. The woman's husband, Heinz, asked everyone he knows for money but could only collect $1,000. He offered this to the druggist but the druggist refused. Desperate, Heinz broke into the lab and stole the drug for his wife. Should he have done this?"

This is the famous Heinz dilemma, created by Lawrence Kohlberg in *The Heinz Dilemma and Kohlberg's 6 Stages of Moral Development,* [1] to analyze how people think through a moral dilemma.

Kohlberg was not interested in whether people thought Heinz acted morally. He wanted to know how they justified their answer. From their responses, he was able to construct a six-stage theory of moral development proposing that throughout a lifetime, people move from a pre-conventional self-centered morality based on obedience or self-interest to a more conventional group-oriented morality in which they value conformity to rules and the importance of law and order. Some people move past this conventional morality to a post-conventional humanistic morality based on human rights and universal human ethics.

Kohlberg proposed that "these are universal stages of moral judgment that anyone in any culture may go through, but still allowed for a wide range of cultural variation." In his studies, just 2% of people responded in a way that reflected a model of morality based on universal human ethics, and in practice, he reserved the highest stage of moral development for moral luminaries like Gandhi and Mother Theresa.

However, some saw Kohlberg's universal morality as biased toward a very specific model of morality that was culturally and politically biased in favor of liberal American values. By placing this humanistic morality as beyond and more developed than morality based on conformity to law and order he was placing his cultural values at the pinnacle of human moral achievement.

When children were asked whether it was okay to wear regular clothes to a school that requires school uniforms, kids said no, except in cases in which the teacher allowed it. The kids recognized that these rules were based on social conventions. But if you asked them if it was okay if a girl pushed a boy off a swing, the kids said no, and held to that answer even in cases in which the teacher allowed it or there were explicitly no rules against it. In this case, the kids were not basing their moral reasoning on social conventions. This suggests that these were moral rules, not conventional rules, and moral rules were based on a universal moral truth: harming someone is wrong. ABC News, Lee Dye, *Do we need God to be Moral?* [2]

This moral truth of these children reflects the wisdom of the Golden Rule, which is found in religious traditions all over the world. The words of Jesus; "Do unto others what you would have them do unto you" in Luke 6:31, seems to reveal that we humans are innately aware of this morality. Humans know right and wrong; it is embedded into our very conscience. These ingrained values have been present in humans since creation, not because morality evolved. On the contrary, God created Adam and Eve in His image and therefore with both an understanding of what was good and the choice to obey or disobey their Creator. We should understand that the Creator of all people provided a single standard authoritative yardstick of morality in the Bible.

"This is the new covenant I will make with my people on that day, says the Lord: I will put my laws in their hearts, and I will write them on their minds" (Hebrews 10:16). We need the Word of God to truly know God's authoritative standard by which each of our consciences is judged. As our Creator, God alone has that moral authority.

Where Did Morality Come From?

How can we explain the origin of today's moral standards? Is genuine morality objective? Most of us would admit that the Nazi genocide was inherently evil. Given that genuine morality is not absolute, we must ask where did morality come from?

From an evolutionary point of view, humans are merely insignificant products of random natural processes. As such, humans should have no intrinsic value, deserve no moral consideration, and expect no moral obligations from each other. From a naturalistic viewpoint, morality is derived from evolution with people competing against each other and some people exercising sacrificial behavior to improve group survival.

The more selfless individuals are, the more likely they are to pass on their genes. If this is true, we humans must be suffering from an overly inflated opinion of our goodness.

Science can only describe what is, not what ought to be. Without a divine source of morality, there can be no objective morality, only popular opinions. There can be no absolute standards of right and wrong. Is it true that humans have evolved to know right from wrong? Is it true that everything we do is determined by naturalistic processes anyway, so the idea of choice and free will is an illusion? Would this mean we are morally responsible even for accidents? We can imagine what we ought and ought not do, but are we only fooling ourselves?

Some things are morally right and other things are wrong. Since right and wrong exist, is there a materialistic explanation? Evolutionists try to make a case for morality without ultimate moral authority. Is there such a thing as human morality, or is morality created by a higher power? We must trust in the Word of God, which is authoritative from the very first verse. The question is, can we be good without God?

CHAPTER 16

Christian Morality

Love one another, even love your enemy! The most basic concept of Christian moral life is the recognition that every person bears the dignity of being made in the image of God. We have an immortal soul as well as the gifts of intelligence and reason to help us understand God's laws and commands. We have free will to decide things for ourselves and seek out what is right or wrong. We have within us, the overwhelming desire for good because we are made in the image of God, and the darker urges toward evil because of the effects of sin. Christian morality and God's law are not subjective but are specifically given to us for our happiness and wellbeing. God gave us intelligence and the capacity to act freely. Many people today understand human freedom merely as the ability to make their choice, neglecting to recognize the responsibility they have toward others.

Morality for a Christian is to apply God's laws to our actions and our behavior. When seeking a moral life, a Christian will try to obey the rules decreed by God that are recorded in the Bible. Christians should obey God's moral directives because God's Law is a tremendous gift for us. Unfortunately, some people do not see it that way. They believe that Christian morality is only about rules, faithfully following dos, and don'ts as sort of a divine test we must pass to get into Heaven. But Divine Law is not a test. Jesus Christ reveals that the real meaning of the moral law is more than just following rules. The rules only serve a greater purpose; they are not an end in themselves. True morality then is found, not in the codes established by a society or religion, but in that which is established by the Word of God. Although societies and religions may change, the Word of God never changes and stands forever. This tells us that true morality is unchanging because the Word of God is unchanging. We don't change our standards based on the changes in society, we base our morality on the unchanging moral standards of God. Truth, according to the Word of God, is the measure. Any moral code of conduct established by a society or religion that differs from the truth established in the Word of God is not righteous moral conduct. If any act or behavior can be regarded as moral, it will have to stand to the scrutiny of what God has to say.

The Bible becomes the only source of morality because the Bible is the very Word of God in written form. If the Christian wants to know God's will, they turn to the Bible. If the Christian wants to discern right from wrong, they turn to the Bible. Christians do not rely on the changing views of society, or their political party, to obtain their moral values, they rely only on the word of God.

True morality and true Christianity are joined by the very same foundation, which is the Word of God. Morality is not found in what is right or justified in the eyes of society, but more in the revelation of God's view of right and wrong. We know abortion is wrong because God says, "thall shall not kill." When God says something is wrong, like homosexuality, we believe it and we don't make an excuse to do it anyway. When we talk about the true moral character of a person, it is to be found in that person's life and how it coincides with the instructions given to us in the Word of God. Although there may be some codes of conduct in society that may relate to God's view, it is evident that true morality in society today suffers from a lack of a full inclination to what God has to say about morality. We all hold the individual responsibility to adhere to the Word of God and modify our conduct accordingly to be the instruments of change in our society. We must stand against any code of conduct that is contrary to the Word of God, to establish a true moral compass, if society is to find its way back to God. Only then can we be true Christian individuals, living within the measure of true morality within our society.

The psalmist of ancient Israel said that all have turned aside (from seeking to do good and from seeking God) "they have become corrupt; there is no one who does good, not even one" (Romans 3:10–11). Then he adds this comment to include believers; "all have sinned and fall short of the glory of God" (Romans 3:23). All human beings live and have lived on a battlefield between the righteous God and his rebellious angel Satan, and this battle between God's righteousness and our rebellious desires goes on day after day in everyone's life.

A Pharisee, an expert in the law, asked Jesus, which is the greatest commandment in the Law? And Jesus replied with this answer: "Love the Lord your God with all your heart and with all your soul and with all your mind. This is the first and greatest commandment. And the second is like it: Love your neighbor as yourself" (Matthew 22:37–40). This simplifies the rules for morality, and God's laws for moral behavior. Just love God completely and love everyone else as much as you love yourself. So, the moral life is centered on love. The Bible also says that "God wrote His law on our hearts" (Romans 2:15). This is our conscience. In other words, even without God's revelation in the commandments, we intuitively know God's law because we were created in His image.

If social consensus is our moral compass, then we have built our morality on a foundation of shifting sand. Social consensus is just that, a consensus. It's a picture of the general social values of the day. A generation or two ago, homosexuality, divorce, and adultery were still not accepted, and even considered sinful. Nowadays, both homosexuality and divorce are normal and adultery isn't as stigmatized as it once was. What we have with social consensus is what happened to the Israelites a couple of generations after conquering the Promised Land: "In those days there was no king in Israel; everyone did what was right in his own eyes." (Judges 17:6). The people abandoned God, and within two generations they were doing what was evil in the sight of God.

So why should the Bible be our source of morality? Because without it, we are like ships adrift at sea. At the end of the Sermon on the Mount, Jesus said these words: "Everyone then who hears these words of mine and does them will be like a wise man who built His house on the rock. And the rain fell, and the floods came, and the winds blew and beat on that house, but it did not fall, because it had been founded on the rock." (Matthew 7:25) The Word of God, the Bible, is the only rock upon which to build morality.

CHAPTER 17

Homosexuality

Perhaps no other topic displays the shifting sands of popular belief as does the topic of homosexuality. Only fifty years ago homosexuality held negative connotations for almost all of society, today however homosexuality is widely accepted. It's interesting how culture can make such a dramatic shift in values in such a short period. During the last century laws regarding homosexuals have changed significantly. During the 1960s, homosexuality was a criminal offense. Today it is not. Before 1962, all fifty states criminalized same-sex sexual activity, but by 2015, LGBTQ Americans had won the right to marry nationwide. Recently, the Supreme Court invalidated a state law banning protected class recognition based upon homosexuality, struck down sodomy laws nationwide, struck down Section three of the Defense of Marriage Act, made same-sex marriage legal nationwide, and prohibited employment discrimination against gay and transgender employees.

Adoption of children by same-sex married couples is legal nationwide since June 2015 following the Supreme Court's decision in Obergefell v. Hodges. Policies regarding adoption vary between jurisdictions. Some states allow adoption by all couples, while others ban unmarried couples from adoption.

Hate crimes based on sexual orientation or gender identity are punishable by federal law under the Matthew Shepard and James Byrd, Jr. Hate Crimes Prevention Act of 2009. Law Teacher, *Laws Regarding Homosexuals.* [1]

For much of the twentieth century, the western world lived under the umbrella of the Christian worldview. People, even though they may not have been Christian, generally built their presuppositions about the world on the Christian worldview. For example, marriage would have been rightfully understood to be one man and one woman united in a lifelong covenant under God. However, the western world now rejects the idea that there is one eternal, true, and loving creator God who has revealed himself to his creation and defined what morality, marriage, and sexuality is. The current sexual agenda that is being promoted in our culture is part of a Neopagan view of the world that has shaped the current millennial generation. What is happening now in western culture is not just the influence of secularism but also the return of ancient paganism. Morality has become twisted and corrupted. Heterosexuality celebrates otherness (Greek, héteros = other) whereas homosexuality (Greek, homo = same) celebrates the sameness of everything, which is the now accepted worldview. But what is the impact of these new beliefs?

Data from various research demonstrates that many of those who identify as LGBTQ suffer from mental health issues. Here are a few of the saddening statistics provided by Pink News, Joe Williams, *Depression and low self-esteem rising among gay men.* [2]

- 24% of gay men admitted to trying to kill themselves, while 54% admitted to having suicidal thoughts.
- A further 70% said low self-esteem was the main reason for their depression and suicidal thoughts.
- One in fourteen gay and bisexual men deliberately harmed themselves compared to just one in thirty-three men in general who has ever harmed themselves.
- Other factors included relationship issues (56%), isolation (53%), not feeling attractive (49%).
- 42% of young LGBTQ people have sought medical help for anxiety or depression.
- 52% of young LGBTQ people report self-harm either now or in the past.
- A shocking 15.9% of Generation Z Americans now identify as LGBTQ amid sexual identity indoctrination and a loss of Christian foundation in culture.

In a 1978 study, 43% of homosexuals admitted to having sex with more than five hundred partners, and 28% to having sex with more than 1,000! They also revealed that most of their sexual partners were anonymous persons with whom they only encountered once.

Many accept homosexuality because they think we should all get along without hatred or being judgmental, or because all people should be treated fairly. I think we all should agree with these sentiments; however, it is also important that while we must strive to accept human beings with fairness and openness, we must also be clear that we love all people, including homosexuals, it is the practice of homosexuality that we can disagree with.

The biggest argument that the world poses for why homosexuality cannot be wrong, is that these feelings are real and not chosen. Most people in the LGBTQ community can look back on their lives and honestly say they've felt attraction for people of the same gender for as long as they can remember. If their feelings are sincere and have been present their entire life, shouldn't they be valued rather than condemned?

Recent scientific studies claim that some people are born gay. Could this be? From an evolutionary perspective, it really wouldn't make any sense for homosexuality to have a biological basis. One of the major tenets of evolution is reproduction and passing on one's genes to the next generation. The existence of homosexuality amounts to a profound evolutionary mystery, since failing to pass on your genes means that your genetic fitness is a resounding zero.

The case for a homosexual gene has evaporated. There is no scientific evidence that this exists. And if homosexual behavior has a genetic component, how could it even be passed on to future generations? The question is not, was I born gay? The answer is clear as Jesus replied in John 3:4, "I tell you the truth unless you are born again, you cannot see the Kingdom of God."

Some argue that the Bible does not condemn homosexuality. This is simply not true. Homosexuality is condemned as a sin against God in both the Old and New Testaments. It was one of the sins for which the cities of Sodom and Gomorrah were destroyed. It was specifically singled out in the Mosaic Law as an abomination. In Leviticus 18:22; "You shall not sleep with a male as one sleeps with a female; it is an abomination." The Mosaic Law prescribed the death penalty for such activity. Leviticus 20:13 declares; "If there is a man who sleeps with a male as those who sleep with a woman, both of them have committed a detestable act; they must be put to death. They have brought their deaths upon themselves." It is very clear and evident that God says homosexuality is wrong. As Christians, we must accept this truth. There is no other option. If you are a Christian, and you believe there is nothing wrong with homosexuality you are wrong! Is God your priority or is your priority aligned with the evils of society? God gave you free will, so you can choose however you wish. But I hope you choose wisely. There are always consequences to our immoral decisions and actions.

In the New Testament Paul specifically condemns homosexual activity. Romans 1:26–28 states; "For this reason, God gave them over to degrading passions; for their women exchanged natural relations for that which is contrary to nature, and likewise the men, too, abandoned natural relations with women and burned in their desire toward one another, males with males committing shameful acts and receiving in their persons the due penalty of their error." And just as they did not see fit to acknowledge God, God gave them up to a depraved mind, to do those things that are not proper. Clearly, Paul says it is unrighteous and that it will keep one from inheriting the kingdom of God: Do not be deceived: neither fornicators, nor idolaters, nor adulterers, nor effeminate, nor homosexuals, nor thieves, nor the covetous, nor drunkards, nor revilers, nor swindlers, shall inherit the kingdom of God. (1 Corinthians 6:9-10)

In his first letter to Timothy, Paul again refers to the sin of homosexuality. He classifies homosexuals with those who are lawless and rebellious, ungodly, unholy, and profane. 1 Timothy 1:9–10 goes on to say; "realizing the fact that law is not made for a righteous person but for those who are lawless and rebellious, for the ungodly and sinners, for the unholy and worldly, for those who kill their fathers or mothers, for murderers, for the sexually immoral, homosexuals, slave traders, liars, perjurers, and whatever else is contrary to sound teaching." Can it be any clearer than that? Homosexuality is condemned in the Bible. I hear many people say that Jesus never talked about homosexuality. This statement is not true.

First, we must realize that God within the Trinity, exists in complete unity. There is never disagreement or differing opinions between the Father, the Son, and the Holy Spirit. If God states something in the Bible, whether it's in the Old Testament or the New Testament, then it is said by the Father, the Son, and the Holy Spirit. Don't forget that Jesus Himself, is the author of the entire Bible.

Second, the fact is that Jesus had a lot to say about sexual morality, and what He had to say rules out homosexuality as an acceptable lifestyle before God. Jesus taught that all sexual unions must be judged by God. Jesus proceeded to point out that God's original intention was that "a man shall leave his father and mother and shall cleave to his wife, and the two shall become one flesh" (Matthew 19:5). In other words, Jesus taught that the only moral sexual relationship is the one that occurs within marriage, between a man and a woman. Perhaps the most important distinction for human sexuality is God's creation of humankind: God created humankind in his image, in the image of God He created him; male and female He created them.

There are several things about the distinction between male and female that are important for us to understand as they are being eroded by the Neopagan worldview. The distinction between male and female is a biological reality and not self-constructed. What made Adam and Eve male and female is that they were told to be fruitful and multiply and fill the earth. The fact that the man and woman can procreate tells us what God means by male and female as this is what their reproductive systems have been designed to do. When God sought a helper fit for Adam, he chose neither an animal nor an exact duplicate of the man, but instead, He created a woman, uniquely formed for intimacy, companionship, co-workmanship, and procreation. Only a woman and a man can join together to become one flesh. The distinction between male-ness and female-ness is not self-constructed but rather is constructed by God and is to be celebrated as being very good. Nowhere in the Bible is homosexual behavior affirmed, but multiple times it is declared to be sinful and unnatural. The Bible's standard regarding homosexual acts is clear. Here are a few verses from Scripture that deal with homosexuality.

- "Therefore, a man shall leave his father and mother and be joined to his wife, and they shall become one flesh." (Genesis 2:24)
- "You must not lie down with a male in the same way that you lie down with a woman." (Leviticus 18:22).
- "If a man lies with a male as he lies with a woman, both of them have committed an abomination. They shall surely be put to death." (Leviticus 20:13)
- "Therefore, God gave them up to vile impurity in the lusts of their hearts, so that their bodies would be dishonored among

them. For they exchanged the truth of God for falsehood, and worshiped and served the creature rather than the Creator, who is blessed forever." (Romans 1:24–25)

- "Do you not know that the unrighteous will not inherit the kingdom of God? Do not be deceived. Neither fornicators, nor idolaters, nor adulterers, nor homosexuals, nor sodomites, nor thieves, nor covetous, nor drunkards, nor revilers, nor extortioners will inherit the kingdom of God." (1 Corinthians 6:9–10)
- "Run from sexual sin! No other sin so clearly affects the body as this one does. Sexual sin goes against your own body. Don't you realize that your body is the temple of the Holy Spirit, who lives in you and was given to you by God? You do not belong to yourself, for God bought you at a high price. So, you must honor God with your body." (1 Corinthians 6:13–20)
- "The law is not made for a righteous person, but for ... fornicators, for sodomites, for kidnappers, for liars, for perjurers, and if there is any other thing that is contrary to sound doctrine." (1 Timothy 1:9–10)
- It is clear from these verses in the Bible that homosexual behavior is a sin, and approving of sin is also a sin.
- Homosexuality "exchanges glory for corruption" (Romans 1:23), it "exchanges truth for lies" (Romans 1:25), and it "exchanges the creation ordinance for dysfunctional sexuality that is against nature" (Romans 1:26–28).

The act of homosexuality is clearly against God's teaching, there is no way anyone can deny that. It is a clear disregard for how humans were created by God, and it goes against nature itself. If you are practicing homosexual conduct, I urge you to re-examine your viewpoint, especially if you see yourself as a Christian. Homosexuality is a clear rebellion against God. It is out of love that I make this plea, I simply ask that you trust in God's Word and follow His commands. Make God the number one priority. We are called to follow God's will, not our own will. It may be difficult, and I can't claim that I know how difficult it is because I can't. But trust in God and He can pull you through. Like He does for all the negative experiences we go through in life. Remember God wants to help you.

The Bible says in Colossians 3:5: "Don't be controlled by your body. Kill every desire for the wrong kind of sex." If you regularly fill your mind with wholesome thoughts, you can more readily dismiss wrong desires (Philippians 4:8). While you may struggle greatly at first, it can become easier. God promises to help you to be made new in the force actuating your mind.

We know that we are made in the image of God. We are much more than the sum of our genes. We know that we have a will and can make choices for or against God. God's Word makes it clear that homosexual behavior is sinful but so are many other things like alcoholism, drug addiction, promiscuity, lying, cheating, stealing, and many other sins.

Is there hope for homosexuals? Yes, there is. The hope is Jesus Christ. As Jesus said, one must be born again to inherit the Kingdom of God. We all must die to our current or old selves and be made new, with a heart and desire for God and His ways. I ask you to be born again ... become a new creation. Through the power of His Spirit, homosexuals can be delivered from bondage to their sin. The first act is to recognize that homosexuality is a sin, it opposes God's desire for your life, and opposes His moral character. God created man and woman to have intimate relationships not with each other, but with the opposite gender. If you look at God's creation of the two genders, this makes perfect sense.

Do not be deceived: neither fornicators, nor idolaters, nor adulterers, nor effeminate, nor homosexuals, nor thieves, nor the covetous, nor drunkards, nor revilers, nor swindlers, shall inherit the kingdom of God. Paul minces no words in this statement, and the impact is devastating. Homosexuals are condemned with the worst of sinners. But in the very next verse, Paul provides a wonderful glimpse of hope: And such were some of you but you were washed, but you were sanctified, but you were justified in the name of the Lord Jesus Christ, and the Spirit of our God. (1 Corinthians 6:11) JW.org, *Is Homosexuality Wrong?*[3]

Isn't that wonderful? Those words were addressed to saved children of God! Paul says, "and such were some of you." Yes, some of the Christians at Corinth had been sexually immoral, but they had been delivered from their bondage by the power of God in Christ Jesus. Their sins had been forgiven and forgotten by a God who does not wish that any should perish. Like all sinners, homosexuals can find forgiveness and deliverance when they get on their knees and repent of their sins. He will also find acceptance in the Church.

CHAPTER 18

Marriage

The changing values in culture have led to a new cultural definition of marriage. Marriage used to be defined as the union of one woman and one man. Now, after the 2015 Supreme Court ruling states must license and recognize same-sex marriages. Consequently, same-sex marriage is legal in all fifty states.

Society has embraced same-sex marriage, so what's next? Will you soon be able to marry your pet and claim them as a dependent and have them covered on your medical plan? How about marrying your mother or your father, your aunt or uncle, your brother or sister ... where will it end? Will men be able to marry young boys or young girls? This may seem utterly ridiculous, but it wasn't that many years ago we thought the same thing about a man marrying a man, and a woman marrying a woman!

You can certainly love your same-sex friend, but sexual relationships are only permitted between a married man and woman. Today's culture has completely misapplied the word love in their relationships. The correct term for sexual desires is lust, not love. Love is a healthy expression not to be confused with lustful expressions of physical sex.

When married the two individuals become one flesh. The only way to create this one flesh is through diversification. A male and a female join to form one flesh. This combination of the two different elements of humanity will form one whole being. Per the Bible, marriage is a covenant between one man, one woman, and God. It represents God in the Trinity, Father, Son, and Holy Spirit. It represents humans, body, soul, and spirit. This is a very sacred holy union created by God. Man cannot redefine what God created. You can never combine a male with another male because you will be missing the female component, and you can never combine a female with another female because you will be missing the male component. Same-sex unions can never become one flesh.

As we have noted earlier, one of the clear discoveries that cause some people to be gay is their upbringing and environment. This highlights one of the huge risks of married gay people bringing up adopted children, namely the vulnerability of the children to be confused about their own sexual identity. To put it simply, if one's environment contributes to homosexuality, gay marriage will tend to increase the likelihood of the next generation being gay.

Jesus who created us and therefore owns us and has the authority to determine right and wrong did deal directly with the gay marriage issue, in the Bible's New Testament, Jesus answered and said to them, "Have you not read that He who made them at the beginning made them male and female, and said, for this cause, a man shall leave father and mother and shall cling to his wife, and the two of them shall be one flesh? So then, they are no longer two but one flesh. Therefore, what God has joined together, let not man separate" (Matthew 19:4–6).

Christ quoted directly from the book of Genesis to explain the doctrine of marriage as being one man and one woman. Thus, marriage cannot be a man and a man, or a woman and a woman. Jesus dealt quite directly with the gay marriage issue when He explained the doctrine of marriage. In Leviticus 18:22, Jesus deals directly with the homosexual issue, and thus the gay marriage issue. Law Teacher, *Definition of Marriage*.[1]

Because Jesus is the author of the entire Bible, whenever Scripture deals with marriage and/or the homosexual issue, Jesus himself is directly dealing with these issues. The Bible is the Word of our Creator, its science and history can be trusted. We have an absolute authority that determines marriage. The Church must return to the absolute authority of the Bible. Then and only then will there be a true foundation for the correct doctrine of marriage, one man for one woman for life. These Bible scriptures should be studied to help us remember the definition and purpose of marriage:

Again, we can learn what the Bible says about homosexual behavior and gay marriage from the following verses:

- Genesis 2:18–25 – Then the Lord God said, "it is not good for the man to be alone; I will make him a helper suitable for him. So, the Lord God caused a deep sleep to fall upon the man, and he slept; then He took one of his ribs and closed up the flesh at that place. And the Lord God fashioned into a woman the rib which He had taken from the man and brought her to the man. Then the man said, at last this is bone of my bones, and flesh of my flesh; She shall be called 'woman,' Because she was taken out of man. For this reason, a man shall leave his father and his mother, and be joined to his wife; and they shall become one flesh. And the man and his wife were both naked, but they were not ashamed."
- Leviticus 18:22 – "You shall not sleep with a male as one sleeps with a female; it is an abomination."
- Mark 10:6 – "But from the beginning of creation, God created them male and female."
- Romans 1:26–28 – "For this reason God gave them over to degrading passions; for their women exchanged natural relations for that which is contrary to nature, and likewise the men, too, abandoned natural relations with women and burned in their desire toward one another, males with males committing shameful acts and receiving in their persons the due penalty of their error."
- 1 Corinthians 6:9–10 – "Or do you not know that the unrighteous will not inherit the kingdom of God? Do not be deceived; neither the sexually immoral, nor idolaters, nor adulterers, nor homosexuals, nor thieves, nor the greedy, nor those habitually drunk, nor verbal abusers, nor swindlers, will inherit the kingdom of God."
- 1 Timothy 1:9–10 – "Realizing the fact that law is not made for a righteous person but for those who are lawless and rebellious, for the ungodly and sinners, for the unholy and worldly, for those who kill their fathers or mothers, for murderers, for the sexually immoral, homosexuals, slave traders, liars, perjurers, and whatever else is contrary to sound teaching."
- Jude 1:7 – "Just as Sodom and Gomorrah and the cities around them, since in the same way as these angels indulged in sexual

perversion and went after strange flesh, are exhibited as an example in undergoing the punishment of eternal fire."
- Matthew 19:3–6 – "Some Pharisees came to Jesus, testing Him and asking, is it lawful for a man to divorce his wife for any reason at all? And He answered and said, have you not read that He who created them from the beginning made them male and female, and said, for this reason, a man shall leave his father and his mother and be joined to his wife, and the two shall become one flesh. So, they are no longer two, but one flesh. Therefore, what God has joined together, no person is to separate."

God made the first man and woman, the first marriage. Thus, marriage can only be between a man and a woman because we are accountable to the One who made marriage in the first place.

CHAPTER 19

Family Values

The family is considered the focal point for individual connection within most societies. The family is the most basic unit of social organization and one which carries out important functions, such as supporting marriage, rearing children, and supporting all the individuals within the family unit. However today it seems as though the definition and meaning of the family structure are under much attack.

The attack is coming from those who build their thinking on the anti-God beliefs that are destroying society and the family unit. Society says that a child is raised by the village instead of by the family. Families have been redefined by supporting same-sex parents, and single moms. Unfortunately for single moms, many fathers have abandoned their families, causing fathers to be almost regarded as nonessential. This has led to the demise of the family unit; the very unit God uses to transmit the knowledge of himself to every generation.

Satan is using a barrage of tactics to try to bring down your child and your family. Three of the most destructive are; one) secular humanism, two) peer pressure, and three) compromise.

The nuclear family of the '50s epitomized the economically stable family unit. The idea of the middle-class, child-centered families that were headed by wage-earning husbands became the ideal, although making that family model the norm for most Americans took decades and (even) then was short-lived. Today, the male breadwinner, female housewife family represents only a small percentage of American households. In addition, single-parent families headed by mothers, families formed through remarriage, and empty-nest families have all become part of the norm.

Along with these shifts have come declining marriage and birth rates and a rising divorce rate. The American birthrate is half of what it was in 1960. In addition, the number of cohabiting couples increased from less than half a million in 1960 to 4.9 million in the 2000 census. Today it is estimated that more than 50% of households in America are headed by an unmarried person and almost 40% of children were born to unmarried, adult mothers. One reason for these developments is that marriage has been repositioned and redefined. It is viewed as an event that should happen after finishing college and establishing a career.

The Supreme Court extended constitutional protections for various forms of reproductive freedom through its ruling in Griswold v. Connecticut. There were also medical advances in contraception, including the invention of the birth control pill in 1960. As a result, the way children were brought into families became more varied than ever before. Divorce changed during the '1960s as well. In 1969, California became the first state to adopt no-fault divorce, permitting parties to end their marriage simply upon showing irreconcilable differences. And within sixteen years, every other state had followed suit.

Included in these trends is the expansion of rights granted to same-sex couples. With the decline of barriers to lesbian and gay unions and the increase in legal protections, the number of lesbian and gay people living openly and forming families has expanded.

Humanists argue that the family is negative and the extended family is reproducing conflict between classes. The Humanist perspective argues that the family reproduces patriarchy where men benefit from the family. They also argue that men oppress women through domestic violence. Humanists have also highlighted women's oppression in domestic duties due to gender distinctions within the family. Radical Humanists think that men benefit from women's oppression. They think that gender distinction is politically and socially constructed and that in family life, choices and decisions are not our own but political. Humanists paint a very negative picture of family life and they portray women as passive victims of capitalist and patriarchal exploitation.

The Marxist perspective of the family is that family is a negative social construct, thus reproducing conflict between classes. It also benefits the elite by creating a labor force and working-class exploitation.

The nuclear family they view has developed as an instrument to help solve the problems of inheritance of private property from father to son then to son, keeping wealth in the family. The family is designed to control women and protect property. They continue with the view that the family only benefits men, and is designed to guarantee and preserve male power through inheritance of property, serving the interest of capitalism.

With many fatherless families, and single mothers raising families, many family units have eliminated the role, or at least the importance, of the father in today's family structure. Father responsibilities and mother responsibilities are no longer separated into two distinct roles, now it seems there is only the parent role. No longer is there a male role and a female role, the new parenting role has no gender distinctions. With that said, no longer are boys being brought up to be men, and girls are no longer being brought up to be women, children are now untrained in gender roles and simply chose their gender identity based on their feelings.

Christians view the family as a positive union in which family members receive unconditional love, nurturing, and care. Not all family units live up to these standards, yet the family unit when working as designed is a very positive union for individuals in that family. Christians believe that each part of society has a specific function to make sure that society runs smoothly and everything stays in harmony. Christians believe that the family has equal benefit to everyone within the family and the goal of the family is to make all members a positive influence on others in society. A good Christian family lives its life based on biblical principles and one in which each member understands and fulfills his or her God-given role. The family is not an institution designed by humans, it was created by God for the benefit of humans, and humans have been given stewardship over it. The basic biblical family unit is comprised of one man, one woman, (married spouses), and their offspring or adopted children. The extended family can include relatives by blood or marriage such as grandparents, nieces, nephews, cousins, aunts, and uncles. One of the primary principles of the family unit is that it involves a commitment ordained by God for the lifetime of the members. The husband and wife are responsible for holding the family together. Although divorce is sought and granted much too easily in our society, the Bible tells us that "God hates divorce" (Malachi 2:16).

The husband is required to love and cherish his wife as Christ loved the church, and a wife should respect her husband and willingly submit to his leadership in the family. The husband's leadership role should start with his spiritual relationship with God and then flow to instructing his wife and children in scriptural values, leading the family into biblical truth. "Fathers are instructed to bring up their children in the training and instruction of the Lord" (Ephesians 6:4). "A father is also to provide for his family. If he does not, he denies the faith and is worse than an unbeliever" (1 Timothy 5:8).

The husband and wife in a Christian marriage are to remain faithful to one another for a lifetime. God declares equality of worth in that men and women are created in God's image and are therefore equally valuable in His eyes. This does not mean, however, that men and women have identical roles in life. Women are more adept at nurturing and caring for the young, while men are better equipped to provide for and protect the family. Thus, they are equal in status, but each has a different role to play in a Christian marriage.

The Bible disagrees with the cultural view that divorce, living together without being married, and same-sex marriage are acceptable in God's eyes. Sexuality expressed according to biblical standards is a beautiful expression of love and commitment. Outside of marriage, it is sin.

Children are given two primary responsibilities: "to obey their parents and to honor them" (Ephesians 6:1–2). Obeying parents is the duty of children until they reach adulthood, but honoring parents is their responsibility for a lifetime. God promises His blessings to those who honor their parents.

Ideally, a Christian family will have all members committed to Christ and His service. When a husband, wife, and children all fulfill their God-appointed roles, then peace and harmony reign in the home. But, if we try to have a Christian family without Christ as Head or without adhering to the biblical principles the Lord has lovingly provided for us, the family home will suffer.

The family is God's idea. Families are close to God's heart. From the beginning, when God created humans, He said, it is not good for man to be alone, so He created woman as a helpmate, suitable for him. Then, He blessed them and told them, be fruitful, and multiply, and replenish the earth. Throughout the ages, God's plan and desire have always been for parents to raise their children to know and love Him and walk in His ways. In Deuteronomy 6:6, God told the Israelites; "These words, which I am commanding you today, shall be on your hearts."

Many families today are in deep trouble because they have not been diligently teaching their children in God's ways. Instead, they have left it to the schools, media, museums, and others to do the job of teaching their children. We've often heard, I'm not going to shove the Bible down my kids' throats. When they are old enough, they can decide for themselves. The problem is, these parents forget that while they are not teaching their kids the Bible, the world is teaching its evolutionary, humanistic, atheistic, or New Age religion down their throats. While these parents may think they are doing the best for their children, and that their children will be able to objectively look at all their options and choose for themselves when they are older, they are leaving them defenseless against the anti-god teaching of our modern-day society. No parent would just let kids discover for themselves the dangers of running into a busy street. They would teach, warn, and even discipline their children. In like manner, we need to prepare them to face the challenges of the day by teaching the truth and exposing the lies of a society that has turned its back on God.

Parents are abandoning their role and handing it over to society and the public education system. God's longing is for Godly parents in a Christian family to raise their children in the teachings of Biblical values. We are commanded to have godly offspring and ordered by God to teach our children God's ways so they can grow up to themselves become godly parents. If we don't produce godly offspring, how will the future generations of the world hear the truth about living a righteous life? If godly offspring are not being produced our culture could end up becoming spiritually empty. Not only could it happen, but in many parts of our culture and our world, it is already happening. We have to look no further than Europe to see that the peoples who were once at the center of Christian strength, have now become almost entirely void of the things of God. This is rapidly happening in America as well.

We must produce godly offspring, who in turn will transmit the knowledge they have to the next generation, and to the next, and so on. It is a strategic and eternally vital task and requires considerable work to ensure information is passed on and not lost to succeeding generations. JW.org, *Values*.[1]

CHAPTER 20

Sexual Gender Identity

Until recently, human beings identified themselves as one of two genders: male or female. Today this is changing. The number of transgender adults has grown dramatically in recent years. Many people today now identify themselves with a gender that differs from their birth-identified gender.

Transgender people express their gender identities in many different ways. There are now, at last count, sixty-eight different genders transgender people who can identify themselves as. Some people use their dress, behavior, and mannerisms to live as the gender that feels right for them. Some people take hormones and may have surgery to change their body so it matches their gender identity. Some transgender people reject the traditional understanding of gender as divided between just male and female, so they identify just as transgender, or many other gender identities.

Normally, a person's gender, which is defined by the sex chromosomes in their DNA which is present in every cell of their body, is defined when they became a fertilized ovum. That is, it happened at conception when human life forms -- an ovum and a spermatozoon -- combined to produce a new human life with a new, unique DNA. About half the time, the DNA contains a Y chromosome which indicates a male zygote; if it does not have a Y chromosome it is a female zygote. However today, many believe that it is their brain or their emotional state of being, that tells them what their gender identity is.

A recent article in Reuters, Jonathan Allen, *New study estimates 1.6 million in U.S. identify as transgender,*[1] estimate there are 1.6 million people in the United States that identify themselves as transgender.

This diverse population includes individuals whose gender identity or gender expression differs from the cultural norm for their particular biological sex. A biological male who identifies as female and a biological female who identifies as male consider themselves to be transgender.

Transgender issues – like transgender people – are diverse, complex, and evolving. What's certain is that the transgender experience is distinct from the lesbian, gay and bisexual experience. That's because transgender issues have to do with gender identity rather than sexual orientation. Transgender people may be lesbian, gay, bisexual, heterosexual, or asexual, but that is beside the point. What's special about transgender people is their self-understanding and self-expression regarding gender and how they understand themselves as masculine, feminine, or transgender.

Younger adults are more likely to identify as transgender than older adults. This may be a result of a new wider acceptance of transgender people from the communities, allowing for those who identify as transgender to have a greater voice. Even more recently young children now identify themselves as a different gender than their birth gender, and some parents influence their children that they are a different gender than their birth gender.

Overall, the public is more uncomfortable with male-to-female transgender individuals using female-designated bathrooms than they are with female-to-male transgender individuals using male bathrooms. Men are much more likely to report being uncomfortable with a male-to-female transgender individual using a female designated bathroom.

At the same time a solid majority of Americans endorse transgender military service, they favor restrictions on transgender athletes' ability to play on teams that correspond with their gender identity. The issue is being debated in dozens of state legislatures, and five U.S. states have banned transgender girls, who were born male, from playing on girls' sports teams.

A majority of Americans (62%) say trans athletes should only be allowed to play on sports teams that correspond with their birth gender, while 34% say they should be able to play on teams that match their gender identity.

There's gender identity, which is how you, in your head, define your gender, based on how much you align (or don't align) with what you understand to be the options for gender.

The second characteristic is gender expression, which is the way you present gender, through your actions, dress, and demeanor. In addition to feminine or masculine, the options are butch, femme, androgynous, or gender-neutral.

The third is biological sex, defined as the physical sex characteristics you're born with and develop, including genitalia, body shape, voice pitch, body hair, hormones, chromosomes, etc.

The final two characteristics concern sexual orientation: sexually attracted to and romantically attracted to. The options include Women/Females/Femininity and Men/Males/Masculinity.

They claim that the real self is something other than the physical body, in a new form of Gnostic dualism, yet at the same time, they embrace a materialist philosophy in which only the material world exists. They say that gender is purely a social construct while asserting that a person can be trapped in the wrong gender.

They promote a radical expressive individualism in which people are free to do whatever they want and define the truth however they wish, yet they try ruthlessly to enforce acceptance of transgender ideology.

It's hard to see how these contradictory positions can be combined. If you pull too hard on any one thread of transgender ideology, the whole tapestry comes unraveled. But here are some questions we can pose:

If gender is a social construct, how can gender identity be innate and immutable? How can one identity concerning a social construct be determined by biology in the womb? How can one identity be unchangeable concerning an ever-changing social construct? And if gender identity is innate, how can it be fluid? If the categories of man and woman are objective enough that people can identify as, and be men and women, how can gender also be identified as both, or neither, or somewhere in between?

The American public is sharply divided along religious lines over whether someone can be a gender different from their sex at birth. Most Christians in the United States say that whether someone is a man or a woman is determined by their sex at birth. Those who identify religiously as atheist, agnostic, or nothing in particular – about 60% say they think a person's gender is not necessarily determined by the sex they are given at birth.

The different sexual identities that are being promoted and celebrated by many in our culture today, are another example that society has adopted a pagan worldview.

What should Christians do about sexual gender identity?

First, we should recognize that we are witnessing moral rebellion against God's design, abandoning all semblance of biblical authority. God is not honored or obeyed. The rates of suicide among transgender people show the brokenness this choice causes. Paul McHugh, the former Johns Hopkins University psychiatrist in chief, has noted in the Wall Street Journal article, *Transgender Surgery Isn't the Solution*,[2] that the suicide rate among transgender individuals is twenty times higher than in the normal population. Embracing transgender identity at the cultural level does not produce happiness and wholeness.

Second, we should celebrate the beauty of God's creative design. The Christian church and the godly family should be a celebration of happiness. We should rejoice that God in His sovereign wisdom has opened our eyes to see that He made us according to His perfect design. Manhood and womanhood aren't Plan B. God Himself has made us as we are, the pinnacle of His creation.

Third, we should recommit ourselves to training our children. The bodily differences between men and women are real. They speak to differences in our makeup, specifically designed by our Creator. In practical form, we must teach these differences to our children. They must see that being a boy or a girl is a matter of God's glory. There should be no shame in boys liking boyish things or in girls adopting girlish behaviors. Christians should encourage this kind of awareness. David said to his son Solomon, "and prove yourself a man" (1 Kings 2:2). If we do not teach our kids about gender and sexuality, we can be assured that our unbiblical culture will.

Fourth, we should reach out in compassion and call for repentance. We must reach out to those cursed by Adam's fall just as we are. We may feel pulled to sin and its effects, but we should show mercy to all lost people. Transgender individuals will be increasingly common in our neighborhoods and communities. We have a choice: we can sinfully avoid them, or we can seek to reach out to them in kindness and evangelize to them.

Conversion for transgender individuals will not be neat and clean. It will be messy. It will involve the recognition that "sin has corrupted us in every fiber of our being" (Isaiah 64:6). But the gospel is stronger than sin. Christ's death washes us clean, and Christ's Resurrection gives us life. The Resurrection raised Christ's spirit even as it renewed His body.

Pastors should preach on the implications of the Resurrection for all people, including transgender ones. The gospel makes sense of our humanity. It restores our dignity. It calls us to be people who see our body as a gift for us to give glory to our Maker and Redeemer. We are a wonderful creation.

CHAPTER 21

The Sanctity of Human Life

We mentioned earlier how explosive the topic of homosexuality can be, but perhaps even more explosive is the topic of the sanctity of human life, and more specifically the procedure of abortion. There is a big controversy in today's society on pro-life vs ... pro-choice (abortion).

Abortion is the process of a pregnant woman deciding that she does not want to give birth to the child, then decides to have a procedure to physically remove that child, which terminates the life of that child.

There are a lot of reasons for a woman making such a crucial, devastating decision in her life. One main reason is that she doesn't believe she is ready to take on the role of becoming responsible for another human being, or she is not financially ready to help support a child and give them the love and the care that they may need to progress in life. She may even feel pressured by her family, her father, her husband, or her boyfriend to have the abortion. Men may be one of the primary reasons for abortion.

It's important to realize that there are other options. If a mother feels as though she cannot bear responsibility for another child, she can always place that child up for adoption, instead of ending that child's life. That child should still have the opportunity to be born and live a life like any other human being.

Whatever the reason, the act of abortion not only ends the life of the child, it also creates a devastating impact on the life of the woman as well. Many women grieve after abortion because they know deep down that they have indeed lost a baby. Later in life, the women experience long-term physical complications, emotional devastation, or psychological traumas that result from their abortion. Many women suffer feelings of grief at a higher intensity level and for a prolonged period; sometimes twenty, thirty, or fifty years later.

Even though most researchers claim to have shown a high incidence of depression in people who have had an abortion, the culture has rejected such views, claiming that it is more important that others have the right to choose. The argument that abortion kills people is an important one because most people still accept the basic biblical prohibition against taking innocent human life. We should ensure that people know that the baby is human. As so many people like to say, just follow the science, if they follow the science and medical experts, they will learn, and know without a doubt, that abortion is the killing of a human being. Do not listen to the lies thrown around by many who say it is only tissue that is being removed. That is clearly false. The baby in the womb, no matter how old, is a human being with human DNA. The fetus is not tissue or a lesser animal, it is fully human. Those who support abortion teach this lie often, but the scientific data clearly proves that a fetus is a human being. Human life begins at conception which is proven by medical science, and abortion is ending a human life. Compelling Truth, *What is the sanctity of life? Why do Christians believe in the sanctity of life?*[1]

Some evolutionists popularized the concept that babies in the womb are actually undergoing animal developmental stages, such as a frog stage and so on. This idea has come to be known as ontogeny recapitulates phylogeny. However, this discredited idea has been used repeatedly for a hundred years! Textbooks today still use this concept and museums around the world teach it. Through this deception, many women have been convinced that the babies they are carrying in their wombs are simply going through an animal phase and can be aborted. Some abortion clinics in America have taken women aside to explain to them that what is being aborted is just an embryo in the fish stage of evolution and that the embryo must not be thought of as human. These women are being fed outright lies.

Evolutionary views have decreased the value of human life. Throughout the world, the casualties of the war on children are staggering. Though deaths of children and the unborn did exist before the evolution revolution, they have increased exponentially after the promotion of these teachings. In this day and age, governments readily promote and fund the killing of children, both boys and girls, and sometimes command it, through abortion.

Medical facts state that within three weeks, the brain, heart, and spinal cord are developing. Through a sonogram, you can even hear the baby's heartbeat at five to seven weeks.

Life begins at fertilization, and all human life is precious and made in the image of God. Feminist groups and Christians in the nineteenth century were strongly against the act of killing unborn babies because of the belief in the worth of all human beings. However, today feminist groups see abortion as a positive choice instead of prioritizing the value of the life being aborted.

Whose choice is it to end an innocent life? Do humans have the right to make this choice, to end the life of another human being? The clear answer is no. Only God has the right to make this choice. It is not the right of the government or any individual to make this decision. Society believes that the woman has the right because it is her body, but that removes any responsibility of the father, the family, and certainly the child.

As one of the Ten Commandments clearly states, "thou shall not kill" (Exodus 20:13). Abortion is not done by accident it is done as a choice. In God's eyes, this is wrong. Killing another human being, no matter what age, is against God's moral law.

We must speak of the value, dignity, and goal of human life, even with its imperfections and struggles. Human life, as a profound unity of physical and spiritual dimensions, is sacred. It is distinct from all other forms of life since it alone is imprinted with the very image of our Creator God.

The practice of abortion is nothing more than the practice of child sacrifice, it is killing a human being in the name of convenience. It is detestable, and it has nothing to do with women's rights, after all, half of the children killed by abortion are females. Abortion is evil, disguised as a choice. All Christians should stand together to oppose this horrible practice.

Democrats, liberals, humanists, and evolutionists claim they are for the people, but really only care about votes. They have misled millions of people into believing that there is nothing wrong with abortion. Abortion is wrong and yet the Democratic party supports this evil act.

If you are a Christian, how can you support abortion and how can you be affiliated with a political party that does? Abortion is a practice that goes against every law from God. If you support abortion, then you are rebelling against God. How can you possibly vote for a person who supports abortion? If you vote for a person who supports abortion, then you are just as guilty of the act of abortion as the so-called doctor that performs the procedure. You have the blood of millions of children on your hands! This does not sit well with God. Killing His human creation which is made in the image of God Himself, is as evil as you can get. I urge you to put some serious thought into this matter and reconsider your stand and rearrange your priorities. Are you really a Christian or a fake Christian? Are you a friend of God, or just a casual Christian who doesn't give much thought to God or give God the respect He deserves? Christians should strongly oppose abortion at all costs. How can you be both close to God, and yet support abortion? It's very uncomfortable for me to be so critical, but I can think of no other way to convince you how terrible an offense to God that abortion truly is. You must change your ways and choose to follow God's commands. You cannot serve two masters with such differing views on abortion. It's time to make God the priority, not your worldly political party. You must see the evil for what it is! One day, we will all be judged, and I urge you to make the right decision before that day comes.

 The Bible proclaims the status of human life before birth. In Jeremiah 1:4–5, we read: "Then the word of the LORD came to me, saying: Before I formed you in the womb, I knew you; Before you were born, I sanctified you; I ordained you a prophet to the nations." First, God says that He knew Jeremiah when he was in the womb. Second, He makes clear that He knew Jeremiah even before He was formed in the womb. Third, He tells Jeremiah that his growth in the womb is a result of being formed by God Himself. Psalm 139:13–16 states; "For You formed my inward parts; You covered me in my mother's womb. I will praise You, for I am fearfully and wonderfully made; Marvelous are Your works, and that my soul knows very well. My frame was not hidden from You, When I was made in secret, and skillfully wrought in the lowest parts of the earth. Your eyes saw my substance, being yet unformed. And in Your book, they all were written, the days fashioned for me, when as yet there were none of them." Even in this unborn state, it is clear that the baby is human, as God has already determined the days fashioned for the baby.

Scripture makes clear that both Jesus and John the Baptist were human before their birth. Jesus was given a name, and His birth was foretold to Mary, at the time of His conception. In Luke 1:41–44 it says, "When Elizabeth heard Mary's greeting, the baby leaped in her womb, and Elizabeth was filled with the Holy Spirit. And she cried out with a loud voice and said, Blessed *are* you among women, and blessed *is* the fruit of your womb! And how has it happened to me that the mother of my Lord would come to me? For behold, when the sound of your greeting reached my ears, the baby leaped in my womb for joy." Elizabeth was immediately able to ascertain that Mary was pregnant with the Messiah. What is interesting about this passage is that the unborn John joins in the celebration. John was fully human before his birth. The bible makes it clear enough that abortion is murder because the unborn baby is human.

The Bible's position is clear, we did not evolve through millions of years of death, disease, and bloodshed; we are not just animals. We are special because we are made in the image of God. We have the assurance that we are human, and that our humanity began at the moment of conception. It is for that reason that we oppose abortion because it is a denial of the humanity of the unborn baby.

CHAPTER 22

Values

We've looked at some of the moral issues in society and discovered that many issues cause strife and friction. The same is also true for the values in our society. These values are more defined by political values, governance, and cultural values and beliefs. As individual values are influenced by the groups, we chose to involve ourselves. For instance, we frame our beliefs based on our political party, social clubs, special interests, and other groups we chose to align ourselves with. As we align ourselves with these groups, we become like-minded and our opinions and values come into agreement with other members of the group. Different groups push different belief systems out into the world and even if you don't align necessarily with that group, your values can still be influenced by what they teach. Let's shift to looking at a few of these values to determine how we should understand them and how they impact our society. After all, these values can stretch from one extreme to another, so we must understand these values, then compare them to the teaching in the Bible so we can arrange our values properly and make the best decisions possible. PNAS, Francisco Ayala, *The difference of being human.*[1]

CHAPTER 23

Ethics

Both morals and ethics have to do with what's right and wrong. Morality is seen by some as personal while ethics refer to the standards of a community. For example, your community may not view premarital sex as a problem. But on a personal level, you might consider it immoral. By this definition, your morality would contradict the ethics of your community.

Morals and laws are designed to normalize behavior so people can live in harmony. This way people can still be independent but also avoid harming others.

Some people argue that laws and morality are independent, meaning that laws can't be unheeded simply because they're morally indefensible. Others believe law and morality are interdependent. These thinkers believe that laws that claim to regulate behavior must be in accord with moral norms.

All laws must protect the welfare of the individual and be in place for the good of the entire community.

For instance, adultery may be considered immoral by some, but it's legal in most states. Additionally, it's illegal to drive slightly over the speed limit but it isn't necessarily considered immoral to do so.

There may be times when some people argue that breaking the law is the moral thing to do. Stealing food to feed a starving person, for example, might be illegal but it also might be considered the right thing to do if it's the only way to prevent someone from starving. Very Well Mind, Brittany Loggins, *Morality vs. Ethics: What's the Difference?* [1]

People have moral values and they accept standards according to which their conduct is judged as being either right or wrong, good, or evil. The particular norms by which moral actions are judged vary to some extent from individual to individual and from culture to culture, but value judgments concerning human behavior are accepted in all cultures. This presents two questions: (one) whether the moral sense is part of human nature, one more dimension of our biological make-up; and (two) whether ethical values may be products of biological evolution rather than being given by religious and other cultural traditions.

CHAPTER 24

Liberalism

Liberalism is rapidly taking over our country so it's vastly important to understand liberalism before it's too late. Liberalism claims that they are not judgmental against any lifestyle or worldview, except of course religion, especially the Christian religion, and conservatism. Liberals, in general, don't believe in absolute evil or absolute good. So, any viewpoint that does believe in absolute right and wrong, is a challenge to their viewpoint. Most liberals have great contempt for Christians and conservatives. Christian liberals are even laughed at behind their backs, except when the non-Christian liberals need their votes.

To be a liberal Christian means you either have to completely abandon your religious beliefs to make them compatible with your political beliefs, or you have to have more value for your political beliefs than you do for God.

Hollywood and Liberal entertainers continually attack the Christian faith and its followers. Hollywood has become very comfortable hating Christians. There's a reason they do that: Christianity, with its absolute moral values, is a huge threat to liberalism. If you're a Christian with staunch morals who's not in favor of abortion, gay marriage, or banning schools from mentioning Christ over Christmas, you conflict with liberalism.

Liberals love to mock, challenge, and disrespect Christians and conservatives at every opportunity, except when there's an election coming up. New American, Thomas Sowell *The High Cost of Liberalism*.[1]

In the Townhall article by John Hawkins, *The Left's War on*

Christianity,[2] "Barack Obama, won the Catholic vote by nine points in 2008, then demanded that Catholic hospitals provide free birth control and abortion-inducing drugs, even though that violates their religious beliefs. Every Catholic bishop in America has spoken out against the policy, but of course, the Democratic Party is unmoved.

This should shock no one who has seen the left enthusiastically support government-sponsored anti-Christian art, sue Christians who want to mention Christ in schools or courthouses, and even fight to remove the World Trade Center Cross from the National September 11th Memorial and Museum.

The massive movement by the left to dismantle religion and banish God from our civil society continues at a rapid pace.

Another interesting thing is that liberals only attack Christianity, not other religions such as Hinduism, Buddhism, or Islam — the latter being far more intolerant and bloodthirsty than the others? Schools in Baltimore, Maryland, recently joined those in New York, Detroit, and other districts throughout the country in closing for so-called holy days on the Muslim calendar, even though no other religious holidays are recognized. Buddhism and Hinduism are promoted in different ways. For more than a decade, U.S. public schools have been indoctrinating children with Far East mystical practices, masked under so-called Mindfulness programs to supposedly promote stress management. Youngsters are made to sit on classroom floors in the lotus position, eyes closed, hands resting on knees with palms raised, meditating or chanting Hindu mantras. Schools have been transformed into anti-American, Marxist boot camps.

Liberals have legitimized sodomy with same-sex marriage, justified willful murder by calling it abortion, and subverted marriage — the sacred institution created by God for the propagation of the human race and the rearing of children.

Christians must fight back, or our children and generations to come will live in fear of expressing their faith. Liberalism is engaging in a war against Christianity and it's time for people to call it what it is and start picking sides. TGS, Andrew Hoffecker *Liberal Theology.*[3]

The Democratic party has been around since the time of the election of Andrew Jackson in 1828. Its platform at that time was mainly against big government. They supported slavery then, as they do abortion today. It presented itself as the champion of individual liberty advocating the right to own slaves. Democrats gained the support of impoverished farmers by freeing up land through the violent persecution of Native Americans and immigrants.

Later, even though FDR was credited with the economic recovery, it is universally recognized that Hitler and the war had much more influence on the economic recovery.

After FDR's death, Harry Truman's attempted to continue Roosevelt's reforms but was defeated by the Southern Democrats. Only collaboration with Republicans on anti-communist policy secured his reelection in 1948. Following a landslide defeat in 1952, the party regained control of Congress by bargaining with Southern Democrats, selling out black Americans yet again. These powerful Southern Democrats, in coalition with conservative Republicans since FDR's second term, worked to block progressive legislation well into the 1970s.

But wait, didn't the Democrats pass the civil rights legislation to help improve the lives of Black Americans in the mid-1960s? The truth is that only the southern Democrats opposed this legislation. The republican party had a higher approval vote for the legislation than the Democratic party.

Instead of representing all Democrats, the party caters to the far left, pushing an agenda it describes as compassionate, inclusive, and empowering, but is anything but. It paints minorities as victims who cannot do for themselves and need the party to save them. It promotes both limiting and compelling speech by force; punishing people for either saying what's deemed politically incorrect or not saying what hard-liner progressives demand. The Democratic party has a long history against God and voting against Christian and Godly values. That's why pro-life Democrats like Bart Stupak had to throw the babies under the bus when push came to shove over Obamacare.

The Democratic party strongly supported the separation of Church and State which they drew into law in 1947. (All nine Democratic Supreme Court members voted for the proposal.) Since this term did not exist in the congressional records, they used it from the private letter of Thomas Jefferson to the Danbury Baptist Association. Subsequently, the Supreme Court ruled that a wall of separation between church and state exists based on that personal letter rather than the constitution. The constitution states that religion should be protected from government, not that government should be protected from religion.

In 1952, the Lyndon Johnson amendment forbade pastors to speak politics in the pulpit. Perhaps the most restrictive of First Amendment rights for churches and faith-based organizations is the Johnson Amendment, which prevents pastors, ministers, and leaders of corporations with 501c3 tax exemption from using their office to express a political opinion about a candidate or an issue. Any other corporation, labor union, school or university, or public entity can voice their support for any candidate they choose ... but not the Church. How unfair is this?

The Democrats then removed prayer and Bible reading from public schools in 1962-1963. On June 25th, 1962, the United States Supreme Court decided in Engel v. Vitale that a prayer approved by the New York Board of Regents for use in schools violated the First Amendment by constituting an establishment of religion. The following year, in 1963, in Abington School District v. Schempp, the Court found Bible readings in public schools also in violation of the First Amendment. However, atheists are free to teach their religion of Humanism and Naturalism, in any public school.

Then Democrats passed a resolution in which they framed religious liberty as a risk to civil rights. The Democratic National Committee unanimously passed this resolution which represents atheists, agnostics, and humanists and assists these groups regarding policies. Democrats rejoiced as this meant that for the first time, a leading political Party embraced American nonbelievers.

Under the Obama administration, Democratic politicians sought to eliminate public funding from Christian colleges, making it harder for poor and minority students to attend. They created hate lists of Christian and Catholic schools. They also threatened to deny Christian schools their tax-exempt status. They also sought to remove all Christian and Catholic colleges from the NCAA.

Democrats have made it clear that Christian morals and values have no place within their party. Democrat senators Kamala Harris and Mazie Hirono implied that Judge Buescher's membership in a Catholic service organization makes him unfit for the federal courts. Democrats also opposed Mike Pompeo's nomination as secretary of state because of how his Christian faith impacts his politics. Pompeo indicated that he believes in what the Bible says about life, sex, and marriage.

Democrats sponsored bills such as House Bill 2696 to allow leaving babies born alive after attempted abortions alone to die without life-saving medical care.

Democrats maintain a pro-socialist agenda with their attacks on private property ownership. Their support for the welfare state has led to the punishment of many minorities. Going back to the time after the civil war, Democrats were against the 13th Amendment, which abolished slavery; the 14th Amendment, which gave blacks citizenship; and the 15th Amendment, which gave blacks the right to vote. Remember it was a Democrat that created the KKK. Democrats have also supported anti-family legislation by redefinition Marriage.

Now Democrats are fighting against the 1st Amendment - While Democrats claim to promote tolerance, they continually silence those who hold values they disagree with.

Religiously unaffiliated Americans overwhelmingly share the Democratic Party's values. 70% of religiously unaffiliated Americans voted Democrat and under the Obama administration, the Democratic Party forced taxpayers to fund abortions, even if it violated their conscience. Democrats do not support Christian values and have made efforts to censor the Bible's moral influence on society. Christians are increasingly silenced and punished for living according to their beliefs. Unfortunately, many good people have been fooled by the Democratic party. The truth is they have never helped minorities, they keep them subjugated to living at a minimum wage, and the welfare state, as they continue raising taxes and imparting hardships for the poor.

If you are a Democratic party Christian, how does this make sense to you? You are supporting the party that wants to eliminate your religious faith. You have allowed your hate to overpower your wisdom and love for God. All Christians need to decide which master they will follow. Will, they choose to follow God or chose to follow their Democratic political party that is doing everything in its power to eliminate your faith. I urge you to do your research if you want to know the truth. Don't choose your political party based on your emotions. You need to choose your party based on how they align their values to God's values. If you are a democrat and are working to influence others in the party to oppose abortion and support Christianity, then I commend you. Keep it up! Just be careful not to vote for Democratic candidates that support abortion and who fight against Christian faith and values. My intent is not to destroy the Democrat party, but to influence Democrats to support God's values on pro-life, homosexuality, and Christian values. The current Democratic party doesn't align its party platform with Biblical, Godly values, they are instead at war with Christianity. Take it from me, a former Democrat. It is possible to learn the truth and follow God in the process. The question is, who do you love more, God or the Democratic party?

CHAPTER 25

Socialism

Socialism is a fast-growing political value that is gaining strong support from liberals in the Democratic party, as well as many younger adults according to the Heritage Foundation, Samuel Gregg, Ph.D., *Young Americans Increasingly Prefer Socialism; Here's How to Change Their Minds.*[1]

The reason for the rapid growth stems from the envy of people becoming more hostile to the individuals with wealth and the resentment of large corporations. They want to see a shift away from very rich individuals having most of the wealth, and the growing number of poor people in this country. I can agree with this, however, socialism is not the answer.

The problem is that socialists believe the solution to this problem is through the redistribution of wealth. They want the government to seize the assets of rich people and distribute those assets to the poor. This is a huge problem. No one, not even the government, has the right to seize anyone's property or possessions. This is stealing. We should never be envious of what others possess because this is greed and the Bible warns us not to be envious or greedy. Taking what belongs to someone is stealing, and we all know that stealing is wrong, even from the rich.

We in America, live in a Democratic society that supports a free marketplace where people are allowed to create companies that in turn hire and pay employees and sell products or services. Employees then use their income to buy other services and products. This interchange forms the strength of our economy. The government should have little to no influence in this system other than to make sure that the system is regulated, runs fairly, and doesn't negatively impact individuals.

On the other hand, Democrats are beginning to turn away from this system and are becoming more and more socialist. These people tend to be more liberal as well. They believe the government should have total control of the economy and other areas in people's lives, like social reforms and other values of society. In the economic system of socialism, the government has complete control and authority, with no publicly owned companies or corporations. The government sets the price on most, if not all products and services, as well as wages for individual workers.

It's important to note that socialists claim that 'citizens' own all the wealth and assets in the country, but just look at any socialist or communist country and you will find that it is the government that holds all the power, not the people. Just look at these two countries, 'The Peoples Republic of China and the Democratic People's Republic of Korea? Do you believe the people have any control or even any say in how the government is run? Of course not. These are dictatorship-controlled governments that suppress the voice of the people. The people have no say whatsoever. These countries have huge numbers of poor people struggling to earn enough wages to support themselves.

The ruling dictatorship controls all means of distribution and the citizens are left to the decisions made by this dictatorship as to how much of a salary they earn. The reason so much production has been moved to China is because of the low wage's workers earn there. If you want to earn low wages, the answer is a socialist economy. Capitalism is not perfect, but at least it allows competition from various companies to drive up wages and earnings for workers. Without competition, as with a socialist-controlled government, there is nothing that allows wages to increase. There are no countries in the world that are 100% socialist, according to the Socialist Party of the United Kingdom website, Socialist Party of the United Kingdom, *OECD report: A system in crisis*.[2] Most have mixed economies that incorporate socialism with capitalism, communism, or both.

The five Nordic countries—Norway, Finland, Sweden, Denmark, and Iceland have strongly socialist systems. Many of its workers are unionized, granting them greater power. However, these countries are democracies, allowing the general population input into decision-making by electing their officials. These countries are known for having high taxes on income. According to the OECD, Denmark (26.4%), Norway (19.7%), and Sweden (22.1%) all raise a high amount of tax revenue as a percent of GDP from individual income taxes and payroll taxes. This is compared to the (15%) of GDP raised by the United States through its income taxes and payroll taxes. To raise a lot of income tax revenue, income tax rates in Scandinavian countries are rather high. Denmark's top marginal effective income tax rate is 60.4%, Sweden's is 56.4%, and Norway's top marginal tax rate is 39%. Yes, you may have almost free healthcare but every product you buy will cost more than 25% more during your lifetime. Just add it up and see which is the better arrangement.

More extreme forms of socialism would include China, Cuba, Laos, Vietnam, and Venezuela. China, in particular, and Vietnam have some free-market aspects to their economies, even though their governments remain under the sole control of their country's Communist Parties. The People's Republic of China has the second-largest economy because in the late 1970s Deng Xiaoping abandoned the rigid excesses of Maoist socialism thought and adopted a form of communism that allowed foreign investments and even a stock market while underwriting SOEs (state-owned enterprises). At the same time, Deng ensured strict political control of China through the Communist Party and the People's Liberation Army. The Chinese economy has grown rapidly because of the low wages paid to workers, which attract businesses from outside of China, like Apple, Microsoft, Boeing, GM, Nike, Coca-Cola, Procter & Gamble, Intel, and many others. Our own American companies are the main reason that the Chinese economy has grown so much.

Once ranked as the richest South American country thanks to its oil reserves, in 1998 Venezuela elected a socialist leader, Hugo Chávez. Chávez centralized power in his increasingly authoritarian grip and spent billions on social programs from profits from oil. Under Chavez's successor, Nicolás Maduro, global oil prices plummeted and Venezuela's petroleum-dependent economy collapsed.

After the collapse of the Soviet Union, Russia changed its constitution to remove references to communism. It describes itself as a Democratic republic.

For socialists' economies to work, several components must fall into place. These include:

- Depends on people being cooperative. (People are by nature competitive)
- Human greed must be limited. (Good luck with this one)
- Fewer rewards for entrepreneurship and innovation. (No incentive to do better or grow)
- Government can't abuse its greater power. (But it always does)
- People must be pushed harder to work and earn more. (People want more independence)

The biggest disadvantage of socialism is that it relies on the cooperative nature of humans for it to work. Capitalism can take advantage of the Greed is good drive. Socialism pretends greed doesn't exist. Socialism doesn't reward people for being entrepreneurial. It struggles to be as innovative as a capitalistic society. Another disadvantage is that the government has a lot of power. Government leaders can abuse this position and claim more power for themselves.

America's Founding Fathers included the promotion of the general welfare in the Constitution to balance capitalism's flaws. It instructed the government to protect the rights of all to pursue their idea of happiness. In American democracy, it's the government's role, directed by the vote of the people, to create a level playing field to allow that to happen.

Another disturbing factor about socialism is that most socialists choose to become atheists? In a real sense, they view the government as their god. In a time when 26% of Americans are unaffiliated with any religion, and the number of atheists and agnostics in the U.S. has doubled in the last ten years, many see atheism as their instrument of liberation. This declaration of atheism allowed them to embrace sexual hedonism and socialism. Society desired liberation from certain political and economic systems and liberation from any system of morality. They objected to morality because it interfered with their sexual freedom; they objected to the political and economic system because it was unjust. Atheists embrace absurd doctrines like communism or fascism to satisfy their hunger for meaning.

Socialist countries have been weak in distributing wealth to the poor. Socialism is not the answer. We must educate the rising generation about the true costs of socialism, and not just in dollars and cents. Would millennials be willing to accept communism with its denial of free speech, no free press, no free assembly, the imprisonment and often execution of dissidents, no open elections, no independent judiciary or rule of law, the dictatorship of the Communist Party in all matters and on all occasions? Socialism has failed in every country where it has been tried, from the Soviet Union and the People's Republic of China to three non-communist countries that tried but ultimately rejected socialism. All three of those countries Israel, India, and the United Kingdom adhered to socialist principles and practices for more than 20 years, only to change direction and adopt capitalism as the better way to economic prosperity. As a result, India today has the largest middle class in the free world.

Ten Reasons to Reject Socialism

1. Socialism and Communism are the same ideology. Communism is but an extreme form of socialism. From an ideological standpoint, there is no substantial difference between the two.
2. Socialism violates personal freedom. Socialism seeks to eliminate injustice by transferring rights and responsibilities from individuals to the State government. In the process, socialism creates injustice. It destroys liberty.
3. Socialism violates human nature. Socialism is anti-natural. It destroys personal initiative and replaces it with State control. It leads to totalitarianism, with its government and police repression, wherever it is implemented.
4. Socialism violates private property. Socialism calls for redistributing the wealth by taking from the rich to give to the poor. It uses taxation to promote economic and social egalitarianism.
5. Socialism opposes the traditional marriage. Socialism sees no moral reason for people to restrict sex to marriage, that is, to an indissoluble union between a man and a woman.
6. Socialism opposes parental rights in education. Socialism has the State, and not parents, control the education of children. Almost from birth, children are to be handed over to public

institutions, where they will be taught what the State wants, regardless of parental views. Evolution must be taught. School prayer must be forbidden.
7. Socialism promotes radical equality. Supposed absolute equality among humans is the fundamental assumption of socialism. It sees any inequality as unjust in itself. Private employers are quickly portrayed as exploiters whose profits belong to their employees.
8. Socialism promotes atheism. Belief in God clashes head-on with the principle of absolute equality. Socialism rejects the spiritual, claiming that only matter exists. God, the soul, and the next life are illusions according to socialism.
9. Socialism promotes relativism. For socialism there are no absolute truths or revealed morals that establish standards of conduct that apply to everyone, everywhere, and always. Everything evolves, including right and wrong, good, and evil.
10. Socialism mocks religion. According to Karl Marx, from Learn Religions, Austin Cline, *Religion as Opium of the People,* [3] Lenin said the same. Religion is a sort of spiritual booze in which the slaves of capitalism drown their human image, their demand for a life more or less worthy of a human.

Have you ever thought about what would happen if America become a socialist nation? The first is the redistribution of wealth. Not only is this the goal of the liberal left, but many in society will celebrate this event because of their lack of understanding of what redistribution of wealth entails and what socialism is. Because of the resentment, many have for the wealthy, this will be celebrated in the beginning. But where do you draw the line? Many believe this is all about helping the poor and giving equal rights to everyone. Well not so fast. Everyone will be required to hand over their possessions to the government. Anyone owning a house will have to give up ownership of that house. Socialism allows no ownership of real estate. The government will then have full authority to redistribute these assets in any manner it sees fit. The government has control, not the people. Second, the socialist government will ban the citizens from gun ownership. When citizens are no longer able to bear arms, the government has limitless control. Then we lose free speech. No criticizing the government unless you look forward to imprisonment.

Also lost is the right of citizens to vote. Democracy as we know it will no longer exist. Individuals will no longer have any rights. The U.S. will then be just like China and North Korea. Wages will go down as the state retains more of your money. Soon the economy will begin a slow and painful collapse as the lower wages create less spending to support the economy.

Socialism can't motivate the people to succeed because no matter how hard they work they will only receive the wages that the government allocates. Then the economy completely collapses and taxes go up with no end in sight

Socialism is a true utopia where no one owns property, or their own business, or earns a decent wage. With low income and higher taxes, it will be difficult to save money and provide yourself with a better future. There's simply no way to ever get ahead. This is the reality of socialism, it is not about getting something for free, as so many people falsely believe, it is only about giving up your freedom. Socialism has never benefited the people; it only benefits the very small ruling class. Beware, socialism is just around the corner.

CHAPTER 26

Censorship and the Cancel Culture

We are currently living in a culture that no longer values the concept of free speech. That may be hard to conceive but with the recent political developments, it's apparent that our society believes silencing others is more important than allowing people with different opinions to be heard. And this is coming from the liberal side, the side that used to value free speech at all costs. I am reminded of one of the liberal mottos you used to hear from time to time that says: *I may Disapprove of What You Say, But I Will Defend to the Death Your Right to Say It,*[1] from Quote Investigator website. As you can see from what's going on in the world today, liberals have abandoned this right to free speech and have replaced it with censorship. Liberals need to silence any thought, idea, or person who disagrees with their platform. But why do you suppose this is? Do they need to keep their followers in line? Are they afraid their followers will turn ship if they hear a better viewpoint? Are they trying to hide the truth?

Opinions, if different than that of the ruling authorities, the media, or social media platforms, are no longer valued or tolerated. The right to freely speak your opinion is under extreme attack. We now see something that we have never seen before in the history of our country, and that is the fight to eliminate free speech. News outlets and social media now practice censorship of speech daily. Post something on Facebook that Mark Zuckerberg disagrees with and your post is deleted. Do it more than once, your account gets removed. The question is, what are they so afraid of?

They are afraid of the truth. The liberal agenda is more important to them than the right to free speech. They know if the truth gets out, they will lose their influence and power. They believe in their power to shut people up. They do not care about people; they only care about power and their beliefs. They like to say that they are concerned about disinformation, but this is merely an excuse to hold on to their power and authority.

The social left doesn't even know what they are getting themselves into. They are gladly giving up their rights as citizens because they believe in the lie. They believe everything they hear from the Democratic party and the news media, and they are unwilling to research the facts for themselves. Soon we all will be second-class citizens controlled by a totalitarian government that liberals helped put in place.

Freedom of speech has been a right that has allowed America to thrive past and present. We should do everything we can to protect freedom of speech for all American citizens, even if it is used to criticize Christians and America itself.

Just think, the liberals are now using the same tactics as Hitler, Stalin, and Lenin. Removing free speech is nothing more than a power grab, to seize control of what people say and think.

Then there are cancellation attacks, which involve mobs denouncing people, publicly humiliating them, and attempting to punish them for legitimate ideas or political positions, or for minor mistakes and missteps. People have been attacked and/or fired for statements made that disagree with the censors of society. What happened to our respect for others? Treating others with kindness? People in society are now less important than ideas and ideology. This is completely different than God's values. We as Christians are called to love other people as much as we love ourselves.

Today's cancel culture cracks down on free speech by crushing an individual's right to use a platform to present their point of view. Ideas can't be thwarted by trying to snuff them out, choke them, murder them. Ideas simply cannot be killed that way.

Cancel culture is a new term permeating public conversation, which at its core is simply censorship dressed up in woke clothing and it's rampant in today's culture. This Cancel Culture attempts to harm the reputation, livelihood, and social presence of people, products, TV shows, celebrities, employees, etc., for violating a particular ideological standard. Cancel Culture warriors will use ridicule and shame others to get them fired from jobs and get others to not support them. It can be an oppressive means of attempted control of others. CARM, Matt Slick, *What is Cancel Culture?* [2]

Social media has given rise to a kind of unaccountable mob rule that punishes the so-called guilty for all sorts of moral violations. Cancelling can occur for not being on the right side of such topics as:

- Black Lives Matter – A leftist, anti-family, pro-Marxism, socialist ideology.
- Critical Race Theory – Examining society as it relates to race and power by judging people by their skin color.
- Gender Identity – A person's sense of his or her gender regardless of biology.
- Intersectionality – How discrimination and privilege manifest in a person's social framework.
- LGBTQ – An acronym symbolizing many sexual deviations.
- Race/Racism – Discrimination or privilege based on a person's skin color.
- Sexism – Discrimination of privilege based on a person's sexual orientation.
- Socialism – Increased governmental oversight with a decrease in personal freedom.
- Transsexuality – The surgical alteration to change a person's birth sex.
- White Privilege – The inherent privilege in society due to being white.

In today's world, the standard that describes what is acceptable and what is not is a liberal, pro-LGBTQ, pro-abortion, anti-racism, and anti-conservative attitude. If you do not agree with the leftist agenda, you can lose your reputation, popularity, or even your job. The Cancel Culture of the left is a hypocritical attitude of intolerance while demanding tolerance. Its depths and tentacles are varied and deeply interwoven into today's society. Americans say the political climate these days prevents them from saying things they believe because others might find them offensive. Nearly a third of employed Americans say they are worried about missing out on career opportunities or losing their job if their political opinions became known. CATO Institute, Todd Zywicki, *Extending the Culture Wars.* [3]

The liberal, self-righteous, online, Brownshirt, social police will take to Twitter, Facebook, chat forums, etc., to denounce and attack people who, for example, say anything bad about transgenderism, homosexuality, gender identity, LGBTQ, or have been deemed racist, or even support the wrong political candidate. This is Cancel Culture run amuck. Conservativism, Biblically-based morals, and non-politically correct attitudes are no longer welcome!

Of course, Christian ideals are not allowed, and the result is a denial of free speech for people with whom cancel culture warriors disagree.

Those in the cancel culture cannot logically or philosophically establish a means by which their view is the right one. They assume they have the ideological high ground, and all who oppose them must be silenced. But, on what do they base their moral standard? If you want to examine who is morally right, just look at abortion. Leftists have the self-centered view that killing a baby is good and they have the right to kill just for the sake of convenience. If that is not evil, then nothing is! Forbes, Evan Gerstmann, *What Is Cancel Culture?* [4]

Ultimately, we as Christians, answer to God, not to those who hold to politically correct ideology. Christians are obligated to fight unrighteousness in all of its forms. What do we do as Christians? It's simple:

- Pray (Ephesians 6:18)
- Be courteous (Colossians 4:5–6)
- Love your neighbor (Leviticus 19:18)
- Love them by speaking the truth, even if they don't (1 Corinthians 13:6)
- Quote scripture, when necessary, even if they don't affirm it (Isaiah 55:11)
- Be prepared to support your views with logic and documentation (1 Peter 3:15)
- Be prepared to be hated (Luke 21:17).

What if people complain and call you names? Just respond with kindness and patience and when the opportunity arises, speak the truth in love. Trust God through it all. God ultimately wins through love and Christians should always reach out to others in love. Just because liberals rage in hatred is no excuse for us to sink to their level. We stand on higher ground. We love our haters and we pray for them. That is the correct Christian response. We must obey God. God is always our priority and following Him and obeying Him is the true mark of a faithful Christian.

CHAPTER 27

Liberalism in the Christian Church

Today's Christian Church has become very diverse. Almost every Christian denomination has branches and divisions within the Church that have adopted a liberal bias. Perhaps because unity is preached so much, as well as our teachings to love all people, many Christians assume that we need to be all-inclusive for this to happen. What we must understand is that liberal doctrine is waging war against Christian beliefs. The Christian Church has an enemy, not just outside the Church, but within the Church as well. The liberal element within the Church is preaching a type of faith and practice that is anti-Christian to the core. Every true Christian must recognize this false religion of liberalism, yet many do not. It is strange how in the interests of an utterly false kindness to people, Christians are sometimes willing to relinquish their loyalty to God.

Liberalism denies the supernatural nature of Christianity; rejects the Bible as the inerrant Word of God, and focuses on this world, while it refuses to contemplate eternity.

Liberals have rejected Christian doctrine and Christian ethics. Theological liberalism believes that true religion is not based on external authority - liberal Christian thinkers have argued that religion should be modern and progressive and that the meaning of Christianity should be interpreted from the standpoint of modern knowledge and experience. They also believe that Christianity should be more focused on social issues rather than the teachings of God. Liberalism also believes truth can be known only through social change, not through the unchanging character of God. Many liberal views are directly opposed to biblical beliefs. For instance, most Christians would strongly agree that abortion is not supported by the Christian doctrine. However, many liberal Christians are now teaching otherwise. Recently, a Maryland United Church of Christ pastor said in an article by LifeNews.com, Micaiah Bilger, *United Church of Christ Pastor Celebrates Her Abortion,*[1] that she "never felt more loved by God" than when she walked into an abortion facility to abort her unborn baby. Can you believe this? Christian pastors are teaching unchristian values in our churches. Liberalism has invaded the values of our Christian faith and distorted its teaching. This must stop! We cannot allow false teaching to rear its ugly head and distort the Christian faith. Yet this is being accepted more and more, and many Christians are being led astray. Liberalism differs significantly from historic teaching. Liberals believe they are making Christianity relevant, credible, beneficial, and humane. However true believers understand that liberal teachings are making Christianity something other than Christianity.

So how can we know the differences between the traditional conservative Churches and the liberal Churches? It's important to know the difference because as a Christian you need to be grounded in the teachings of solid Biblical and Godly values.

Perhaps you attend a liberal Church and feel something not quite right. Or perhaps you struggle with why you feel strongly in favor of issues that are contrary to your understanding of Christian values. You may vote Democrat but you consider yourself a Christian. Might I suggest that you have been taught these unbiblical values for so long you just don't know what to believe in anymore? Take a look at the table below to see just how different a Conservative Church is from a Liberal Church. If you truly want to be a follower of Christ, instead of a follower of society's values, perhaps this may change your thinking. If not, then perhaps you should accept the fact that you may not value God as highly as you thought, but instead value the values of society more.

WORLDVIEW OF THE CHRISTIAN FAITH

Conservative Church	Liberal Church
Separation of Church and State - Conservatives believe in the power of God over the State.	Separation of Church and State - Liberals believe in the power of the State over God
Society Viewpoints - Mostly supports the Republican party. Supports the values of Western Civilization, Does Not Support Gay Marriage, Supports Pro-Life, believes in a government based on Democracy.	Society Viewpoint - Mostly supports the Democratic party. Does not support the values of Western Civilization, Supports Gay Marriage, Supports Abortion, believes in a government based on Socialism.
Evangelism - Conservative evangelicalism tends to focus on sin, repentance, and salvation. Believes in the purpose of reaching and saving the lost.	Evangelism - Liberal evangelism tends to focus on Christ's love and inclusion for marginalized people as the focus of their faith. Doesn't want to talk about their religious beliefs outside of their Church family.
God's Sovereignty and Will - God is utterly sovereign and omnipotent; he has revealed his will fully and finally in Scripture, and we need to obey it.	God's Sovereignty and Will - If God can be said to exist, he is dynamic, mysterious, other, largely, or wholly unknowable; but he is best known as love and goodness, and best seen in human beings. God may not be particularly strong or in control. His will is love, freedom, mercy.
Salvation - By means of Christ's atonement, being saved from our sins and their penalty – eternal punishment in hell. Salvation is only received by those who repent of their sins and make a commitment to follow Christ.	Salvation - Becoming fully human, free, alive, who we were meant to be; the redemption and restoration of all humanity, all creation, and the whole cosmos. This redemption is open to all, and all will (hopefully) ultimately enter into it.
The Gospel - Focus on crucifixion and divinity of Christ. Christ died on the cross for our sins, to save us from hell and bring us to eternal life if we repent and believe in him. Base all their practices on the unadulterated gospel of Christ (Mathew. 28:18; 2 Timothy 3:16-17).	The Gospel - Focus on incarnation and humanity of Christ. Christ came as one of us to model true humanity, freedom, and love, that we might learn how to become fully human, fully alive, fully free. Base many of their practices on the silence of the Scriptures, and appeal to the traditions of the past.
Mission - Primarily evangelism: preaching 'the gospel' to convert people, saving them from hell and making them disciples of Christ. Have no missionary, benevolent and educational organizations to execute the work of the church. They believe the local church is God's only organization to do his work (Philippians 1:1; Acts 14:23).	Mission - Active care for people, poor and planet; striving for a just society. Have missionary, benevolent, and educational organizations to execute the work of the church. Emphasize society and the physical man by appealing to the carnal nature with "church banquets," "church kitchens," "church camps," "fellowship halls," and all kinds of parties.

Conservative Church	Liberal Church
Pastors/Clergy/Elders - Have evangelists, elders (pastors) and teachers (Ephesians 4:11). Reject all such titles as unscriptural (Matthew 23:7-12). Do not expect their preachers to leave the work of God to serve tables (Acts 6:20). They have deacons and godly women to take care of the "physical needs" of the congregation and elders to do the planning (Acts 20:28). The preacher is left free to study, meditate, pray, and carry on the work of preaching the gospel to the lost (2 Timothy 2:15; 1 Timothy 4:12-16). The preacher is to visit the sick because he is a Christian (Matthew 25:36), not as a "preacher duty."	Pastors/Clergy/Elders - Have "educational directors," "associate ministers," "youth directors," and "superintendents" over their human organizations. Elevate their preachers above the rest of the members by using such titles as "doctor." Expect their preachers to be modern-day "pastors," running after the members and visiting the hospitals on a regular basis and to be the "head planner" of all their projects and promotions.
Sex/Sexuality - Dangerous, prime area of sin and temptation; only proper expression is within Christian marriage.	Sex/Sexuality - Broadly good and wholesome, and a range of expressions are valid; not something to get hung up over.
The Bible - The inspired, inerrant Word of God; literally true and factually accurate; the ultimate authority and final arbiter on all matters of truth, faith, doctrine, and Christian practice. Believe following God's Word explicitly is commanded by God's Word (Deuteronomy 4:2, Proverbs 30:6; 1 Corinthians 4:6; Galatians 1:6-9; 1 Peter 4:11; Revelation 22:18,19). Believe that all scripture is given by the inspiration of God and will judge us all (2 Timothy 3:16;17; John 12:48).	The Bible - Good and important, even (to an extent) inspired, but at least partly human; not flawless or inerrant; not the final word in all matters. Tradition, reason, and experience have equal weighting in decisions about doctrine and practice. Believe following God's Word explicitly is equated to being a hypocrite (Legalism). Do not believe that all scripture is given by the inspiration of God.
Hell - Real place or state of eternal conscious torment for all who have not accepted Christ as their Savior in their lifetime; just and everlasting punishment for all who have died in their sins.	Hell - If real at all, an existential state of profound alienation from one's true self or from reality and goodness; a rejection of the image of God in self and others; a loss of self; dehumanization. Not necessarily permanent, and not the automatic destination of non-Christians.
Attitude to other Traditions / Religions - Suspicion, fearfulness, even hostility; only evangelical Christianity is truly faithful to Christ's truth as revealed in Scripture; others are mostly heretics, apostates or unbelievers destined for hell unless they repent.	Attitude to other Traditions / Religions - Positive attitude, willingness to learn from other faiths and traditions. See most other faiths as valid and inspired, and all on basically the same path.
Satan - Very real, powerful being who is constantly seeking to attack, tempt, distract, and disrupt the life and ministry of the true believer, leading him/her astray into sin or heresy.	Satan - Metaphor for all the forces and powers in the world and in humanity that dehumanize and mar the image of God in people and creation, that oppress and enslave and abuse people and planet.

Conservative Church	Liberal Church
Christ - The divine Son of God, second person of the eternal Holy Trinity, begotten of God not created; the Lord, Savior, and redeemer of the world (or at least of the elect, of true believers).	Christ - The perfect example and expression of humanity, and of the divine potential and spark within all humanity.
Miracles and the Supernatural - Real and true in the Bible. Miracles continue today.	Miracles and the Supernatural - Miracles and the supernatural may or may not be real but aren't particularly important. Biblical miracles are mainly metaphorical and symbolic, carrying deeper meanings but not necessarily literally true. This may even extend to the Resurrection, and almost definitely the Virgin Birth.
The Cross and Atonement - Penal substitution: Christ's perfect sacrifice in our place and on our behalf, bearing the just punishment for our sins and so turning aside God's wrath from us.	The Cross and Atonement - Christ's identification with oppressed and suffering humanity in the face of brutality and evil, modelling for us the way of love and self-sacrifice.
Truth - Truth is primarily factual, propositional, binary (right/wrong, true/false, good/bad). The Bible is the final source of eternal and unchanging truth, which we must obey by an act of intellectually and then will.	Truth - Truth is deep, complex, mysterious, paradoxical, unpredictable, dynamic; it cannot simply be read from a book. Relational, interpersonal, and experiential truth are as important as (or more important than) factual, logical truth.

The more religious a person is, the more conservative they are, and this relationship is strongly mediated by the value placed on tradition and respect for customs and institutions. Liberals place their value on universalism and social tolerance. As with previous studies, conservatives were more conscientious, while liberals were more agreeable and more open to new ideas and experiences.

In a recent study, it has been discovered that many liberal Churches are dying at an extremely rapid pace. Practically every liberal denomination — Methodist, Lutheran, Presbyterian — that has tried to adapt itself to contemporary liberal values has seen a drastic plunge in church attendance. Within the Catholic Church, too, the most progressive-minded religious orders have often failed to sustain themselves. Liberal churches are in trouble: A 2015 report by the Pew Research Center found that these congregations are now shrinking by about one million members annually. Faced with this troubling development, clergy members have made various efforts to revive church attendance. It was almost twenty years ago that John Shelby Spong, a U.S. bishop in the Episcopalian Church, published his book *Why Christianity Must Change or Die*. Harvey Cox, a theological liberal, comments on Spong's book in the Whosoever, Rev. Candice Chellew, article *Why Christianity Must Change or Die*, [2] said congregations would grow if they abandoned their literal interpretation of the Bible and adapt to the changing times. Harvard Divinity professor and liberal theologian Harvey Cox said Bishop Spong's work is a significant accomplishment, and indeed, Cox himself has been involved with shifting Christianity to meet the needs of the modern world. Thus, liberal theology has been taught for decades in mainline seminaries and preached from many mainline pulpits. Its enduring appeal to embattled clergy members is that it gives intellectual respectability to religious ideas that, on the surface, might appear far-fetched to modern audiences.

But the liberal turn in mainline churches doesn't appear to have solved their problem of decline. Over the last five years, a comparison study was performed between growing mainline congregations to those that were declining. The survey received responses from over 2,200 congregants. The results of the study came to a counterintuitive discovery: Conservative Protestant theology, with its more literal view of the Bible, is a significant predictor of church growth while liberal theology leads to decline. The results were published in the peer-reviewed journal, Review of Religious Research.

Also found by the study, on Springer Link, David Millard Haskel, *Theology Matters: Comparing the Traits of Growing and Declining Mainline Protestant Church Attendees and Clergy*, [3] growing church clergy members were most conservative theologically, followed by their congregants, who were themselves followed by the congregants of the declining churches and then the declining church clergy members. In other words, growing church clergy members are the most theologically conservative, while declining church clergy members are the least.

For example, the study found that 93% of clergy members and 83% of worshipers from growing churches agreed with the statement, Jesus rose from the dead with a real flesh-and-blood body leaving behind an empty tomb. This compared with 67% of worshipers and 56% of clergy members from declining liberal churches. Also growing church clergy members and 90% of their worshipers agreed that God performs miracles in answer to prayers, compared with 80% of worshipers and a mere 44% of clergy members from declining churches.

Growing churches have been identified as almost exclusively conservative in doctrine. What explains the growth gap between liberal and conservative congregations? Because of their conservative outlook, the growing church clergy members in the study took Jesus' command to go make disciples literally. Thus, they all held the conviction it's very important to encourage non-Christians to become Christians, and thus likely put effort into converting non-Christians. Conversely, because of their liberal leanings, half the clergy members at the declining churches held the opposite conviction, believing it is not desirable to convert non-Christians. Some of them felt, for instance, that peddling their religion outside of their immediate faith community is culturally insensitive. But don't you think that if you truly love God and love people, wouldn't you want to share God with others so that they too can have eternal life? It seems as though liberals do not love God, or people, enough to share the good news. Consider what the early church did to spread the gospel all around the world, but it appears that liberals are ashamed of their religion and their God.

The views of liberal Christians are quite alarming. Rachel Held Evans, a liberal Christian, shares her beliefs on; First Things, David T. Koyzis, *LIBERAL AND CONSERVATIVE CHRISTIANITY ... AND IN BETWEEN,*[4] where Rachel Held Evans – *Post her beliefs,*[5]

- I do not fit in the conservative evangelical church.
- I believe in evolution.
- I vote for Democrats.
- I doubt.
- I enjoy interfaith dialog and cooperation.
- I like smells, bells, liturgy, and rituals particularly when it comes to the Eucharist.
- I'm passionate about gender equality in marriage and church leadership.
- I'm tired of the culture wars.
- I want to become a better advocate for social justice.
- I want my LGBTQ friends to feel welcome and accepted in their churches.

Unfortunately, Rachel Evans has since pasted, but if she had loved her friends, she would have shown them in love, how immoral their sexual actions were, and how those actions separated them from God. Without change, her friends will never follow Christ, who makes it clear that sexual relations are only to take place between a man and a woman in marriage. When your views stray so far away from Biblical values, it's no wonder the liberal church is failing. Their social views are more important to them than Biblical or Godly values. Faith cannot survive with these convoluted beliefs. As Jesus stated in Matthew 6:24; "No one can serve two masters. For you will hate one and love the other; you will be devoted to one and despise the other."

Liberals are trying to serve two masters, one is God, and one is society. They will eventually be forced to make a choice. Which master will they choose? It should be obvious which of these two convictions is more likely to generate church growth.

While the research helps explains the dwindling ranks of liberal mainline congregations, it isn't likely to bring much joy to the world of mainliners, especially those on the theological left. But, if it's any consolation, when it comes to growth in mainline churches, Spong and other liberals are right to claim that Christianity must change or die. They just get the direction of the change wrong.

SECTION 4
Science and Religion

There is a huge battle going on in our country today between those who seek out science, and those who seek God. For some, science motivates their beliefs and understanding of all things, while others are motivated by their faith. But must science and religion be at odds?

All the arguments that we make are based on our worldview. The scientific method is anchored in the ideas of repeatability, falsifiability, and testability. Each of these ideas assumes that there is a uniformity to the world that we live in. But on what grounds can we assume that the universe should operate uniformly? Only because God has created the universe to function according to specific laws.

Science is the systematic study of things to gain knowledge that is generated by the study. In the past, the supernatural origins of the universe and everything in the universe were assumed to be true because they are revealed in the Bible. Today, this is no longer the case, as there is now a wide schism between science and religion. Atheistic and Humanistic thought today drive the path of science, while completely ignoring the supernatural and removing God from the equation.

Because God created the universe, it follows that certain natural laws were put into place by Him. God created the laws of nature to guide the universe along a stable and predictable path. God created a universe that operates within His established laws proving again that science and the Bible work together.

We see the principle of uniformity present in the early chapters of the Bible where God created the various kinds of plants and animals to reproduce after their kind. More specifically, (Genesis 8:22) communicates God's intention to uphold the earth consistently. Connecting this to passages like (Hebrews 1:3) provides a solid foundation for understanding why the universe is the way it is.

Someone who rejects the Bible can believe that there is uniformity in the universe, but they have no reason to believe that the universe should be a place of order. He is making an arbitrary assumption about the universe with no reasoning to support that assumption. This doctrine is often summarized in the phrase the present is the key to the past. However, the present is not the key to understanding the past. The earth has undergone many changes in its history, and the current state is nowhere near its past state.

Many people claim that those who have a naturalistic, atheistic scientific worldview are neutral and approach their study of the world objectively. But, if you don't believe in supernatural events, you are biased against the supernatural.

The question is: which bias is the best bias to be biased by? Which worldview provides the true foundation for examining the world we live in? Every person takes these starting assumptions on faith. Whether it is faith in science or faith in God.

If we start from a biblical perspective, "we understand that the worlds were framed by the word of God, so that the things which are seen were not made of visible things" (Hebrews 11:3). Christians trust that God created the universe out of nothing because He has told us that He did, not because we have seen or experienced the origin of the universe.

Those whose faith is in science without the possibility of supernatural events, do so with a faith that rests on many assumptions. It takes a lot of faith to believe in the naturalistic origins of the universe, our planet, and all the life on it. Voddie Baucham, *Why I Choose to Believe the Bible.* [1]

Many so-called scientific facts are not facts at all. In science, a fact typically refers to an observation, measurement, or another form of evidence that can be tested or expected to occur the same way under similar circumstances. However, many scientific theories have never been observed, tested, or validated. That is the difference between a theory and a law. A theory has not gone through this verification process as the law has. Thus, the theory of evolution, is not a law, it is a theory not proven by the testing of science.

CHAPTER 28

Astronomy

Astronomy studies the laws of the stars, celestial objects, and other phenomena. It uses mathematics, physics, and chemistry to explain their origin and evolution. Objects of interest include planets, moons, stars, nebulae, galaxies, and comets. Relevant phenomena include Supernova explosions, gamma-ray bursts, quasars, blazars, pulsars, and cosmic microwave background radiation. More generally, astronomy studies everything that originates beyond Earth's atmosphere. Within the scientific community, astronomers have estimated the age of the earth to be about 4.6 billion years old with the universe being even older, around 13.7 billion years. These ages are based on two fundamental assumptions. (one) Naturalism, the belief that nature is all there is, and (two) uniformitarianism, the belief that current rates and conditions are the same as past rates and conditions. Both assumptions are false, even the scientific community admits that the rate of expansion of the universe is slowing down. Ruling out supernatural activity from God eliminates many possibilities. If these starting assumptions are not correct, then there is no reason to trust their conclusions. Modern science has limited itself by its artificial limitation to naturalism, or secularism, without any consideration for the supernatural. Space.com, Jamie Carter, *What is astronomy?*[1] As we look at the following points of evidence from Answers in Genesis, Dr. Jason Lisle, *The New Answer Book 3, Chapter 19, Does Astronomy Confirm a Young Universe?*[2] we will learn that the earth and universe are much younger than suggested.

- Galaxies: Spiral galaxies pose a problem for the secular time scale. Spiral galaxies contain blue stars in their arms. But blue stars are very luminous and expend their fuel quickly. They cannot last billions of years. Secular astronomers realize this and so they simply assume that new blue stars form continuously (from collapsing clouds of gas) to replenish the supply. However, star formation is riddled with theoretical problems. It has never been observed, nor could it truly be observed since the process is supposed to take hundreds of thousands of years. The spiral arms of galaxies rotate differentially—meaning the inner portions rotate faster than the outer portions. Every spiral galaxy is essentially twisting itself up—becoming tighter and tighter with time. In far less than one billion years, the galaxy should be twisted to the point where the arms are no longer recognizable. Many galaxies are supposed to be ten billion years old in the secular view, yet their spiral arms are easily recognizable. The spiral structure of galaxies strongly suggests that they are much younger than generally accepted. We have assumed hypothetically that both naturalism and uniformitarianism are true, and yet we still find that the estimated ages come out much younger than the old-universe view requires. This shows that the billions of years the old-universe view is internally inconsistent.
- The Stars: Current models predict very gradual changes. The sun, for example, is predicted to pass through several stages in the coming ages. Each stage is assumed to last for millions of years. Observations suggest that some stars may age much more rapidly than generally believed. For example, consider Sirius, the brightest nighttime star. At a distance of 8.6 light-years from earth, it is known as the Dog Star, prominent in the Canis Major constellation. Sirius has a dwarf companion star, and there is intriguing evidence that this dwarf may have formed from a red giant in just the past 1,000 years. Historical records, including those of Ptolemy, describe Sirius as red or pink. The suggestion is that the red giant companion dominated the pair at this early time. Today, Sirius is a brilliant blue-white color and its dwarf companion is invisible. Other stars also occasionally show unexpected color changes, indicating possible rapid aging

WORLDVIEW OF THE CHRISTIAN FAITH

processes. Such events call into question the fundamental time scale of current stellar evolution models.

- <u>Comets</u>: Comets don't last forever. They could be ejected from the solar system or collide with other objects as they rotate around the sun. As time goes by, there are fewer and fewer comets. The question is: why do comets still exist? On a time scale of multiple billions of years, they should all be long gone by now. The average number of solar revolutions before a comet dissipates is estimated to be about forty trips. Based on the rate at which comets are destroyed today, it is surprising (from an old-universe perspective) that comets are still present. The supply should have been depleted billions of years ago. How then do secular astronomers explain these apparently young comets in a solar system that they believe to be billions of years old? The presence of comets is evidence that the solar system is not nearly as old as is often assumed.

- <u>The Sun</u>: Astronomers use the term stellar evolution for the aging process of stars. Our sun is assumed to be in its midlife stage, 4.6 billion years of age, as it gradually converts its hydrogen to helium via nuclear fusion reactions in its core. However, a basic time problem arises. Computer modeling of the sun on an evolutionary time scale predicts that the sun must gradually brighten. If true, the sun would be 30% dimmer during the period 3.8–2.5 billion years ago. Geologic evidence points to an earth that was warmer in the past (irrespective of the time scale). This means that there is a fundamental problem with the unlimited extrapolation back in the time of solar energy output. The alternative is that the sun was placed in the heavens much more recently than billions of years ago.

- <u>The Earth</u>: Prevailing winds are caused by two phenomena. The sun's heat causes north-south or south-north winds, depending on latitude. The rotation of the earth causes the winds to shift east or west—clockwise north of the equator and counterclockwise to the south. This Coriolis effect is proportional to the speed of the earth's rotation: the greater the rotational speed, the greater the Coriolis effect. Due to these prevailing winds, the Sahara Desert is in the process of desertification, expanding approximately four miles per year. Calculations based on the rate of the Sahara's expansion show the desert to be 4,000 years old. This young age of the Sahara Desert fits quite well in the creationist timeline, beginning its desertification process soon after the global Flood. The current slowing rate of the earth's rotation, and its relationship with the Coriolis effect, allows for a variety of climates around the world without creating a menacing environment. Following the evolutionist timeline throughout millions of years, the Sahara Desert should have already expanded to its maximum size. However, since the earth's rotational speed is decreasing measurably, the Coriolis effect would have been far greater millions of years ago, exacerbating the evolutionists' difficulty explaining the Sahara Desert's young age. Studies over the past 140 years show a consistent decay rate in the earth's magnetic field. At this rate, as few as 25,000 years ago, the earth would have been unable to support life because of the heat from the electric current.

- <u>The Moon</u>: The current scientific opinion declares that the moon was created by an ancient collision of the earth with a Mars-size space object. Consider the gravitational tide force between the earth and moon. This interaction results in a very gradually receding moon, and a slowing of the earth's rotation. A slight delay in the earth's high tides results in a forward pull on the moon, causing it to slowly spiral outward from the earth. In turn, the moon's gravity pulls back on the earth, slightly decreasing its spin. Currently, the moon is drifting away from the earth by 3.82 cm/yr. (1.5 in/yr.). However, this recession is highly nonlinear and would have been greater in the past. If one assumes unlimited extrapolation back in time, gravity theory shows the moon in direct physical contact (in the same location) with earth about 1.55 billion years ago. The tides lead to a limited time scale for the moon, far less than 1.55 billion years. However, evolutionists assume that the moon and solar system are 4.6 billion years old. Life, they assume, originated on earth about 3.5 billion years ago. The fundamental problem with the evolutionary time scale is obvious. The moon has moved outward by only about 755 feet (230 m) since its creation. The moon was placed in orbit close to its present earth's distance. On a larger time, scale, of 1.55 to 4.6 billion years, the earth and moon would have to occupy the same physical space which is impossible. For the earth and the moon to be in their current positions, and drifting apart at the current rate, would require a much shorter time scale, in the thousands of years, not billions of years.

CHAPTER 29

Cosmology

Cosmology is a branch of astronomy that studies the universe as a whole. Cosmologists puzzle over exotic concepts like string theory, dark matter, and dark energy and whether there is one universe or many (sometimes called the multiverse). Earth was regarded as the center of all things, with planets and stars orbiting it. In the 16th century, Polish scientist Nicolaus Copernicus suggested that Earth and the other planets in the solar system orbited the sun. Albert Einstein proposed the unification of space and time in his General Theory of Relativity. In the early 1900s, scientists were debating whether the Milky Way contained the whole universe within its span, or whether it was simply one of many collections of stars. Most secular scientists today think that the earth formed about the same time as the sun and everything else in the solar system—about 4.6 billion years ago. However, there are many problems with the scientific, evolutionary ideas of cosmology which include the following from, Answers in Genesis, Dr, Danny R. Faulkner, *What About Cosmology?*[1]

- <u>Missing Monopoles</u> - Most people know something about magnets—like the kind found in a compass or the kind that sticks to a refrigerator. We often say that magnets have two "poles"—a north pole and a south pole. Poles that are alike will repel each other, while opposites attract. A "monopole" is a hypothetical massive particle that is just like a magnet but has only one pole. So, a monopole would have either a north pole or a south pole, but not both. Particle physicists claim that many magnetic monopoles should have been created in the high temperature conditions of the big bang. Since monopoles are stable, they should have lasted to this day. Yet, despite considerable search efforts, monopoles have not been found. Where are the monopoles? The fact that we don't find any monopoles suggests that the universe never was that hot. This indicates that there never was a big bang, but it is perfectly consistent with the Bible's account of creation, since the universe did not start infinitely hot.

- <u>The Flatness Problem</u> - Another serious challenge to the big-bang model is called the flatness problem. The expansion rate of the universe appears to be very finely balanced with the force of gravity; this condition is known as flat. If the universe were the accidental by-product of a big bang, it is difficult to imagine how such a fantastic coincidence could occur. Big-bang cosmology cannot explain why the matter density in the universe isn't greater, causing it to collapse upon itself (closed universe), or less, causing the universe to rapidly fly apart (open universe). The problem is even more severe when we extrapolate into the past. Since any deviation from perfect flatness tends to increase as time moves forward, it logically follows that the universe must have been *even more* precisely balanced in the past than it is today. Thus, at the moment of the big bang, the universe would have been virtually flat to an extremely high precision. This must have been the case (assuming the big bang), despite the fact that the laws of physics allow for an *infinite* range of values. This is a coincidence that stretches credulity to the breaking point. Of course, in the creation model, "balance" is expected since the Lord has fine-tuned the universe for life.
- <u>Inflating the Complexities</u> - Many secular astronomers have come up with an idea called "inflation" in an attempt to address the flatness and monopole problems (as well as other problems not addressed in detail here, such as the horizon problem). Inflation proposes that the universe temporarily went through a period of accelerated expansion. Amazingly, there is no real supporting evidence for inflation; it appears to be nothing more than an unsubstantiated conjecture—much like the big bang

itself. Moreover, the inflation idea has difficulties of its own, such as what would start it and how it would stop smoothly. In addition, other problems with the big bang are not solved, even if inflation were true. These are examined below.

- <u>Where Is the Antimatter?</u> - Consider the "baryon number problem." Recall that the big bang supposes that matter (hydrogen and helium gas) was created from energy as the universe expanded. However, experimental physics tells us that whenever matter is created from energy, such a reaction also produces *antimatter*. Antimatter has similar properties to matter, except the charges of the particles are reversed. (So, whereas a proton has a positive charge, an antiproton has a negative charge.) Any reaction where energy is transformed into matter produces an exactly equal amount of antimatter; there are no known exceptions. The big bang (which has no matter to begin with, only energy) should have produced exactly equal amounts of matter and antimatter, and that should be what we see today. But we do not. The visible universe is comprised almost entirely of matter—with only trace amounts of antimatter anywhere. This devastating problem for the big bang is actually consistent with biblical creation; it is a design feature. God created the universe to be essentially matter only—and it's a good thing He did. When matter and antimatter come together, they violently destroy each other. If the universe had equal amounts of matter and antimatter (as the big bang requires), life would not be possible.
- <u>Missing Population III Stars</u> - The big-bang model by itself can only account for the existence of the three lightest elements (hydrogen, helium, and trace amounts of lithium). This leaves about 90 or so of the other naturally occurring elements to be explained. Since the conditions in the big bang are not right to form these heavier elements (as big-bang supporters readily concede), secular astronomers believe that stars have produced the remaining elements by nuclear fusion in the core. This is thought to occur in the final stages of a massive star as it explodes (a supernova). The explosion then distributes the heavier elements into space. Second- and third-generation stars are thus "contaminated" with small amounts of these heavier elements. If this story were true, then the *first* stars would have

been comprised of only the three lightest elements (since these would have been the only elements in existence initially). Some such stars should still be around today since their potential life span is calculated to exceed the (big bang) age of the universe. Such stars would be called "Population III" stars. Amazingly (to those who believe in the big bang), Population III stars have not been found anywhere. All known stars have at least trace amounts of heavy elements in them. It is amazing to think that our galaxy alone is estimated to have over 100 billion stars in it, yet not one star has been discovered that is comprised of only the three lightest elements.

With all the problems listed above, as well as many others too numerous to include, it is not surprising that quite a few secular astronomers are beginning to abandon the big bang. Although it is still the dominant model at present, increasing numbers of physicists and astronomers are realizing that the big bang simply is not a good explanation of how the universe began. In the May 22, 2004, issue of *New Scientist*, there appeared an open letter to the scientific community written primarily by *secular scientists* who challenge the big bang. These scientists pointed out that the copious arbitrary assumptions and the lack of successful big-bang predictions challenge the legitimacy of the model. Among other things, they state:

The big bang today relies on a growing number of hypothetical entities, things that we have never observed—inflation, dark matter and dark energy are the most prominent examples. Without them, there would be a fatal contradiction between the observations made by astronomers and the predictions of the big bang theory. In no other field of physics would this continual recourse to new hypothetical objects be accepted as a way of bridging the gap between theory and observation. It would, at the least, raise serious questions about the validity of the underlying theory.

This statement has since been signed by hundreds of other scientists and professors at various institutions. The big bang seems to be losing considerable popularity. Secular scientists are increasingly rejecting the big bang in favor of other models. If the big bang is abandoned, what will happen to all the Christians who compromised and claimed that the Bible is compatible with the big bang? What will they say? Will they claim that the Bible actually does not teach the big bang, but instead that it teaches the latest secular model? Secular models come and go, but God's Word does not need to be changed because God got it exactly right the first time.

The big bang has many scientific problems. These problems are symptomatic of the underlying incorrect worldview. The big bang erroneously assumes that the universe was *not* supernaturally created, but that it came about by natural processes billions of years ago. However, reality does not line up with this notion. Biblical creation explains the evidence in a more straightforward way without the ubiquitous speculations prevalent in secular models. But ultimately, the best reason to reject the big bang is that it goes against what the Creator of the universe himself has taught: "In the beginning God created the heaven and the earth" (Genesis 1:1).

CHAPTER 30

Evolution

The theory of evolution states that species change over time and become new species. Charles Darwin proposed that individuals with traits most suitable to their environments lived long enough to reproduce and passed down those desirable traits to their offspring. Over time, only the fittest traits of the species survived. Eventually, after enough time passed, these small adaptations would add up to create new species. Primate evolution and the idea that humans evolved from monkeys has been a major point of friction between scientific and religious communities. Evolutionists look at three options for the beginning of life: Option one is the most popular. Life spontaneously originated in a simple form inside a primordial soup. Option two is similar to option one, except instead of primordial soup, life originated from non-life in an underwater hydrothermal vent. Lastly, option three is called panspermia. That's where life originated in another part of the universe and was delivered by a comet (or even an advanced alien civilization) to early earth when conditions were just right for life to evolve. Evolution is taken as fact by both unbelievers and many Christians. The story of evolution leaves no room for a supernatural Creator.

Evolutionary processes are supposed to be purely naturalistic. Evolutionists begin with the assumption that humans evolved from apes. Evolutionists generally do not believe that humans evolved from an ape that is now living, so they look to fossils of humans and apes to provide them with their desired evidence. Fossil apes having such features are declared to be ancestral to humans (or at least collateral relatives) and are called hominids. Living apes, on the other hand, are not considered to be hominids, but rather are called hominoids because they are only similar to humans but did not evolve into them. If evolution were true, then where is the evidence of different types of animals now evolving into other types? Where is the evidence of cats, dogs, and horses gradually turning into something else? We do see changes within species, but we do not see any changes into other species. And, as mentioned, we see no evidence of gradual change in the fossil record either. The only historical evidence that could support the ape ancestry of humans must come from fossils. Unfortunately, the fossil record of humans and apes is very sparse. Approximately 95% of all known fossils are marine invertebrates, about 4.7% are algae and plants, about 0.2% are insects and other invertebrates, and only about 0.1% are vertebrates (animals with bones). Because of the rarity of fossil hominids, even many of those who specialize in the evolution of humans have never actually seen an original hominid fossil. Teeth and jaw fragments are the most frequently found primate fossils. Thus, much of the evidence for the ape ancestry of humans is based on similarities of teeth and jaws. The problem in declaring a fossil ape to be a human ancestor based on certain humanlike features of the teeth is that some living apes have these same features and they are not considered to be ancestors of humans. Thick enamel is one of the most commonly cited criteria for declaring an ape fossil to be a hominid. Artistic imagination has been used to illustrate entire ape-human from nothing more than a single tooth. In the early 1920s, the ape-man Hesperopithecus (which consisted of a single tooth) was pictured in the London Illustrated News complete with the tooth's wife, children, domestic animals, and cave! Experts used this tooth, known as Nebraska Man, as proof of human evolution. Later, Nebraska man was found to be an extinct peccary (wild pig)!

Skulls are perhaps the most interesting primate fossils. However, the skulls of apes and the skulls of humans are vastly different.

The most eagerly sought-after evidence in fossil hominids is an anatomical feature that might suggest bipedality (the ability to walk on two legs). Since humans walk on two legs, any evidence of bipedality in fossil apes is considered by evolutionists to be compelling evidence for human ancestry. But we should bear in mind that the way an ape walks on two legs is entirely different from the way a human walks on two legs. The distinctive human gait requires the complex integration of many skeletal and muscular features in our hips, legs, and feet. Thus, evolutionists closely examine the hipbones (pelvis), thighbones (femur), leg bones (tibia and fibula), and foot bones of fossil apes to detect any anatomical features that might suggest bipedality. Humans can keep their weight over their feet while walking because their femurs converge toward the knees, forming a carrying angle of approximately nine degrees with the tibia. In contrast, chimps and gorillas have widely separated, straight legs with a carrying angle of essentially zero degrees. These animals manage to keep their weight over their feet when walking by swinging their body from side to side in the familiar ape walk. Evolutionists assume that fossil apes with a high carrying angle (humanlike) were bipedal and thus evolved into humans. The point is that there are living tree-dwelling apes and monkeys with some of the same anatomical features that evolutionists consider to be definitive evidence for bipedality, yet none of these animals walks like a human and no one suggests they are our ancestors or descendants. Charles Dawson, a medical doctor, and an amateur paleontologist discovered a mandible (lower jawbone) and part of a skull in a gravel pit near Piltdown, England. The jawbone was apelike but had teeth that showed wear similar to the human pattern. The skull, on the other hand, was very humanlike. These two specimens were combined to form what was called Dawn man, which was calculated to be 500,000 years old. The whole thing turned out to be an elaborate hoax. The skull was indeed human (about five hundred years old), while the jaw was that of a modern female orangutan whose teeth had been filed to crudely resemble the human wear pattern. The success of this hoax for over fifty years, despite the scrutiny of the best authorities in the world, led the human evolutionist, Sir Solly Zuckerman, to declare: "It is doubtful if there is any science at all in the search for human's fossil ancestry." Religio-Political Talk (RPT), *Imagination and Plaster of Paris = Lucy*. Man, and the apes have never had an ancestor in common. Assuming they did, for the sake of analyzing the argument, then forty million separate mutation events would have had to take place and become fixed in the population in only 300,000 generations.

Evolution's Hoaxes

Evolutionists have had difficulty in finding evidence and proof that their theory is valid. So in an attempt to prove their evolutionary theory, some evolutionists have resorted to falsifying the records to create their desired results. Below are some of the well-known cases that were used to try and prove evolution as fact, but were later proven to be fake:

- Nebraska Man: How many skeletons do you think were found of Nebraska Man? One hundred? Twenty-five? five? How about one? It turns out that Nebraska man was reconstructed from a single tooth. What is even more amazing-the tooth turned out later to be a pig's tooth!
- Java Man: How many skeletons do you think were found of Java Man? Java Man was reconstructed from a skullcap, thighbone, and two molar teeth. Dr. Eugene DuBois found the thighbone fifty feet away from the skullcap but assumed it was the same individual. After discovering human skulls at the same level as his Java Man discovery, he hid the skulls under the floorboards of his bedroom for twenty-six years. Before his death, DuBois confessed that he had not found the missing link and admitted that Java Man was probably a giant gibbon.
- Piltdown Man: In 1912 Charles Dawson reconstructed Piltdown Man out of a jaw, two molar teeth, and a piece of skull. In 1953 the hoax was exposed. The jawbone turned out to be that of a modern orangutan, the teeth had been filed down and the bones artificially colored to deceive the public. For over forty years evolutionists promoted his findings as fact.
- Orce Man: Found in the southern Spanish town of Orce in 1982, and hailed as the oldest fossilized human remains ever found in Europe. One year later officials admitted the skull fragment was not human, but probably came from a four-month-old donkey. Scientists had said the skull belonged to a seventeen-year-old man who lived 900,000 to 1.6 million years ago and even had very detailed drawings done to represent what he would have looked like.
- The Taung Child: A fossil skull discovered by Raymond Dart in South Africa in 1924 was initially depicted as a supposed ancestor of humans. However, contemporary evolutionists can no longer maintain that it represents such an ancestor—because it subsequently transpired that the skull belonged to a young gorilla!

- Ramapithecus: A partial jawbone, consisting of two parts, was discovered by G.E. Lewis in India in the 1930s. Based on these two jaw bone fragments, claimed to be fourteen million years old, evolutionists reconstructed Ramapithecus's family and supposed natural habitat. For fifty years, the fossil was portrayed as an ancestor of Man but following the results of a 1981 anatomical comparison with a baboon skeleton, evolutionists were forced to quietly set it aside.
- Boule's Neanderthal Man: Reconstructed in 1915. Marcellin Boule wrongly arranged the foot bones so that the big toe diverged from the other toes to look like an opposing thumb. The knee joint was misplaced to give a bent knee look. The spine was misshapen so it couldn't stand upright and the head was placed in an unbalanced position too far forward. Boule's model of Neanderthal man was placed on display in the Field Museum of Natural History in Chicago for forty-four years before the mistakes were discovered.
- The Neanderthal Fraud: After a skull was discovered in the Neander Valley in 1856 by Prof. Protsch, evolutionists suggested that Neanderthals were primitive ape-human. To make matters worse, the skull was dated at 36,000 years old, allowing it to fall neatly into the evolutionists' timeline between Neanderthals and modern human. Later it was found that the fossil was the remains of a modern human afflicted with rickets and osteoporosis.
- Lucy the Hominid: This fossil, discovered in Africa in 1974, was widely esteemed by evolutionists and was the subject of some of the most intensive speculation. Recently it has been revealed that Lucy (A. afarensis) had an anatomy ideally suited to climbing trees and was no different from other apes we are familiar with. Yet Lucy has been Evolution's poster child. Very creatively designed sculptures of Lucy appear in museums, and these sculptures are hoaxes, not following the obvious ape-like bone structures, but rather dishonestly presenting Lucy as if she had human-like bone structures. Religio-Political Talk (RPT), *IOmagination and Plaster of Paris = Lucy.*[1]
- Earnst Haeckels evolution Embryo: The Haeckel embryo sequence has long been said to demonstrate that humans share a common ancestry with animals and thus prove the theory of

evolution. Pictures were designed by Ernst Haeckel. For example, the dog embryo and human embryo, in his book, are completely identical. Haeckel maintained that he faithfully copied the dog embryo from Bischoff (forth week). They then reprinted the original drawing made by Bischoff of the dog embryo at four weeks and the original of a human embryo at four weeks made by Haeckel. The originals were completely different! Elsewhere in Haeckel's book, that same fraud is used to portray a dog, a chicken, and a tortoise! He was charged with fraud by five professors and convicted by a university court. His deceit was exposed in *Haeckel's Frauds and Forgeries*, a 1915 book by J. Assmuth and Ernest R. Hull, Creationism, *Haeckel's Frauds and Forgeries*,[2] who quoted nineteen leading authorities of the day. Haeckel's drawings are still printed in some of today's school science textbooks with full knowledge that they are wrong.

- Pithecanthropus Erectus: After years of excavations with the assistance of forced laborers, they dug up a tooth and skullcap. The skullcap was ape-like having a low forehead and large eyebrow ridges. The following year and about forty feet away, the workmen uncovered a human thigh bone. Due to the proximity of the find, they assumed they belonged to the same creature. In 1907, they hired seventy-five workers and sent forty-three crates of fossil material back to the place, but no evidence of Pithecanthropus could be found. Instead, they found modern flora and fauna in the strata where they had found the Pithecanthropus. Two other skullcaps were uncovered which were human. The man who found it failed to display the human skullcaps when parading his Pithecanthropus. He kept the skulls hidden under the floorboards of his house for thirty years, then finally made them known in the 1920s. Professor Reiner Protsch von Zieten: He was famous for finding missing links suggesting the interbreeding of Neanderthals with humans—until he was exposed in 2005. The Guardian newspaper's correspondent in Berlin, Luke Harding, wrote about this in his article "History of Modern Man Unravels as German Scholar Is Exposed as a Fraud": The Guardian, David Adam, *History of Modern Man Unravels as German Scholar Is Exposed as a Fraud*, Luke Harding.[3] His discovery appeared to show that Neanderthals

had spread much further north than was previously known. But ... a crucial Hamburg skull fragment, which was believed to have come from the world's oldest German, a Neanderthal known as Hahnhöfersand Man, was a mere 7,500 years old, according to Oxford University's radiocarbon dating unit. The unit established those other skulls had been wrongly dated as well. Another of the professor's sensational finds, Binshof-Speyer woman, lived in 1,300 B.C. and not 21,300 years ago, as he had claimed, while 'Paderborn-Sande man' (dated at 27,400 B.C.) only died a couple of hundred years ago, in 1750.
- <u>Charles Darwin</u>: Darwin became the figurehead for a system of thought that was one catch-all explanation for how things are in nature. Richard Dawkins said that "Darwin made it possible to be an intellectually satisfied atheist." Conservapedia, *Essay: Is Richard Dawkins an intellectually fulfilled atheist?*[4]

Today many people idolize Darwin as a great revolutionary scientist because of his theory of evolution and natural selection. However, Darwin's reputation was already fading as early as the 1890s. The theory of evolution was an idea that had been current for at least fifty years before Darwin began his work. Darwin wanted to be the Man Who Invented Evolution, so he tried to remove his predecessors from the story. Darwin claimed to have never read the evolutionary theories from Goethe, Cuvier, Matthew, Lamarck, Erasmus Darwin (Charles Darwin's grandfather), and many others who believed that life forms evolve through myriad mutations. Darwin lied! But for 154 years the scientific community simply took his word for it. In the book, Dr Mike Sutton, *Nullius in Verba: Darwin's greatest secret,*[5] further proves that Darwin told six deliberate lies in order to achieve primacy over Matthew and reveals for the first time his desperate attempt to have the codified rules of scientific priority changed so that better known scientists such as he would be awarded priority over lesser known first discoverers such as Matthew. Moreover, all eight of Darwin's excuses for why he supposedly had no prior-knowledge of Matthew's prior-published discovery are all proven to be completely fallacious.

Having destroyed the myth of Darwin the honest gentleman of science, 'Nullius' examines further new bombshell discoveries in light of earlier discoveries of Darwin's dishonesty in stealing the ideas, given in confidence, of his Edinburgh tutor, Grant, and his notorious editing of the second edition of the 'Voyages of the Beagle', which fueled the myth that he discovered natural selection on the Galapagos Islands rather than a year or two later where he really found it – inside books between 1837 and 1838."

Darwin in his writings has been proven to be a racist. Darwin refers to many groups as savages including, Australians, Mongolians, Africans, Indians, South Americans, Polynesians, and Eskimos. What is Merging. com, Josie Glausiusz, *SAVAGES AND CANNIBALS: REVISITING CHARLES DARWIN'S VOYAGE OF THE BEAGLE.*[6] Darwin asks, "How little can the hard-worked wife of a degraded Australian savage, who uses hardly any abstract words and cannot count above four, exert her self-consciousness, or reflect on the nature of her existence?" These savages, according to Darwin, also had lower mortality, a lack of ability to reason, and less self-control. And, quite naturally, given the survival of the fittest and the ruthlessness of the evolutionary process, the superior whites should conquer and colonize the savage's lands.

These many hoaxes should be a wake-up! Contrary to popular belief, anthropologists are not unbiased in their interpretations.

CHAPTER 31

DNA

DNA is the chemical name for the molecule that carries genetic instructions in all living things. The DNA molecule consists of two strands that wind around one another to form a shape known as a double helix. Each strand has a backbone made of alternating sugar (deoxyribose) and phosphate groups. Attached to each sugar is one of four bases--adenine (A), cytosine (C), guanine (G), and thymine (T). The two strands are held together by bonds between the bases; adenine bonds with thymine, and cytosine bonds with guanine. The sequence of the bases along the backbones serves as instructions for assembling protein and RNA molecules. DNA is a remarkably simple structure, but it allows enormous complexity to be encoded by the pattern of those bases, one after another. DNA is organized structurally into chromosomes and then wound around nucleosomes as part of those chromosomes. Functionally, it's organized into genes, which are pieces of DNA, which lead to observable traits. And those traits come not from the DNA itself, but actually from the RNA that is made from the DNA Genes that are made of DNA, are then made into messengers, and lastly made into proteins. Life is built upon information. CDC, *Frequently Asked Questions About Research Using NHANES DNA Samples.* [1]

In fact, in just one of the trillions of cells that make up the human body, the amount of information in its genes would fill at least one thousand books of five hundred pages of type written information. Scientists now think this is hugely underestimated. Information cannot come from mutations, a so-called mechanism of evolution, but is there any other possible way information could arise from matter? Dr. Werner Gitt makes it clear that one of the things we know for sure from science is that information cannot arise from disorder or by chance. Hyper Physics, Werner Gitt, *In the Beginning Was Information,* 1997.[2]

It always takes greater information to produce information, and ultimately information is the result of intelligence. A code system is always the result of a mental process (it requires an intelligent origin or inventor or creator).

It should be emphasized that matter as such is unable to generate any code. All experiences indicate that a thinking being voluntarily exercising his own free will, cognition, and creativity, is required. There is no known natural law through which matter can give rise to information. There is no known law of nature, no known process, and no known sequence of events which can cause the information to originate by itself in the matter. The most powerful reason for science's reluctance to embrace a theory of intelligent design is also based on philosophical considerations. Many people, including many important and well-respected scientists, just don't want there to be anything beyond nature. They don't want a supernatural being to affect nature, no matter how brief or constructive the interaction may have been. In other words, ... they bring a philosophical commitment to their science that restricts what kinds of explanations they will accept about the physical world by eliminating any supernatural events.

During the initial stages of DNA science in the early 1970s, very crude and indirect techniques were utilized to unzip mixtures of human and chimpanzee DNA. Based on these studies, it was declared that human and chimpanzee DNA was 98.5% similar. But only the most similar protein-coding regions of the genome (called single-copy DNA) were compared, which is an extremely small portion—less than 3%—of the total genome. It was later discovered by an evolutionary colleague that the authors of these studies had manipulated the data to make the chimpanzee DNA appear more similar to humans than it was. These initial studies not only established a fraudulent gold standard of 98.5% DNA similarity between humans and chimps but also the shady practice of cherry-picking only the most similar data. The idea of nearly identical human-chimp DNA similarity was born and used to bolster the myth of human evolution, something that the lack of fossil evidence was unable to accomplish.

As DNA sequencing became more advanced, scientists were able to compare the actual order of DNA bases (nucleotides) between DNA sequences from different creatures. Three papers were published to describe the amount of non-similar data that was thrown out. When those missing data were included in the original numbers, and overall DNA similarity between humans and chimpanzees was only about 81% to 87%, depending on the paper!

What does 81% to 87% DNA similarity mean? First of all, it is important to note that for human evolution to be plausible, a DNA similarity of 99% is required. This is based on known current mutation rates in humans and an alleged splitting of humans from a common ancestor with chimpanzees about three to six million years ago. This length of time is a mere second on the evolutionary timescale. Any level of similarity less than 99% is evolutionarily impossible. This is why evolutionists rely on all sorts of monkey business when it comes to comparing human and chimpanzee DNA—they must achieve a figure close to 99% or evolution collapses.

As scientists began to decode the human DNA molecule, they found something quite unexpected—an exquisite 'language' composed of some three billion genetic letters. The coding regions of DNA, explains Dr. Stephen Meyer, "have the same relevant properties as a computer code or language." Stephen C. Meyer.com, Dr. Stephen Meyer, *Three Major Scientific Discoveries in the Past Century that Point to God*.[3]

Up to now, Darwinian evolutionists could try to counter their detractors with some possible explanations for the complexity of life. But now they have to face the information dilemma: How can meaningful, precise information be created by accident and by mutation and natural selection? None of these contain the mechanism of intelligence, a requirement for creating complex information such as that found in the genetic code.

Evolution is increasingly being challenged by a growing number of scientists. As recently as twenty-five years ago, says former atheist Patrick Glynn, "a reasonable person weighing the purely scientific evidence on the issue would likely have come down on the side of skepticism regarding a Creator. Rational Wiki, Patrick Glynn, *God: The Evidence*.[4] That is no longer the case." He adds: "Today the concrete data points strongly in the direction of the God hypothesis. It is the simplest and most obvious solution ... " Academic Atheism, Patrick Glynn, *Reviewing the Case for a Creator: Chapter 6.* [5]

Dr. Stephen Meyer considers the recent discoveries about DNA as the Achilles heel of evolutionary theory. He observes: "Evolutionists are still trying to apply Darwin's nineteenth-century thinking to a twenty-first-century reality, and it's not working ... I think the information revolution taking place in biology is sounding the death knell for Darwinism and chemical evolutionary theories." Dr. Stephen Meyer, *SIGNATURE IN THE CELL.* [6]

Dr. Stephen Meyer's conclusion? "I believe that the testimony of science supports theism. While there will always be points of tension or unresolved conflict, the major developments in science in the past five decades have been running in a strongly theistic direction." Dr. Stephen Meyer, *Return of the God Hypothesis.* [7]

Dean Kenyon, a biology professor who repudiated his earlier book on Darwinian evolution—mostly due to the discoveries of the information found in DNA—states: "This new realm of molecular genetics is where we see the most compelling evidence of design on the Earth." Zion Christian Ministry, Shawn Stevens *Microbiology: Hard Evidence for Intelligent Design.* [8]

Just recently, one of the world's most famous atheists, Professor Antony Flew, admitted he couldn't explain how DNA was created and developed through evolution. He now accepts the need for an intelligent source to have been involved in the making of the DNA code. Beyond Today, Mario Seiglie, *The Tiny Code That's Toppling Evolution,* [9] Professor Antony Flew.

"What I think the DNA material has done is show that intelligence must have been involved in getting these extraordinary diverse elements together," he said (quoted by Richard Ostling, WWRN World-Wide Religious News, Richard N. Ostling, *Famous atheist now believes in God* (AP, December 9, 2004). [10]

Evolution has had its run for almost 150 years in schools and universities and the press. But now, with the discovery of what the DNA code is all about, the complexity of the cell, and the fact that information is something vastly different from matter and energy, evolution can no longer dodge the outcome. The evidence certainly points to a resounding doom for evolution!

The more we learn scientifically, the more we learn about God our creator!

CHAPTER 32

Archeology

Archaeology is the study of human activity through the discovery and analysis of ancient artifacts. Archaeologists study human history to understand cultural history. Wikipedia, *Archeology.* Wikipedia, *Archeology.*[1]

Archaeology is important for biblical studies because the Bible mentions many places, people, and events. Archeology has proven the Bible to be amazingly accurate in its writings on these topics. Archeology shows that the Bible can be counted on more than any other history book to shed light on the true events of history. We would expect to find supporting evidence of the Biblical record through archaeology. And once again, we are not disappointed. Archeology proves the Bible is accurate in many areas: Crossway, John D. Currid, *10 Crucial Archaeological Discoveries Related to the Bible.*[2]

Evidence that Archeology Supports the Bible can be found in the following examples from the Armstrong Institute of Biblical Archaeology, Christopher Eames, *Proof: Archaeology Proves the Bible Archaeology unearths historical fact—and proves the biblical record at the same time,* May 12, 2019:[3]

Evidence of Biblical Accuracy:

- Dead Sea Scrolls: Several scrolls in clay pots were found in 1947, either almost complete scrolls or thousands of fragments of more than nine hundred ancient texts were discovered. Every book in the Old Testament except Esther was represented by at least a fragment. These scrolls date back as much as 2,200 years old to 200 B.C. These scrolls verify the accuracy of the Bible. Our modern Old Testament comes from Hebrew copies that date back only to about AD 1,000. Now we have a reliable and objective method to compare these Old Testament texts. The Dead Sea scrolls verified the accuracy of our biblical texts. An Isaiah scroll was found with the same content as our sixty-six chapters. The text did not change over time. This is true for most of the Old Testament as well.

- The Ketef Hinnom Scrolls: Two small silver scrolls covered with very delicately etched characters. The first word they were able to decipher was the name Yahweh. After much work, they were able to read the entire scroll. It contained the priestly benediction from (Numbers 6).
- The papyri from those Egyptian talking crocodiles have demonstrated that the New Testament documents are remarkable records. A flood of evidence shows the continuity between the New Testament documents (e.g., the Rylands Papyrus with parts of John 18:31–33 on one side and John 18:37–38 on the other) and the abundant evidence from the secular Roman writers and the early church fathers.

Evidence of Individuals:

- Jesus: Problems about the census at the time of our Lord's birth have been resolved by the findings of important papyrus documents. These documents were found in Egypt inside sacred, embalmed crocodiles. The documents were the Jewish priestly writings that were written immediately before, during, and just after New Testament times.
- King Hezekiah's Seal: A tunnel, which most believe to be the very one Hezekiah had dug, was discovered by Sir Charles Warren in 1867. In the rubbish heap outside a royal building in Jerusalem, a tiny seal impression, called a bulla, was discovered., Barely half an inch wide, this seal reads, Belonging to Hezekiah son of Ahaz, king of Judah.
- The Pilate Stone: Many Bible critics claimed that Pilate was a fictional character. They said that there was no evidence in other

books for his existence as an important governor in Judah. In 1961 a team led by Dr. Fora discovered an important inscription on a stone in Caesarea. It has since been dubbed the Pilate Stone. It dates to the time of Jesus and translated from Latin reads: To the Divine Augusti Tiberieum ... Pontius Pilate ... prefect of Judea.
- King David: The Tel Dan Inscription Discovery: In 1993, excavators at Tel Da uncovered an inscription with the word *BYTDWD* on it. The words mean house of David and date to the ninth century BC. King David has been a sticking point for critics. They suppose that he was only a mythical king, yet when the Tel Dan Stele, called the victory stone, was found in 1993, their skepticism collapsed. The inscription also mentions the names of Kings Ahaziah and Joram. Following the discovery of the Ugaritic library, it has become clear that the Psalms of David should be dated to his times and not to the Maccabean period, eight hundred years later
- The Mesha Stele: a ninth-century BC large stone inscription that parallels a biblical story about King David.
- The Egyptian Negev inscription: (10th century BC). Beyond just finding the name of King David, we have also found several constructions that the Bible attributes to him.
- Abraham's negotiations with the Hittites.
- Jacob: The Dead Sea Scrolls make the number of the people of Jacob seventy-five, not seventy, in Genesis 46:27, thus correcting a scribal error and showing that Stephen's figure was right (Acts 7:14).
- Joseph's installation as vizier (chief minister) is very similar to other recorded ceremonies. His new name was Zaphnath-Paaneah, meaning head of the sacred college.
- The Law of Moses was written by a man raised in the courts of the pharaoh, and it was greatly superior to other law codes, such as those of the Babylonian king Hammurabi, and the Eshnunna code that was found near modern Baghdad.
- The covenant forms of the writings of Moses follow the same format as those of the Hittites, as endorsed by Professor George Mendenhall. The law code is a unity, dating to about 1500 B.C. (the time of Moses). These writings come from one source only, and there is no one to fit this requirement at this time except Moses.

- Known Egyptian titles such as captain of the guard, overseer, chief of the butlers and chief of the bakers, and father to the Pharaoh.
- Other Kings: Verified through archaeology are many Kings including, Pharaohs Shishak, Tirhakah, Necho, and Hophra. The Syrian kings Hadadezer, Ben-hadad, Hazael and Rezin. The Moabite King Mesha. Assyrian kings Tiglath-Pileser, Shalmaneser, Sargon, Sennacherib, and Esarhaddon. Babylonian kings Merodach-Baladan, Nebuchadnezzar, Evil-Merodach and Belshazzar. Persian kings Cyrus, Darius I, Xerxes, Artaxerxes, and Darius II. Biblical princes, such as Jehucal and Gedaliah. There is also evidence of the Prophet Isaiah, the false prophet Balaam and even a tantalizing artifact that may well refer to the prophet Elisha.
- King Saul: head and armor were put into two temples at Beth-Shan. Both Philistine and Canaanite temples were found.
- Tatnai: governor on this side of the river (Ezra 6:13). This man and his office have likewise been confirmed through several inscriptions, recorded as Tattenai, Governor of Across-the-River. An unusual title— yet extraordinary archaeological corroboration of the biblical account. Or is it so extraordinary, if the Bible is a legitimate, factual document?
- Long-living Kings at Kish (Sumer)—These kings supposedly lived from 10,000 to 64,000 years ago.
- Sanballat and Geshem: Both are mentioned in (Nehemiah 2:19), though it was claimed by many writers that Sanballat was much later than Nehemiah. Several Sanballat's are now known, and recovered letters even refer to Joiakim. Despite longstanding criticisms, Nehemiah is an accurate record of an actual historical situation.
- Luke: The findings of Sir William Ramsay and his successors in Asia Minor reestablished the veracity of Luke the historian and other New Testament writers.

<u>Evidence of Cities:</u>

- Jericho: The walls of Jericho that came tumbling down? The remains of those crumbled city walls have been discovered.

- Jerusalem: The famous tunnel of Hezekiah, the palace of King David, The Jerusalem wall of King Solomon, the wall that Nehemiah constructed in the fifth century BC.
- Israelite cities such as Samaria, Megiddo, Shechem, Dan, Beth Shean, Jericho, Gezer, and Shiloh. Judean cities like Jerusalem, Hebron, Lachish, and Beersheba. The five Philistine cities of Gath, Ashdod, Ashkelon, Ekron, and Gaza. Egyptian cities. Assyrian cities. Babylonian cities. Persian cities. There are dozens more biblical cities that have been discovered archaeologically—along with an accurate representation of what happened in them including Mari, Boghazkoi, and Nineveh.
- Nineveh: Various details about Nineveh point to the Bible's historicity. The symbol of Nineveh was a pregnant woman with a fish in her womb.
- Ur: Abraham's home city of Ur was excavated by Sir Leonard Woolley, with surprising evidence of near-luxury.

Evidence of Civilizations:

- The Moabite Stone - In 1868, a missionary in Jerusalem found a stone tablet for sale that appeared to be from ancient times. On the tablet is a text written in Moabite dating to the ninth century BC. The text begins, I am Mesha's son of Chemosh, king of Moab.
- The Hittite civilization: Historians said it probably never existed.
- The Canaanites, Egyptians, Assyrians, Babylonians, Persians, Philistines, Moabites, Edomites, Ammonites, Syrians, and more have been corroborated by archaeology.
- Enuma Elish—This is the Babylonian Creation Record. We also have the Ebla Creation Tablet.
- The Epic of Gilgamesh includes the Babylonian Flood Story.
- The ten plagues or judgments against the leading gods of Egypt (Exodus 12:12) are seen as real judgments, with a leading god of Egypt selected for judgment with each of the plagues.
- The Assyrians: King Sargon's palace has been recovered at Khorsabad, including a wall inscription and a library record endorsing the battle against the Philistine city of Ashdod (mentioned in Isaiah 20:1). Assyrian titles such as tartan

(commander-in-chief), and several others, are used casually yet confidently by Bible writers. The death of Sennacherib recorded in (Isaiah 37:38) is confirmed in the records of Sennacherib's son, Esarhaddon. It was later added by Esarhaddon's son Ashur-bani-pal.

- The Babylonians: This was unknown to modern historians until it was confirmed by the German professor Koldewey, who excavated Babylon approximately one hundred years ago. We now know from the Babylonian Chronicle that the date of Nebuchadnezzar's capture of Jerusalem was the night of March 15/16, 597 B.C. We also know that Belshazzar was the king of Babylon at this time because his father Nabonidus was away from Babylon for about ten years.
- The Medes and the Persians: Cyrus became king over the Medes and Persians.

Archaeology proves the Bible to be historically accurate in every sense of the word. Archaeology should cause people to take the Bible seriously because no other book has received as much criticism, yet over and over it proves the skeptics wrong. No other book is like the Bible, written so long ago yet completely accurate.

CHAPTER 33

Geology

G eology is commonly known for the study of the earth's materials, solid rocks, and minerals. Britannica, *Geology*. From this study, scientists calculated, in 1903, the age of the earth to be in the hundreds of millions of years. Radiometric dating methods now have the age of the earth at 4.5 billion years today. These scientists believe it takes long periods to allow rocks to harden. Britannica, *"Geology*.[1]

But is this true? In the last half-century, flaws in the old-age theories began to emerge. Then Derek Ager (1923–1993), a prominent British geologist, and others increasingly challenged these assumptions and argued that much of the rock record shows evidence of rapid catastrophic erosion or sedimentation, drastically reducing the time involved in the formation of many geological deposits. The Other Side, Derek Ager, *The Age of the Earth*.[2]

On May 18, 1980, Mount St. Helens violently erupted. It was one of the most well-studied and scientifically documented volcanic eruptions in earth's history. One of the most fascinating discoveries following the eruption was that some of these pyroclastic deposits, those that contained fine volcanic ash particles, were thinly laminated. When geologists see thin layers like this, they usually assume that slow, delicate processes formed the layers. However, in this case, the layers were formed during a catastrophic volcanic eruption in a very short period. Many geologists still hold on to the slow steady-state model because they have ruled God out of the equation. However, this is flawed because it does not consider the ramifications of the great flood, written in the first book of the Bible,

Genesis. The flood is the greatest geological event in the history of the world, yet it is ignored by many geologists. What can we learn about the age of the earth from geology? From Answers in Genesis, *The 10 Best Evidences from Science That Confirm a Young Earth* [3] we can learn the following:

- Erosion: Modern erosion rates are so fast that according to secular geologists the continents themselves should have been reduced to sea level long ago. A recent study confirmed that outcrops (rocks visible above ground) erode at an average rate of about forty feet every one million years. This means the time needed to completely erode most continents would be less than fifty million years. Erosion can happen catastrophically, at scales that are difficult for us to imagine. When standing along the edge of a canyon and seeing a river at the bottom, one is inclined to imagine that the very river at the bottom of the gorge has cut the canyon over long periods of time. However, geologists are realizing that many canyons have been cut by processes other than rivers that currently occupy canyons. Massive erosion during catastrophic flooding occurs through several processes. This includes abrasion, hydraulic action, and cavitation. The Little Grand Canyon of the Toutle River was cut by a mudflow on March 19, 1982, that originated from the crater of Mount St. Helens. The abrasive mud-flow cut through rockslide and pumice deposits from the 1980 eruptions. Parts of the new canyon system are up to 140 feet deep.
- Bent Rock Layers: There's a lack of time between layers. Secular scientists often place hundreds of thousands or millions of years between parallel sedimentary units, such as the boundary between the Hermit Shale in the Grand Canyon and the overlying Coconino Sandstone. But when you examine the contact between these particular layers, it is nearly perfectly planar in all directions for tens of miles. There may be small, smooth undulations of a few feet in some locations, but for the most part, it's level with sharp contacts from one rock type to the next. Where are the gullies and the uneven topography that should have resulted from erosion over hundreds of thousands of years? In many mountainous areas, rock layers thousands of

feet thick have been bent and folded without fracturing. How can that happen if they were laid down separately over hundreds of millions of years and already hardened? Hardened rock layers are brittle. Try bending a slab of concrete some time to see what happens! But if the concrete is still wet, it can easily be shaped and molded before the cement sets. The same principle applies to sedimentary rock layers. They can be bent and folded soon after the sediment is deposited before the natural cement has a chance to bind the particles together into hard, brittle rocks. The Grand Canyon now cuts through many rock layers. Previously, all these layers were raised to their current elevation (a raised, flat region known as the Kaibab Plateau). Somehow this whole sequence was bent and folded without fracturing. That's impossible if the first layer, the Tapeats Sandstone, was deposited over North America 460 million years before being folded. But all the layers would still be relatively soft and pliable if it all happened during the recent, global Flood. The only viable scientific explanation is that the whole sequence was deposited very quickly.

- Soft Tissue in Fossils: If animals died millions of years ago, why do fossils still contain soft tissue? In 2005, a team of scientists led by paleontologist Mary Schweitzer published a paper in which they described an unusual femur (upper leg bone) of a *Tyrannosaurus rex*. While the outer bone was completely fossilized, the interior regions were somehow sealed off from fossilizing fluids. Inside the *T. rex* femur were intact blood vessels and red blood cells. Once freed from the bones, the blood vessels could be stretched—and even snapped back into place! In early 2009, Schweitzer and colleagues struck again with a new paper. Now a duck-billed dinosaur from the Judith River Formation (below the Hell Creek, and supposedly eighty million years old was described with a host of soft-tissue structures. Furthermore, the analyses of this fossil were done by multiple, independent labs. Several vertebrate-specific proteins (collagen, elastin, and hemoglobin) were discovered. No experimental results support long-age survival, as the last paper by Schweitzer's team readily admits. The only and obvious conclusion is that these bones are not sixty-five million years old, but much, much, younger.

- <u>Helium in Radioactive Rocks</u>: Helium diffuses so rapidly that all the helium should have leaked out in less than 100,000 years. So why are these rocks still full of helium atoms? The hotter the rocks, the faster the helium should escape, so researchers were surprised to find that the deepest, and therefore hottest, zircon's (at 387°F or 197°C) contained far more helium than expected. The only possible explanation: the helium hasn't had time to escape! The helium leakage rate has been determined in several experiments. All measurements agree. The fact that so much helium is still there means they cannot be 1.5 billion years old, as uranium-lead dating suggests.
- <u>Shale and Limestone Deposits</u>: Secular science has long taught that many of Earth's sedimentary rocks were deposited slowly over vast ages. Clay, Earth's most common sediment, doesn't slowly settle out of still water to form rocks. Clay-rich rocks like shale and mud-stones often exhibit fine lamination or thin-bedded layers that only form through moving, not stagnant, water. How do we know? Recent empirical evidence demonstrates that laminated clay must be deposited in energetic settings by moving water. Flume studies verified that carbonate mud is not deposited slowly but instead is laid down rapidly by wave and current action. Laboratory experiments demonstrate that water flowing between ten and twenty inches per second creates ripples and laminated carbonate mud layers identical to those observed in carbonate rocks.
- <u>Carbon-14 in Fossils, Coal, and Diamonds</u>: Carbon-14 (or radiocarbon) is a radioactive form of carbon that scientists use to date fossils. But it decays quickly, with a half-life of only 5,730 years — that none is expected to remain in fossils after only a few hundred thousand years. Yet carbon-14 has been detected in ancient fossils — supposedly up to hundreds of millions of years old — ever since the earliest days of radiocarbon dating. Even if every atom in the whole earth were carbon-14, they would decay so quickly that no carbon-14 would be left on earth after only one million years. Contrary to expectations, between 1984 and 1998 alone, the scientific literature reported carbon-14 in seventy samples that came from fossils, coal, oil, natural gas, and marble representing the fossil-bearing portion of the geologic record, supposedly spanning more than five hundred

million years. All contained radiocarbon. Further, analyses of fossilized wood and coal samples, supposedly spanning thirty-two to three hundred and fifty million years in age, yielded ages between 20,000- and 50,000-years using carbon-14 dating. The fossilized sea creature and wood both yield radiocarbon ages of only thousands of years. Diamonds supposedly one to three billion years old similarly yielded carbon-14 ages of only 55,000 years. All these fossils, coal, and diamonds should be reduced to less than 55,000 years or less.

- Very Little Salt in the Sea: Every year, the continents, atmosphere, and seafloor add 458 million tons of salt into the ocean, but only 122 million tons 27% is removed. At this rate, today's saltiness would be reached in forty-two million years. But God created a salty ocean for sea creatures, and the Flood quickly added more salt. If the world's oceans have been around for three billion years as evolutionists believe, they should be filled with vastly more salt than the oceans contain today. Every year rivers, glaciers, underground seepage, and atmospheric and volcanic dust dump large amounts of salts into the oceans. Some 458 million tons of sodium mix into ocean water each year, but only 122 million tons are removed by other natural processes. If seawater originally contained no sodium (salt) and the sodium accumulated at today's rates, then today's ocean saltiness would be reached in only forty-two million years — only about 1/70 of the three billion years evolutionists propose.

- Very Little Sediment on the Seafloor: If sediments have been accumulating on the seafloor for three to four billion years, the seafloor should be choked with sediments many miles deep. Every year, water and wind erode about twenty billion tons of dirt and rock debris from the continents and deposit them on the seafloor. Most of this material accumulates as loose sediments near the continents. Yet the average thickness of all these sediments globally over the whole seafloor is not even 1,300 feet (400 m). The net gain is thus nineteen billion tons per year. At this rate, 1,300 feet of sediment would accumulate in less than twelve million years, not billions of years. This evidence makes sense within the context of the Genesis Flood cataclysm, not the idea of slow and gradual geologic evolution.

Geological evidence more than proves that Earth is not 4.5 billion years old but just a few thousand years old. There is no empirical evidence to the contrary. Only biased interpretations are based on unverifiable assumptions, such as the radioisotope dates that secular science relies on. The rocks do not show great age. The fossils do not show great age. The Earth is much younger than it is claimed to be.

CHAPTER 34

Creationism

Creationism is the religious belief that nature, and aspects such as the universe, earth, life, and humans, were created with supernatural acts by a divine creator. (Wikipedia, *Creationism*) The Christian organization's Answers in Genesis (AiG), Institute for Creation Research (ICR), and the Creation Research Society (CRS) promote young-Earth creationism and believe that God created the Earth within the last ten thousand years, literally as described in the Genesis creation narrative. Creation Ministries International promotes young Earth views in Australia, Canada, South Africa, New Zealand, the United States, and the United Kingdom. Wikipedia, *Creationism*.[1]

So how do we recognize the evidence of intelligence? Dr. Michael Denton, a non-Christian medical doctor, and scientist with a doctorate in molecular biology is quoted in LIB Quotes, *Michael Denton Quotes* as saying:[2] "The complexity of the simplest known type of cell is so great that it is impossible to accept that such an object could have been thrown together suddenly by some kind of freakish, vastly improbable, event. Such an occurrence would be indistinguishable from a miracle." There is no doubt that even the most ardent atheist concedes that design is evident in the animals and plants that inhabit our planet. If Dawkins rejects chance in design, what does he put in place of chance if he does not accept a Creator God? Richard Dawkins, who admits the design in living things, rejects the idea of any kind of a Designer/God. Why? It is because Dawkins attributes the design to what the blind forces of physics. So who then is the Designer? John 1:3 says "All things came into being through Him, and apart from Him not even one thing came into being that has come into being."

The Creation: The Bible teaches God created the universe. In multiple verses in both the Old and New Testaments, it is clear that God created everything that was made. Here is a small listing: "In the beginning, God created the heavens and the earth. For in six days the Lord made Heaven and earth, the sea, and all that is in them, and rested on the seventh day. Therefore the Lord blessed the Sabbath day and made it holy." (Exodus 20:11). "You alone are the LORD. You have made the heavens, The Heaven of heavens with all their lights, The earth and everything that is on it, the seas and everything that is in them. You give life to all of them, And the Heavenly lights bow down before You." (Nehemiah 9:6). All things were made through Him, and without Him was not anything made that was made. "For by Him, all things were created, in Heaven and on earth, visible and invisible, whether thrones or dominions or rulers or authorities—all things were created through Him and for Him" (Colossians 1:16). "Worthy are you, our Lord and God, to receive glory and honor and power, for you created all things, and by your will, they existed and were created" (Revelation 4:11). God, the Creator, created everything out of nothing.

Many Christians think that if we just take each of the days of creation as being figurative, we can harmonize the Bible with the pagan religion of naturalism/evolutionism/humanism and mix it with evolutionary ideas like the big bang and a very old earth. But this only seems reasonable to those who reject the order of events according to (Genesis 1) and buy into the order of events according to evolutionary models. There are good reasons to reject such attempts at harmonization. The clear teaching of the Word of God is important to believe. The chart below outlines the clear differences between creation and evolution from a biblical perspective.

Creation: God's Word	Evolution: Man's Word
"In the beginning God created"	Any alleged God is not necessary; all things came about by natural processes without God.
God's Word is truth.	There is no absolute truth (yet Evolutionists illogically believe that this is the absolute truth!).
God created the universe in six 24-hour days around 6,000 years ago.	The universe was formed over billions of years ago.
God created all living things according to their kinds and told them to reproduce.	All life evolved from a single-celled organism by random chance.
God created man in his image.	Man evolved like every other animal.
God created marriage as one man for one woman for life.	Marriage can be whatever anyone wants.
God decides what is right and wrong.	Man decides what's right and wrong—<u>if right and wrong</u> even exist.
Man, broke God's law and is guilty before him; only God is good.	Man is "basically good"—<u>if such a thing as "good" even exists.</u>
Death, thorns, and disease are a result of man's sin.	Death, thorns, and disease existed millions of years before man and are the hero that drives evolution.

Biblical creation is true because the ultimate authority on the subject, God is true. Many say there are two different accounts of creation in the Bible. However, if you read it for yourself, it is clear that the account in Genesis 1, covers the 6 creation days, while Genesis 2, only covers more detail of the sixth day. Jesus Christ quotes from both (Genesis 1:27 and Genesis 2:24) when referring to the same man and woman in teaching the doctrine of marriage. Jesus saw them as complementary accounts, not contradictory ones.

Because the Bible is true, we expect to see evidence of God's fingerprints all over his creation. Even the building blocks of life—DNA—is a confirmation of what we expect to find because God created all things. This Creator revealed himself to us through his Son Jesus Christ and his Word, the Bible. Biblical creation mattered to the Lord Jesus: "But from the beginning of the creation, God 'made them male and female'" (Mark 10:6). Jesus taught that Adam and Eve were made at the beginning of creation, not billions of years after the beginning. If the universe is billions of years old, Jesus' statement was a lie. But Jesus did not lie. He affirmed creation, reasoned from creation, and taught the truth of biblical creation.

We also learn about creation and evolution from the account of the Fall of Adam and Eve. The Bible is clear, there was no death in the world before Adam and Eve sinned. (Romans 5:12) states: "Therefore, just as through one man's sin entered the world, <u>and death through sin</u>, and thus death spread to all people because all sinned." Genesis 1:31 says: "Then God saw everything that He had made, and indeed it was very good. So, the evening and the morning were the sixth day. At the end of the sixth day of creation, God described the entire creation as very good." However, in the fossil record, there are many examples of diseases in the bones of animals (e.g., tumors [cancer]; arthritis; abscesses, etc.). Such diseases could not be described as very good, when in the rest of the Bible diseases are always viewed as bad and a result of sin and the curse. These diseases simply could not have existed before sin. We can therefore conclude with confidence there was no animal death before sin. Paul makes it clear that the whole creation groans because of sin. If we reject that conclusion and imagine that the whole creation was in bondage to corruption as soon as God created it, then what kind of God would He be to call that corruption very good? The whole originally perfect creation was put into bondage to corruption by God's curse.

Evolution teaches that there were millions of years of death before humans came on the scene. This is in pure contradiction to what the Bible teaches. Evolution relies on dating methods to prove its old age theories. All dating methods suffer, in principle, from many limitations and false assumptions. The public reads almost daily in newspapers and magazines that scientists have dated a particular rock at billions of years old. Most just accept it. However, we must learn to ask questions as to how this data was obtained—what method was used and what assumptions were accepted to develop this method?

Another example of poor dating involves red blood cells and traces of hemoglobin that have been found in T. rex bones, although these should have long decomposed if they were millions of years old. Yet the reaction of the researchers was a perfect illustration of how evolutionary bias can result in trying to explain away hard facts to fit the preconceived framework of millions of years: their opinion stated It was exactly like

WORLDVIEW OF THE CHRISTIAN FAITH

looking at a slice of modern bone. But, of course, I couldn't believe it. I said to the lab technician: The bones, after all, are sixty-five million years old. How could blood cells survive that long? Obviously, blood cells cannot survive that long. It is simply impossible for a blood cell to last sixty-five million years. Whenever you hear a news report that scientists have found another missing link or discovered a fossil millions of years old, try to think about the right questions that need to be asked to challenge the scientist's interpretations.

The reason so many Christian professors (and Christian leaders in general) have rejected the literal creation position from God's Word is that they have blindly accepted the interpretation of the secular world. Then they try to reinterpret the Bible accordingly.

Russ Humphreys, a Ph.D. physicist, has developed (among many other things) a model to compute the present strength of planetary magnetic fields, which enabled him to accurately predict the field strengths of the outer planets. Did a belief in the Bible hinder his research? Not at all. On the contrary, Dr. Humphreys was able to make these predictions precisely because he started from the principles of Scripture. John Baumgardner, a Ph.D. geophysicist, and biblical creationist have a sophisticated computer model of catastrophic plate tectonics, which was reported in the journal Nature; the assumptions for this model are based on the global flood recorded in Genesis. Additionally, think of all the people who have benefited from a magnetic resonance imaging (MRI) scan. The MRI scanner was developed by the creationist Dr. Raymond Damadian. Consider the biblical creationists Georgia Purdom and Andrew Snelling, who work in molecular genetics and geology, respectively. They certainly understand their fields, and yet are convinced that they do not support evolutionary biology and geology. On the contrary, they confirm biblical creation. Dr. Jason Lisle has done extensive research in solar astrophysics and made several discoveries about the nature of near-surface solar flows, including the detection of a never-before-seen polar alignment of super granules, as well as patterns indicative of giant overturning cells. Were these scientists hindered in their research by the conviction that the early chapters of Genesis were true? No, it's just the reverse. It is because a logical God created and ordered the universe that creationists, expect to be able to understand aspects of that universe through logic, careful observation, and experimentation.

Let's look at scientists that have won the Noble Prize. Did you know that over 65% of the overall winners identified as Christian, while over 20% were Jewish, and just under 1% were Muslim? It is certainly significant if the Nobel Laureates identified as such, even though some may have been associating themselves with religion in more of a nominal or cultural sense. The Jewish figure is particularly interesting, as they only represented about 0.02% of the world's population, whereas, by contrast, Muslims made up around 20%. Just under 11% of the winners had no belief in God although, interestingly, far more of them were in the field of literature (around 35% of winners), than in scientific disciplines.

Do not forget, as Christians we need to always build our thinking on the Word of the One who has the answers to all of the questions that could ever be asked—the infinite Creator God. He has revealed the true history of the universe in His Word to enable us to develop the right way of thinking about the present and thus determine the correct interpretations of the evidence of the present.

What does a day mean? Could God Have Created Everything in Six Days? The Bible tells us about the meaning of day. In Genesis 1, we see the Hebrew word for day, Yom is used in the context of Scripture. Consider the following:

- A typical concordance will illustrate that yom can have a range of meanings: a period of light as contrasted to darkness, a twenty-four-hour period, time, a specific point of time, or a year.
- A classic, well-respected Hebrew-English lexicon has seven headings and many subheadings for the meaning of yom—but it defines the creation days as ordinary twenty-four-hour days under the heading day as defined by evening and morning.
- A number and the phrase evening and morning are used with each of the six days of creation.
- Outside of Genesis 1, yom is used with a number 359 times, and each time it means an ordinary day. Why would Genesis 1 be the exception?
- Outside of Genesis 1, yom is used with the word evening or morning twenty-three times. Evening and morning appear in association, but without yom, thirty-eight times. All sixty-one times the text refers to an ordinary day. Why would Genesis 1 be the exception?

- In Genesis 1:5, Yom occurs in context with the word night. Outside of Genesis 1, night is used with yom fifty-three times, and each time it means an ordinary day. Why would (Genesis 1) be the exception? Even the usage of the word light with yom in this passage determines the meaning as an ordinary day.
- The plural of yom, which does not appear in Genesis 1, can be used to communicate a longer time period, such as in those days. Adding a number here would be senseless. Clearly, in Exodus 20:11, a number is used with days, which unambiguously refers to six earth-rotation days.
- There are words in biblical Hebrew (such as olam or qedem) that are very suitable for communicating for long periods of time or indefinite time, but none of these words are used in Genesis 1. Alternatively, the days or years could have been compared with grains of sand if long periods were meant.

If we are prepared to let the words of the language speak to us in accord with the context and normal definitions, without being influenced by outside ideas, then the word for day found in Genesis 1, which is qualified by a number, the phrase evening and morning and for Day 1 the words light and darkness—obviously means an ordinary twenty-four-hour day.

Because God is infinite in power and wisdom, there's no doubt He could have created the universe and its contents in no time at all, or six seconds, or six minutes, or six hours—after all, "with God nothing shall be impossible" (Luke 1:37).

We need to understand that all facts are interpreted. You will find over and over again that the Bible is confirmed by real science.

Remember that, like Job, we need to understand that compared to God we know next to nothing. We won't have all the answers. However, so many answers have come to light now that a Christian can give a credible defense of the Book of Genesis and show it is the correct foundation for thinking about, and interpreting, every aspect of reality.

Let's not jump in a blind-faith way at the startling facts we think we need to prove creation—trying to counter their facts with our facts. (Jesus himself rose from the dead in the most startling possible demonstration of the truth of God's Word. But many still wouldn't believe it. Instead, let's not let apparent facts about evolution intimidate us, but let's understand the right way to think about facts. We can then deal with the same facts the evolutionists use, to show they have the wrong framework of interpretation—and that the facts of the real world do confirm the Bible. In this way, we can battle for a biblical worldview.

SECTION 5
Salvation

Salvation by grace through faith is at the heart of the Christian religion. For it is by grace you have been saved, through faith—and this not from yourselves, it is the gift of God.

The statement has three parts— salvation, grace, and faith—and they are equally important. The three together constitute a basic tenet of Christianity.

The word salvation is defined as the act of being delivered, redeemed, or rescued. The Bible tells us that, since the fall of Adam and Eve in the Garden of Eden, each person is born in sin inherited from Adam: "Therefore, just as through one man's sin entered the world, and death through sin, and thus death spread to all people because all sinned." (Romans 5:12)

Sin is what causes all of us to die. Sin separates us from God. But is sin really that bad?

CHAPTER 35

The Narrow Path

Sin is evil! Without judgment, there would be no end to sin and evil and there would be no Heaven. Evil must end. But who, or what is evil? We are all evil. I know we like to think of ourselves as good, but that simply isn't true. The Bible tells us that all the ways of a man are right in his own eyes. This is just human nature; in our own eyes, we like to think of ourselves as good. You can never judge yourself on your standards or righteousness, but only on God's standards and righteousness. Life, Hope and Truth, Florante Siopan and John Foster, *What is Salvation?*[1]

So how do we stack up to God's righteousness? The difference between us and God is infinite! So what we see as the slightest of sins within ourselves appears, as extreme evil in the eyes of God. We are abhorrently evil. Our lust becomes adultery, and our hate becomes murder. Sin causes an infinite distance between us and God. We know that infinite distance between us and God is hell. The soul is eternal and we will live forever, the question is where?

Sin—disobeying God—produces suffering and pain. God hates sinful attitudes and deeds because of their horrible effects. Sin leads to broken relationships, violence, and misery. It cuts us off from God. Not only does sin harm others, but it destroys the sinner's character and often endangers his life. The cause of trouble, the root of all sorrow, the dread of every human lies in this one small word—sin. We all have this terminal disease and it's far worse than the flu or even cancer. It has crippled the nature of humans and has caused humans to be caught in the devil's trap! People don't willingly expose themselves to the flu virus—people generally run from it. This is what we should do with sin—flee.

At the root of this growing problem is raw, uncontrolled selfishness. How human beings think— with selfish desires, emotions, and feelings dominating too many of our decisions. The real problem lies deep within humans. Sin is bad because it hurts. It hurts you. It hurts me. It separates friends and destroys relationships. It leads to violence, addiction, and untimely death. It locks us in our prisons of heartbreak, suffering, misery, and fear. It never bears good fruit. That's why God hates it. And that's why you and I should hate it too. Sin leads to a short, painful, temporary life compared to the eternal life God wants to give each of us. That's just how bad even the slightest sin is. Yes, sin really is that bad.

Jesus said in Matthew 7:13–14; "Enter through the narrow gate. For wide is the gate and broad is the road that leads to destruction, and many enter through it. But small is the gate and narrow the road that leads to life, and only a few find it." This passage causes some people to question the goodness of God. It sounds as if only a few people go to Heaven, while many will go to Hell. Got Questions, *Why did God make salvation such a narrow path?*[2]

Well first we should be grateful Jesus gives us this warning. Perhaps we have some control over our destiny. A few verses earlier, Jesus had told the same audience, "Ask and it will be given to you; seek and you will find; knock and the door will be opened to you. For everyone who asks receives; the one who seeks finds; and to the one who knocks, the door will be opened" (Matthew 7:7–8). Jesus made it clear: the path to eternal life is open to everyone who asks. However, the gate to Heaven is narrow in the sense of having a particular requirement for entrance. When faced with the choice between a narrow, bumpy road and a wide, paved highway, most people choose the easier road. Human nature gravitates toward comfort and pleasure. God offers salvation to everyone who accepts it. But it is on His terms. We must come the way He has provided. We cannot create our paths or come to a holy God based on our efforts. Compared to His righteousness, we are all filthy. God cannot simply excuse or overlook our sin. He is merciful, but He is also just. Justice requires that sin be paid for. The way to God was completely closed, and sin was the roadblock. No one deserves a second chance. We all deserve to stay on the wide road that leads to destruction.

Satan has paved the highway to hell with fleshly temptations and worldly attractions. Most people allow their passions and desires to dictate the course of their lives. They choose temporary, earthly pleasure. The narrow gate is ignored. So it was with sorrow, not discrimination, that Jesus declared that the road to eternal life is narrow, and only a few find it. Jesus compares the narrow gate to the broad road which leads to destruction (hell) and says that many will be on that road. By contrast, Jesus says that small is the gate and narrow the road that leads to life (Heaven), and only a few find it.

In this sense, the way is narrow because it is the only way, and relatively few people will go through the narrow gate. Entering the narrow gate is so difficult because of the opposition of human pride, our natural love of sin, and the opposition of Satan and the world in his control, all of which battle against us in the pursuit of eternity. God will not give eternal life to anyone who refuses to put the brakes on his or her selfish desires and foolish impulses. Only those who repent of such foolishness and begin building the self-control—the self-discipline—can be trusted with that greatest of all gifts. God asks you to compare your heart and behavior to the fullness of His teachings and make that choice. He hopes you will choose to build good character rather than pursue the temporary, empty pleasures of sin.

We need salvation from sin and its penalty. God explains, "See, I have set before you today life and prosperity, and death and adversity; in that, I, command you today to love the Lord your God, to walk in His ways, and to keep His commandments and His statutes and His judgments, that you may live and multiply, and that the Lord your God may bless you." (Deuteronomy 30:15–16). The good news is that God has provided us with a way to remove this distance from God and a way to avoid the horrors of hell. What each of us needs are to be delivered from that fate. God loved us enough to provide the path to eternal life. However, He also knows that in our self-centered, sin-saturated world there are not many who will desire Him enough to come to Him on His terms. Self-sacrifice is required to follow Jesus. If there are to be no more tears, sorrow, hate, and no more pain, there has to be judgment.

Some people ask if God wants to save everyone, why didn't He make it easier to be saved? Why doesn't He simply let everyone into Heaven? How can we be saved from sin? Most religions throughout history have taught that salvation is achieved by good works and being a good person.

But how do you ever know how much good works are enough? How do you know if you are good enough?

Sin is the great clogger, and the blood of Christ is the great cleanser. We don't need to be crippled any longer by the disease of sin because God has provided the cure. "The blood of Jesus Christ ... cleanses us from all sin" (1 John 1:7) and He will give us the power to turn from sin, through faith in Christ.

We need to understand that Jesus is the Door through which all must enter eternal life. There is no other way because Jesus alone "is the way, the truth, and the life" (John 14:6). The way to eternal life is restricted to just one avenue—Christ. No other religion or god can save us. Only Jesus, yes Jesus is the only way!

Jesus says that the narrow gate leads to a hard road, one that will take us through hardships and difficult decisions. Following Jesus requires crucifying our flesh, living by faith, enduring trials with Christlike patience, and living a lifestyle separate from the world. God, however, has given us the freedom to choose the path we wish to walk! He urges us to choose the right path—but He won't make that choice for us. When faced with the reality of denying themselves to follow Jesus, most people turn away. Jesus never sugar-coated the truth, and the truth is that not many people are willing to pay the price to follow Him.

At great cost to Himself, Jesus paid that price. Without the blood of Jesus covering our sin, we stand guilty before the God we rejected. While there will be relatively few who go through the narrow gate compared to the many on the broad road, there will still be multitudes who will follow the Good Shepherd. The apostle John saw this multitude in his vision in the book of Revelation 7:9–10: "After this I looked, and behold, a great multitude that no one could number, from every nation, from all tribes and peoples and languages, standing before the throne and before the Lamb, clothed in white robes, with palm branches in their hands, and crying out with a loud voice, 'Salvation belongs to our God who sits on the throne, and to the Lamb!'"

Entering the narrow gate is not easy. Jesus made this clear when He instructed His followers to strive to do so. The Greek word translated strive is agonizomai, from which we get the English word to agonize. The implication here is that those who seek to enter the narrow gate must do so by struggle and strain, like a running athlete straining toward the finish line, all muscles taut and giving his all in the effort. Beyond Today, Robert H. Berendt, *Narrow and Difficult*.³

But we must be clear here. No amount of effort saves us; salvation is by the grace of God through the gift of grace. Salvation is found only in the Person of Jesus Christ; He is the only way. We must put our complete faith in Jesus Christ and nothing else.

No one will ever earn Heaven by striving for it. The exhortation to strive to enter is a command to repent and enter the gate and not to just stand and look at it, think about it, or complain that it's too small or too difficult or unjustly narrow. We are not to ask why others are not entering; we are not to make excuses or delay. We are to strive forward and enter! Then we are to exhort others to strive to enter before it's too late.

CHAPTER 36

Hell

According to the Bible, hell is a real place where God judges unrepentant sinners with eternal, conscious punishment. Many people believe hell is the place where bad people go after they die. But this is not entirely true. Hell is the place where people go who have not received Jesus Christ as their Lord and Savior. You see, people do not go to hell because of their sins, they go to hell because of their unbelief in Jesus Christ.

Baker's Evangelical Dictionary of Biblical Theology defines hell as the "Place of God's final retributive punishment." Jesus, however, is most responsible for defining hell. We need to know, what hell really is. There are several ways the Bible describes hell:

- The term Sheol, which is most often translated in English as hell is often used and Sheol sometimes refers to the place of the dead, but sometimes just refers to the grave, highlighting human's mortality.
- Gehenna: According to Strong's Concordance, Gehenna is a valley west and south of Jerusalem, also a symbolic name for the final place of punishment of the ungodly. Jesus used the term gehenna when He said, "But I say to you that everyone who is angry with his brother shall be answerable to the court; and whoever says to his brother, You good-for-nothing, shall be answerable to the supreme court; and whoever says, You fool, shall be guilty *enough to go* into the fiery hell" (Matthew 5:22).

- Hades: According to Strong's Concordance, hades is "the abode of departed spirits." Jesus used "hades" in his account of Lazarus and the rich man. Luke recounts; "the poor man died and was carried by the angels to Abraham's side. The rich man also died and was buried, and in Hades, being in torment, he lifted up his eyes and saw Abraham far off and Lazarus at his side" (Luke 16:22–23).
- Eternal Fire: In addition to naming hell, Jesus also describes hell in other ways. For instance, Matthew recounts Jesus' words on hell when he wrote "Then He will say to those on his left, depart from me, you cursed, into the eternal fire prepared for the devil and his angels" (Matthew 25:41).
- The Lake of Fire and the Second Death: John wrote about another aspect of eternal punishment in Revelation when he recorded; "But as for the cowardly, the faithless, the detestable, as for murderers, the sexually immoral, sorcerers, idolaters, and all liars, their portion will be in the lake that burns with fire and sulfur, which is the second death" (Revelation 21:8). "Then Death and Hades were thrown into the lake of fire. This is the second death, the lake of fire" (Revelation 20:14).
- Eternal Punishment: Matthew records Jesus' words about retributive justice when He spoke of the heartlessness of some professed believers as He condemned them, and "these will go away into eternal punishment, but the righteous into eternal life" (Matthew 25:46).

Why is there punishment in hell? The punishments of hell are directly related to the transcendent holiness of God. Those who face that weight of condemnation have sinned against a God who is truly, purely holy. God's holiness is unable to tolerate anything or anyone that is unholy; his holiness produces a reflex that acts out in wrath against all sin. On the cross, "Jesus cried out with a loud voice, saying, ELI, ELI, LEMA SABAKTANEI? that is, MY GOD, MY GOD, WHY HAVE YOU FORSAKEN ME?" (Matthew 27:46).

People (By Their Very Nature) Are Not Good. We don't have to teach our infants to be selfish, impatient, rude, and self-serving; infants must be taught just the opposite. We don't come into the world equipped automatically with sacrificial goodness. If we are honest with ourselves, each of us must admit we often have difficulty controlling our anger, our lust, or our pride. We are inherently fallen creatures, trying our best to constrain our fallen nature. The Bible simply recognizes the innately fallen nature of humans. We are all sinners, no one is truly good.

God Allows Man to Reap the Consequences of His Deeds. "Whatsoever a man soweth, that shall he also reap" (Galatians 6:7). Jacob sowed lying and deceit and reaped the same in return. King David committed adultery and murder. But even though he repented of these sins and God forgave him, the natural consequences remained. He had trouble in his own family—including adultery and murder—for the rest of his days. People who end up in the lake of fire will be there as a natural consequence of their actions.

Because people are made to last forever, they will either live eternally in Heaven or eternally in hell, forever! The prophet Daniel wrote about the eternal nature of Heaven and hell when he said, "and many of those who sleep in the dust of the earth shall awake, some to everlasting life, and some to shame and everlasting contempt" (Daniel 12:2). Unfortunately, once you make it to hell, there is no turning back. It is too late by then and you can never leave. To make sure you don't go there, you must act in this life, before you die. If not, hell could be your final destination.

The experience of hell is conscious. People in hell are not asleep or annihilated; instead, people are awake and aware of their experiences. Jesus said, while "the sons of the kingdom will be thrown into the outer darkness. In that place there will be weeping and gnashing of teeth" (Matthew 8:12).

Why is punishment conscious? Those who have sinned consciously must also bear their punishment consciously. The Bible tells us that we have not been passive in our rebellion against God but have been willing participants and active rebels. Justice demands conscious punishment, not mere annihilation of the person or his or her sin. What clearer example do we have than Jesus Christ, who consciously bore God's wrath against sin? If Christ's suffering for our sin was conscious, so too will be the suffering of those who bear their sin apart from forgiveness in Christ.

Why is hell eternal? The eternal, never-ending nature of the sinner's punishment is directly related to the infinite and eternal nature of God. When you sin against an infinite God—and all sin is primarily oriented toward God—you accrue an infinite debt. This is the only way to explain the Father's decision not to spare his Son but to deliver Him to suffer in our place. An eternal, infinite being was needed to bear the weight of infinite punishment.

Hell can be a difficult teaching to grasp. Jesus' disciples had a hard time understanding. So there is precedent in the Bible for hearing challenging instruction and acknowledging the gravity of the teaching. Indeed, hell is a hard saying. Despite the emotional difficulty of the doctrine of hell, the Bible records more words Jesus spoke about hell than He did about Heaven. Hell is the just punishment for sin. God will forever punish Satan, his demonic hordes, and all other unrepentant evildoers in the lake of fire. In this way, God underscores his justice against sinful, rebellious creatures considering his infinite holiness.

Would a Loving God Send People to Hell? "*A good and loving God will not send any of His creatures to Hell.*" Many people believe this statement is true and quote it as if it were found in the Bible but unfortunately it is not. One must remember that we have the final choice. The decision to send someone to hell is based on the individual choosing to go to hell. People choose to go to hell by denying God. They choose not to be with God in this life, and they choose not to accept Jesus Christ as their Lord and Savior. If you don't want God now in this life, then God won't force you to be with Him in the next life! Everyone makes that choice! So, we shouldn't blame it on God that people end up in hell. God desires that no one should perish, but He gives each person the right to make that choice.

"God *is* good" (Luke 18:19) and "God *is* love" (1 John 4:8). In His love, God has provided us with a way of escape from the punishment our sin deserves. He sent His only begotten Son—Jesus Christ—to die on the cross in our place, enduring sin's judgment so we can be forgiven. Through the death and resurrection of Jesus Christ, God has made it possible for every man, woman, and child to be saved from eternal punishment in the lake of fire. This gift of salvation is received simply by trusting in the Lord Jesus Christ as one's personal Savior. Even though God, in His love, has provided the way of salvation, He does not force it upon us. He will not drag people kicking and screaming into Heaven. "The one who believes in the Son has eternal life; but the one who does not obey the Son will not see life, but the wrath of God remains on him." (John 3:36).

Today, God is warning sinners to repent, trust in the Lord Jesus Christ, and be saved. Those who reject God's gracious offer of salvation will receive the natural consequences of that rejection. There will be eternal weeping and gnashing of teeth at the realization of what they are missing, and the constant memory of their foolishness in despising, rejecting, or neglecting God's offer of salvation.

Indeed, hell is a real place and some will spend eternity there. What is your choice?

CHAPTER 37

The Plan of Salvation

Salvation means deliverance. All world religions teach that we need to be delivered, but each has a different understanding of what we need to be delivered from, why we need to be delivered, and how that deliverance can be received or achieved. The Bible makes it abundantly clear, however, that there is only one plan of salvation. The most important thing to understand about the plan of salvation is that it is God's plan, not humanity's plan. Humanity's plan of salvation would be observing religious rituals or obeying certain commands or achieving certain levels of spiritual enlightenment. But none of these things are part of God's plan of salvation.

In God's plan of salvation, first, we must understand why we need to be saved. Simply put, we need to be saved because we have sinned. The Bible states "there is not a righteous person on earth who *always* does good and does not *ever* sin." (Ecclesiastes 7:20). Sin is rebellion against God. We all choose to actively do wrong things. Sin harms others, damages us, and, most importantly, dishonors God. The Bible also teaches that, because God is holy and just, He cannot allow sin to go unpunished. The punishment for sin is death and eternal separation from God. Without God's plan of salvation, eternal death is the destiny of every human being.

In God's plan of salvation, God Himself is the only one who can provide for our salvation. There are four parts of salvation included in God's plan of salvation. Ligonier, *"One Way of Salvation."* [1]

- First, God takes the initiative to shine His light upon the individual. In the process of salvation, God always takes the initiative.
- Second, the individual must respond to the initiative of God, and exercise their choice to taste the free gift of God. God offers salvation to us, but we must take the action to receive and accept it. Salvation is always a gift, and there is nothing we can do to earn it.
- Third, Once the individual makes the decision to receive God's free gift, the individual then becomes a partaker of the Holy Spirit. The Holy Spirit comes to indwell and become a part of the believer, making the believer a possessor of the Holy Spirit. This is when we become born again. Thus, salvation is based on the activity and energy of the Holy Spirit.
- Fourth, The Holy Spirit energizes the individual to receive God's Word as something that is good in itself. It is not only God's Word that a person tastes as they are energized by the Holy Spirit, but also the powers of the age to come. They will understand not only that God's Word is good, but also that God's future exercise of power is going to be for the benefit of the believer.

The true believer must undertake all four of these steps. We can't interpret our own decision to follow Christ as salvation, because accepting God's offer of grace is not all there is to salvation. We are truly saved when God sees that the repentance of our sin is genuine and accepts us and makes us part of His body. Salvation only comes with true repentance on our part and such being accepted by God. We must be truly repentant sinners. This is why a true believer can never be lost. However, many accept God's grace, but never truly repent or receive the Holy Spirit. Only these individuals can fall away and be lost.

We are utterly unable to save ourselves because of our sin and its consequences. God became a human being in the Person of Jesus Christ. "Jesus lived a sinless life" (2 Corinthians 5:21) and offered Himself as a perfect sacrifice on our behalf (Colossians 1:22). Since Jesus is God, His death was of infinite and eternal value. The death of Jesus Christ on the cross fully paid for the sins of the entire world. His resurrection from the dead demonstrated that His sacrifice was indeed sufficient and that salvation is now available.

A man asked the apostle Paul how to be saved. Paul's response was, "believe in the Lord Jesus Christ and you will be saved" (Acts 16:31). The way to follow God's plan of salvation is to believe and repent, then God will fill you with the Holy Spirit. That is the requirement for salvation. God has provided for our salvation through Jesus Christ. All we must do is receive it, by faith, fully trusting in Jesus alone as Savior, and truly repent of our sins. That is God's plan of salvation. Learn Religions, Mary Fairchild, *The Plan of Salvation in the Bible.* [2]

Jesus is the way of salvation! Jesus proclaimed; "I am the light of the world. Whoever follows me will never walk in darkness, but will have the light of life" (John 8:12).

Jesus declared; "I am the gate; whoever enters through me will be saved. He will come in and go out, and find pasture" (John 10:9).

Jesus is the way! Jesus said; "I am the good shepherd. The good shepherd lays down his life for the sheep" (John 10:11).

Jesus declared; "I am the resurrection and the life. He who believes in me will live, even though he dies; and whoever lives and believes in me will never die" (John 11:25–26).

Jesus took our sin upon Himself. Jesus died in our place taking the punishment that we deserve. Three days later, Jesus rose from the dead, proving His victory over sin and death. Why did He do it? Jesus answered that question Himself: "Greater love has no one than this, that he lay down his life for his friends" (John 15:13). Jesus died so that we could live. If we place our faith in Jesus, trusting His death as the payment for our sins, all of our sins are forgiven and washed away. We will then have our spiritual hunger satisfied. The lights will be turned on. We will have access to a fulfilling life. We will know our true best friend and good shepherd. We will know that we will have life after we die—a resurrected life in Heaven for eternity with Jesus! If Jesus loves you so much that He died for you, why is it so hard to put your faith and trust in Him?

"The only way to be forgiven of sin and restored to God is to repent and believe in Jesus" (Acts 2:38). "Jesus is the only way to the Father (1 Timothy 2:5)."

When we enter into a right relationship with God through faith in Jesus Christ, we learn who we were created to be and discover the true purpose of our lives: "For we are his workmanship, created in Christ Jesus for good works, which God prepared beforehand, that we should walk in them" (Ephesians 2:10). If you are uncertain if you truly believe in Jesus but you desire to, or if you feel God drawing you to faith in Jesus, the next step is simple. Believe! Trust in Jesus! Rely on Him for your salvation. Allow God to turn you from sin to forgiveness and salvation.

If you are ready to follow God's plan of salvation, continue reading and place your faith in Jesus as your Savior. Change your mind from embracing sin and rejecting God to rejecting sin and embracing God through Jesus Christ. Fully trust in the sacrifice of Jesus as the perfect and complete payment for your sins. If you do this, God's Word promises that you will be saved, your sins will be forgiven, and you will spend eternity in Heaven. There is no more important decision. Place your faith in Jesus Christ as your Savior today!

CHAPTER 38

How Did Jesus' Death Pay Our Penalty?

If we think of Jesus as merely a human, then this question is a natural one to ask. The reason Jesus did not have to spend eternity in hell is that He is not merely a human, but God Himself. Jesus took on flesh and lived among humans in the form of a human. He was a human like no other because His nature was that of God—holy, perfect, and infinite.

In John's gospel we read the following: "In the beginning was the Word, and the Word was with God, and the Word was God. He was with God in the beginning. Through Him all things were made; without Him, nothing was made that has been made. The Word became flesh and made his dwelling among us. We have seen his glory, the glory of the One and Only, who came from the Father, full of grace and truth" (John 1:1–3).

This passage gives clear testimony that the eternal Word, who is co-eternal with God and of the same essence as God, took on human flesh and made His dwelling among us. Paul says regarding Jesus; "For in Christ all the fullness of the Deity lives in bodily form" (Colossians 2:9).

But how can the death of Jesus atone for the sins of every person who has ever lived? This is where the discussion of Jesus being the God-human comes in. Jesus is no mere human; He is God in human flesh. As a perfectly sinless human, He can atone for the sins of humanity without first having to atone for His sin and as God, He can fully satisfy the wrath of God that our sins incur.

Sin against an infinite God must be paid infinitely. That is why payment for our sin must be infinite. There are only two options for infinite payment. Either a finite creature (human) must pay for his sin for an infinite amount of time, or an infinite Being (Jesus) must pay for it once for all humans for all time. There are no other options. A sin against an infinitely holy God requires an equally infinite satisfaction as payment, and even an eternity in hell will not dissipate God's infinite, righteous wrath against sin. Only a divine Being could withstand the infinite wrath of a holy God against our sin. It requires an equally infinite Being as a substitute for humanity to satisfy God's wrath. Jesus, as the God-human, is the only possible Savior.

Jesus' death in our place is what is referred to as substitutionary atonement. Jesus died as a substitute for sinners. Without Christ, we are going to die and spend an eternity in hell as payment for our sins. Death in the Scriptures refers to a separation. Everyone will die, but some will live in Heaven with the Lord for eternity, while others will live a life in hell for eternity. The death spoken of here refers to life in hell. However, the second thing this verse teaches us is that eternal life is available through Jesus Christ. This is His substitutionary atonement.

Jesus Christ died in our place when He was crucified on the cross. We deserved to be the ones placed on that cross to die because we are the ones who live sinful lives. But Christ took the punishment on Himself in our place—He substituted Himself for us.

"He bore our sins in his body on the cross, so that we might die to sins and live for righteousness; by his wounds, you have been healed" (1 Peter 2:24). Here again, we see that Christ took the sins we committed onto Himself to pay the price for us. A few verses later we read; "For Christ died for sins once for all, the righteous for the unrighteous, to bring you to God. He was put to death in the body but made alive by the Spirit" (1 Peter 3:18). Not only do these verses teach us about the substitute that Christ was for us, but they also teach that He was the atonement, meaning He satisfied the payment due for the sinfulness of humanity.

Another passage talks about the substitutionary atonement, about the coming Christ who was to die on the cross for our sins. The prophecy is very detailed, and the crucifixion happened just as it was foretold. "But He was pierced for our transgressions, He was crushed for our iniquities; the punishment that brought us peace was upon Him, and by his wounds, we are healed" (Isaiah 53:5). Notice the substitution. Here again, we see that Christ paid the price for us! Got Questions, *What does it mean that Jesus Christ conquered death?*[1]

We can only pay the price of sin on our own by being punished and placed in hell for all eternity. But God's Son, Jesus Christ, came to earth to pay the price of our sins. Because He did this for us, we now have the opportunity to not only have our sins forgiven but to spend eternity with Him. To do this, we must place our faith in what Christ did on the cross. We cannot save ourselves; we need a substitute to take our place. The death of Jesus Christ is the substitutionary atonement.

CHAPTER 39

How to Receive Jesus Christ?

Many terms used in Christianity can be confusing to new believers or those seeking to know more about Jesus. One such phrase recurs often: Receive Jesus Christ as your Savior. What exactly does it mean to receive Jesus? Since Jesus lived, died, and rose again over two thousand years ago, how can we receive Him now?

Jesus came to all of us, but many did not receive Him. Yet to all who did receive Him, to those who believed in his name, He gave the right to become children of God. John equates receiving Jesus with believing in Him, which results in one's becoming a child of God. Receiving Jesus has to do with faith. We trust who Jesus is and what He has done on our behalf.

When we receive a package, we take it to ourselves. When a running back receives the football, he pulls it to himself and clings to it. When we receive Jesus, we take Him to ourselves and cling to the truth about Him.

To receive Jesus as our Savior means we look to Him and Him alone as the One who forgives our sin, mends our relationship with God and provides us entrance to Heaven. To reject Him as Savior means we either don't believe we need salvation or are looking to another deliverer. Scripture is plain, however, that "salvation is found in no one else, for there is no other name under Heaven given to humankind by which we must be saved" (Acts 4:12). Got Questions, *What is the Christian doctrine of salvation?*[1]

To receive Jesus as our Lord means we let go of the lesser gods we have built our lives around. We cannot receive Jesus as Lord without displacing the idols in our lives—idols such as power, popularity, wealth, or comfort that we trust to provide us with purpose and strength. Jesus described the need to follow Him wholeheartedly in Luke 9:23: "Whoever wants to be my disciple must deny themselves and take up their cross daily and follow me."

Receiving Jesus is more than just acknowledging Him as a good moral teacher, a role model, or even a prophet. We must receive Him as our personal Lord and Savior by faith.

To receive Jesus means we acknowledge that He is who He said He is. "He is the Son of God who took on human form, was born of a virgin, lived a perfect life, and accomplished in full God's plan to rescue humanity from sin. To receive Jesus is to trust that His sacrifice on the cross completely paid for our sin and to believe that God raised Him from the dead" (2 Timothy 2:8). To receive Jesus is to recognize that we are sinners separated from a holy God. To receive Jesus is to call out to Him in faith, trusting that only His blood can cleanse us from sin and restore us to a right relationship with God. Those who receive Jesus by faith are given the right to become children of God—children born not of natural descent, nor human decision or a husband's will, but born of God.

When we receive Jesus as our Savior, and repent of our sins, God sends us the gift of His Holy Spirit who enters our spirits and begins to transform us to be more like Christ. Jesus called this transaction being born again. When a baby is born, a new creature emerges that did not previously exist. Over time, that baby begins to look and act like the parents. So it is when we are born of the Spirit by receiving Jesus. We become children of God and begin to look and act more like our heavenly Father.

Receiving Jesus Christ into our lives is more than adding Him to an already cluttered priority list. He does not offer the option of being only a part of our lives. When we receive Him, we pledge to Him our allegiance and look to Him as the undisputed Lord of our lives. Jesus becomes our number one and our first priority in our lives. Every decision we make, and value we have, is based on Him. We will still disobey His commands at times, but "the Holy Spirit within us draws us to repentance so that our close fellowship with God is restored" (Psalm 51:7). Got Questions, *What Does it Mean to Receive Jesus?*[2]

CHAPTER 40

Having a Relationship with Jesus Christ

A relationship with Jesus is the most important relationship a person could ever have. A relationship with Jesus results in new life, forgiveness, the indwelling of the Holy Spirit, and, in the future, bodily resurrection and a home in Heaven (Philippians 3:20–21). Establishing a relationship with Jesus is not difficult. Jesus Himself came to seek and to save the lost. He has issued the invitation, "come to me, all you who are weary and burdened, and I will give you rest" (Matthew 11:28); He has called for our trust and He has spoken to us as friends. Jesus is certainly willing to have a personal relationship with us.

Having a relationship with Jesus is based on God's grace, through faith. To understand, we need to look at a few relatively simple truths found in the Bible:

The first truth we need to recognize to have a relationship with Jesus is that, naturally, our relationship with God is broken. We have sinned against Him. God's standard is perfection—since He is holy—and we all fall short of that standard. We each need to humble ourselves before God and admit our sins, and repent of our sins.

To have a relationship with Jesus, we also need to understand the biblical truth that the "wages of sin is death" (Romans 6:23). Wages are payment for what we do. The payment or result of our sin is death—this is speaking of spiritual death, eternal separation from God in the place the Bible calls hell.

To have a relationship with Jesus, we also need to grasp the third truth—and this is a wonderful one: God loves us despite our sins, and He sent His Son Jesus Christ to die for us, as our Substitute. God showed his great love for us by sending Christ to die for us while we were still sinners. He didn't wait for us to clean up our act or somehow overcome our sin (an impossibility); rather, He sacrificed Himself for us while we were still estranged from Him. He chose to take the punishment that we deserved. He took our place!

Finally, we need to admit that there's absolutely nothing we can do to save ourselves or to contribute to our salvation. Based on Christ's sacrifice, God forgives our sins by grace, that is, by an undeserved blessing. The Lord Jesus has already done all the work, and He did it perfectly! Salvation is not about what we can do but about what Christ has done.

Knowing these truths, we can have a relationship with Jesus by receiving Him by faith. We turn from our sin, repent, and trust Jesus and His finished work on the cross to have paid for our sins. Call out to Him as the Risen Savior who conquered death once and for all. Accept Him as your Lord and Master. The Bible promises, as many as received Him, to them He gave the right to become children of God, to those who believe in His name.

You can receive Jesus by faith and thus begin a relationship with Him this very moment, right where you are, as you read these words! You can express your faith in Him by praying a prayer similar to this:

God, I know that I am a sinner. I know that I deserve the consequences of my sin. But I am trusting in Jesus Christ as my Savior. I believe that His death and resurrection provided for my forgiveness. I trust in Jesus and Jesus alone as my personal Lord and Savior. Thank you, Lord, for saving me. Lord, I repent of my sins and I thank you for forgiving me! Amen!

God is not as concerned about the exact words you use as He is about the attitude of your heart. He sees your faith; He knows all your sins. Remember the following, Got Questions, *How can I have a relationship with Jesus?*[1]

God loves you and offers a wonderful plan for your life. God's Love - God's Plan - Jesus said; "I came that they might have life, and might have it abundantly" (John 10:10) — that is, that life might be full and meaningful. Why is it that most people are not experiencing abundant life? Because ...

All of us sin, and our sin has separated us from God. We Are Sinful – "All have sinned and fall short of the glory of God" (Romans 3:23).

Jesus Christ is God's only provision for our sin. Through Him, we can know and experience God's love and plan for our lives. Jesus Died in Our Place – "God demonstrates His love toward us, in that while we were yet sinners, Christ died for us. Jesus Rose from the Dead - Christ died for our sins ... He was buried ... He was raised on the third day, according to the Scriptures ... He appeared to Peter, then to the twelve. After that, He appeared to more than five hundred" (1 Corinthians 15:3–6). Jesus is the Only Way to God - Jesus said to him; "I am the way, and the truth, and the life; no one comes to the Father, but through Me" (John 14:6). God has bridged the gap that separates us from Him by sending His Son, Jesus Christ, to die on the cross in our place to pay the penalty for our sins. It is not enough just to know these three principles ...

We must individually receive Jesus Christ as Savior and Lord; then we can know and experience God's love and plan for our lives. We Must Receive Christ, we receive Christ through faith. When we receive Christ, we experience a new birth. We Receive Christ by Personal Invitation - Jesus says, "Behold, I stand at the door and knock; if anyone hears My voice and opens the door, I will come into him" (Revelation 3:20).

CHAPTER 41

Being Born Again

What does it mean to be born again? When a Jewish religious leader named Nicodemus came to talk with Jesus one night, he declared that God was with Jesus because of all the miraculous signs Jesus performed. Jesus had this penetrating response: I tell you the truth, no one can see the kingdom of God unless he is born again.' 'How can a man be born when he is old?' Nicodemus asked. 'Surely, he cannot enter a second time into his mother's womb to be born!' Jesus answered, "I tell you the truth, no one can enter the kingdom of God unless he is born of water and the Spirit. Flesh gives birth to flesh, but the Spirit gives birth to spirit. You should not be surprised at my saying; you must be born again" (John 3:3–7).

The phrase born again in Scripture means to be born from above–a spiritual rebirth. A Christian is a man, woman, or child who has experienced spiritual new birth through the regenerating work of the Holy Spirit. That new birth is a gift of God, through Jesus Christ, given by the grace He freely offers for all. Got Questions, *What does it mean to be a born-again Christian?*[1]

Nicodemus had a real need. He needed a change of his heart—a spiritual transformation. New birth, being born again, is an act of God whereby eternal life is imparted to the person who believes. Being born again also carries the idea of becoming children of God through trust in the name of Jesus Christ.

The question logically comes, "Why does a person need to be born again?" The apostle Paul in Ephesians 2:1 says, "and you He made alive, who were dead in trespasses and sins."

Sinners are spiritually dead; when they receive spiritual life through faith in Christ, the Bible likens it to a rebirth. Only those who are born again have their sins forgiven and have a relationship with God.

How does that come to be? When one is saved, they have been born again, spiritually renewed, and is now a child of God by right of new birth. Trusting in Jesus Christ, the One who paid the penalty of sin when He died on the cross, is the means to be born again. "Therefore, if anyone is in Christ, he is a new creation: the old has gone, the new has come!" (2 Corinthians 5:17). We all need to be born again to get right with God. All About Religion, *Born Again Christianity*.[2]

CHAPTER 42

Mercy and Grace

Mercy and grace are closely related. While the terms have similar meanings, grace and mercy are not the same. Mercy has to do with kindness and compassion; it is often spoken of in the context of God not punishing us as our sins deserve. Grace includes kindness and compassion but also carries the idea of bestowing a gift or favor. It's easy to see it this way:

- Mercy is when you don't get what you deserve (death)
- Grace is when you get what you don't deserve (eternal life).

In Scripture, mercy is often equated with deliverance from judgment and grace is always the extending of a blessing to the unworthy. According to the Bible, we have all sinned. As a result of that sin, we all deserve death and eternal judgment in the lake of fire. Given what we deserve, every day we live is an act of God's mercy. If God gave us all that we deserve, we would all be, right now, condemned for eternity. In (Psalm 51:1–2), David cries out; "Have mercy on me, O God, according to your unfailing love; according to your great compassion blot out my transgressions. Wash away all my iniquity and cleanse me from my sin." Pleading for God's mercy is asking Him to show kindness and withhold the judgment we deserve. Got Questions, *What is the difference between mercy and grace?*[1]

We deserve nothing good from God. God does not owe us any good thing. What good we experience is a result of the grace of God. Grace is simply defined as an unmerited favor. God favors us—He shows us approval and kindness—in blessing us with good things that we do not deserve and could never earn. Common grace refers to the blessings that God bestows on all of humanity regardless of their spiritual standing before Him while saving grace is that special blessing whereby God sovereignly bestows unmerited divine assistance upon His elect for their regeneration and sanctification.

Mercy and grace are evident in the salvation that is available through Jesus Christ. We deserved judgment, but in Christ, we receive mercy from God and are delivered from judgment through grace. In Christ, we receive eternal salvation, the forgiveness of sins, and abundant life, all gifts of grace. Our response to the mercy and grace of God should be to fall on our knees in worship and thanksgiving. Hebrews 4:16 declares, "let us then approach the throne of grace with confidence, so that we may receive mercy and find grace to help us in our time of need."

CHAPTER 43

Can a Christian Lose Salvation?

First, the term Christian must be defined. A Christian is a person who has fully trusted in Jesus Christ as the only Savior and therefore possesses the Holy Spirit. Being a Christian means putting God first over everything else. God is always the number one priority in a Christian's life. A true Christian is a friend of God and obeys everything God teaches in His Word. So are you a friend of God's, or just a casual Christian who does not give much thought to His Word or values? Calling yourself a Christian doesn't make you a Christian. A Christian obeys, follows, and accepts Jesus Christ as their Lord and Savior. Jesus is always our first priority and our worldview is defined by Jesus. With this definition in mind, can a Christian lose salvation? It's a crucially important question. The quick answer is no. However, the problem is that many people consider themselves to be Christian when they are really not!

The best way to know if you are truly a Christian is to examine what the Bible says occurs at salvation and to study what losing salvation would entail. Here are a few points to consider:

- A Christian is a new creation. "Therefore, if anyone is in Christ, he is a new creation; the old has gone, the new has come!" (2 Corinthians 5:17). A Christian is not simply an improved version of a person; a Christian is an entirely new creature. He is in Christ. For a Christian to lose salvation, the new creation would have to be destroyed.

- <u>A Christian is redeemed</u>. "For you know that it was not with perishable things such as silver or gold that you were redeemed from the empty way of life handed down to you from your forefathers, but with the precious blood of Christ, a lamb without blemish or defect" (1 Peter 1:18–19). The word redeemed refers to a purchase being made; a price being paid. We were purchased at the cost of Christ's death. For a Christian to lose salvation, God Himself would have to revoke His purchase of the individual for whom He paid with the precious blood of Christ.
- <u>A Christian is justified.</u> "Therefore, since we have been justified through faith, we have peace with God through our Lord Jesus Christ" (Romans 5:1). To justify is to declare righteousness. All those who receive Jesus as Savior are declared righteous by God. For a Christian to lose salvation, God would have to go back on His Word and un-declare what He had previously declared. Those absolved of guilt would have to be tried again and found guilty. God would have to reverse the sentence handed down from the divine bench.
- <u>A Christian is promised eternal life</u>. Eternal life is the promise of spending forever in Heaven with God. God promises; Believe and you will have eternal life. For a Christian to lose salvation, eternal life would have to be redefined. The Christian is promised to live forever.
- <u>A Christian is marked by God and sealed by the Spirit</u>. "In Him, you also, after listening to the message of truth, the gospel of your salvation—having also believed, you were sealed in Him with the Holy Spirit of the promise, who is a first installment of our inheritance, in regard to the redemption of *God's own* possession, to the praise of His glory." (Ephesians 1:13–14). At the moment of faith, the new Christian is marked and sealed with the Spirit, who was promised to act as a deposit to guarantee the heavenly inheritance. The result is that God's glory is praised. For a Christian to lose salvation, God would have to erase the mark, withdraw the Spirit, cancel the deposit, break His promise, revoke the guarantee, keep the inheritance, forego the praise, and lessen His glory.
- <u>A Christian is guaranteed glorification</u>. "Those He predestined, He also called; those He called, He also justified; those He

justified, He also glorified" (Romans 8:30). Romans 5:1 says, "justification is ours at the moment of faith." Glorification comes with justification. All those whom God justifies are promised to be glorified. This promise will be fulfilled when Christians receive their perfect resurrection bodies in Heaven. If a Christian can lose salvation, then Romans 8:30 is in error, because God could not guarantee glorification for all those whom He predestines, calls, and justifies.

A Christian by the above definitions, cannot lose salvation. This was also discussed in Chapter 37, where it was mentioned that salvation only comes with true repentance on our part and such being accepted by God.

But what about Christians who live a sinful, unrepentant lifestyle? And, what about Christians who reject the faith and deny Christ? Again, not everyone who calls themselves a Christian is a Christian. The Bible declares that a true Christian will not live in a state of continual, unrepentant sin and that they must truly repent of their sin. The Bible also says that any person who departs the faith is demonstrating that they were never truly Christians (1 John 2:19). They may have been religious, they may have put on a good show, but they were never born again by the power of God. "By their fruit, you will recognize them" (Matthew 7:16). "The redeemed of God belongs, to Him who was raised from the dead so that we might bear fruit for God" (Romans 7:4).

Nothing can separate a child of God from the Father's love (Romans 8:38–39). Nothing can remove a Christian from God's hand (John 10:29). God guarantees eternal life and maintains the salvation He has given us. "The Good Shepherd searches for the lost sheep, and, when He finds it, He joyfully puts it on his shoulders and goes home" (Luke 15:5–6). The lamb is found, and the Shepherd gladly bears the burden; our Lord takes full responsibility for bringing the lost one safely home.

Further emphasizes to the goodness and faithfulness of our Savior: "To Him who can keep you from falling and to present you before his glorious presence without fault and with great joy—to the only God our Savior be glory, majesty, power, and authority, through Jesus Christ our Lord, before all ages, now and forevermore! Amen" (Jude 1:24–25).

But how many people are saved? Jesus has much to say about the saved and who will enter the Kingdom of God in Heaven. Jesus uses many parables to teach this lesson so I will list them below and ask that you read these for yourself:

- The Rich Young Man (Matthew 19:16–30): The rich young man thought he had much to lose but didn't think about how much he had to gain. He allowed his possessions to be more important than God. He chose his earthly riches over the eternal riches of God's Kingdom. What would you choose?
- The Camel and the Eye of a Needle (Matthew 19:20–24): It's all about how we prioritize. Sometimes we only see the riches of this life and are unable to see the riches that await us in the Kingdom of God. Jesus says in (Matthew 6:21) "for where your treasure is, there your heart will be also." We need to open our eyes and see the vast treasures that await us in Heaven. (Matthew 6:20) "But store up for yourselves treasures in Heaven, where neither moth nor rust destroys, and where thieves do not break in or steal."
- The Seeds (Matthew 13:3–8): In this passage, Jesus touches on how few people make it to God's Kingdom and Heaven. This is not a good sign for us. We see that the seed only flourishes on the good ground but not on the other three types of ground. If one out of four is any indication at all that's only 25%.
- The Narrow Gate (Matthew 7:13–14): Jesus is again telling us that few will enter into the Kingdom of God. We don't know the number in this parable but it is clearly less than half, and possibly much less. Looking at the world today with many people rejecting God, is it that surprising?
- Two Kinds of People (Matthew 7:24–27): We must obey the teachings of Jesus and "build our house on solid ground, the rock, and not on sand." Jesus is the foundation for what we believe and how we live our lives. We take on Godly values, not the values of our society.
- The Ten Virgins (Matthew 25:1–13): Half of the virgins were prepared the other half were not. The groom came, and those who were ready went in with Him to the wedding feast, and the door was shut. Those not prepared could not get in. Only half enter into the Kingdom and eternal life. The key is to be prepared and ready for when the Lord comes.

- The Talents (Matthew 25:14–30): This parable demonstrates that we are all servants of God and by placing our faith in God we can enter into the Kingdom of God. Two of the servants were faithful, one servant was not. We can only please God by our faith, so you must place your faith in Jesus to enter the Kingdom of God.
- The Sheep and the Goats (Matthew 25:31–46): This parable makes it clear that it's not our works that give us eternal life in the Kingdom, but our faith and relationship with Jesus. Many Christians focus on doing good works to enter into eternal life, but the promise of eternal life rests with our faith and relationship with Jesus. Many people who consider themselves Christian will not enter the Kingdom. They don't put their priority on God, but instead seek society's approval instead of God's approval?

Yes, there are many false Christians in the world. Many of the parables above refer to those who think they are Christians but only a few are. Are you one of the few? If you are, does this change your priorities and make God your priority? Let go of your social values, and your politics and choose God and his values instead! We must take the Bible and God's teaching seriously, we must obey God, not society.

When you think to yourself that you believe in Jesus, how deep does that belief go? Do you have a meaningful relationship with the Most-High God? Are your beliefs and decisions based on God's teachings or do you put more priority on what society has to say? The key is Jesus! Do you love Jesus? Have you placed your faith in Him? Is He priority number one? A true Christian will believe 100% of God's teachings, not just some. Does your worldview or your political party follow the values of God? If not, you must change! Learn Religions, Mary Fairchild, *"The Plan of Salvation in the Bible.*[1]

Many people have good intentions, but you must ask yourself what is my view on abortion, homosexuality, and the other false values of society and my political party? Does your political party and worldview oppose God or uphold God? Do they follow the Bible or oppose the Bible? Do you need to realign your values to match God's values? God's not wrong, because God is never wrong. As Christians, our purpose must be to follow what God has taught us, even if it means being shunned or ridiculed by the people around us. Sadly, there are many today who willfully remain in spiritual darkness. Don't ignore God's warning. People ultimately choose Heaven or Hell. Sinful people ignore and rebel against a perfect and loving God. God gives us free will and we will live with the choices we make forever.

CHAPTER 44

Faith

Faith is confidence or trust in a person, thing, or concept. The word faith is derived from the Latin word fides and the Old French word feed. Wikipedia, *Faith*. In the context of religion, one can define faith as belief in a god or the doctrines or teachings of religion. Religious people often think of faith as confidence based on a perceived degree of warrant, while others who are more skeptical of religion tend to think of faith as simply belief without evidence. Faith is a word we hear thrown around all the time. Keep the faith. Walk by faith. Having faith. So what is faith? Faith has several different definitions: Wikipedia, *Faith*[1] states:

- Complete trust or confidence in someone or something.
- Strong belief in God or the doctrines of a religion, based on spiritual apprehension rather than truth.
- A system of religious belief.
- A firmly held belief or theory

The Bible says that faith is confidence in what we hope for and the assurance that the Lord is working, even though we cannot see it. Faith knows that no matter what the situation, in our lives or someone else's, the Lord is working in it. The Hebrew word for faith is Emunah which means support. This is perfect because faith is like the Lord's support to us because He is working in every situation for his glory. Regardless of what we think, He always knows best, and there are many times we have to see by faith and not our own eyes. Paul E Chapman, *Examples of*

Faith (found in the Bible)[2] on his website mentions many samples from his website.

Examples of Faith:

1. Abel Taught Us Faith Can Save Our Souls. Hebrews 11:4, "By faith Abel offered unto God a more excellent sacrifice than Cain, by which he obtained witness that he was righteous, God testifying of his gifts: and by it he being dead yet speaketh."
2. Enoch Taught Us Faith Pleases God. Hebrews 11:5, "By faith Enoch was translated that he should not see death; and was not found, because God had translated him: for before his translation he had this testimony, that he pleased God."
3. Noah Taught Us Faith Can Save Our Families. Hebrews 11:7, "By faith Noah, being warned of God of things not seen as yet, moved with fear, prepared an ark to the saving of his house; by which he condemned the world, and became heir of the righteousness which is by faith."
4. Abraham Taught Us Faith Can Guide Our Steps. Hebrews 11:8–10, "By faith Abraham, when he was called to go out into a place which he was to receive for an inheritance, obeyed; and he went out, not knowing whither he went. By faith he sojourned in the land of promise, as in a strange country, dwelling in tabernacles with Isaac and Jacob, the heirs with him of the same promise: For he looked for a city which hath foundations, whose builder and maker is God."
5. Sara Taught Us Faith Can Do the Impossible. Hebrews 11:11, "Through faith also Sara herself received strength to conceive seed, and was delivered of a child when she was past age, because she judged Him faithful who had promised."
6. Abraham Taught Us Faith Can Empower Us To Obey In The Most Desperate Situations. Hebrews 11:17–19, "By faith Abraham, when he was tried, offered up Isaac: and he that had received the promises offered up his only begotten Son, Of whom it was said, That in Isaac shall thy seed be called: Accounting that God was able to raise him up, even from the dead; from whence also he received him in a figure."

There are many more examples of faith in the bible, but we may ask; Where Does Faith Come From? "For it is by grace you have been saved, through faith—and this is not from yourselves, it is the gift of God—not by works, so that no one can boast" (Ephesians 2:8–9). Faith can only come from a new heart, regenerated by God; faith is a gift from God. It is the unique way that God uses to bring salvation to his people. We strengthen our faith by reading the Bible and hearing the gospel. The more we immerse ourselves in truth, the more our confidence grows. Everyone who is saved has been gifted faith. It is the ability to believe God is who He says He is, trusting Him in all things for all things. Faith also helps to combat unbelief and motivates us to do what God desires us to do. Not only do we grow our faith by reading Scripture and praying in our own time, but also by hearing the message in church with other believers. Justification by faith means that God has removed the penalty of our sins and has declared us to be righteous. By God's work, we have peace with our Lord Jesus Christ. Since we have been made right in God's sight by faith, we have peace with God because of what Jesus Christ our Lord has done for us.

Faith and belief are often used in the same context, sometimes interchangeably, but they are not quite the same thing. Belief is a strongly held opinion about an idea or worldview. Beliefs are opinions that you form about what you read, hear, or see. Beliefs can change over time, as you grow and learn new things. Faith is not something you start and build from; faith can only be received; it must be given by God. True faith can take on doubts and questions, but it remains intact. We can grow in our faith, but the foundation is always the same. James 2:19 says; "You believe that there is one God. Good! Even the demons believe that-and shudder." You can believe there is a God, even that there is one God, but do you believe He is your God? God produces faith in us by giving us new hearts and opening our eyes to see that He is our God and we need Him. Does your faith in God change the way you live your life? Some say they believe in God, but the way they live their life does not change; they are motivated by other factors. Faith changes how we live our lives, faith motivates us to keep moving in life.

Having faith in the Bible means trusting that God's Word is the truth. The faith that God began in us will grow when exposed to God's Word. It's knowing that every time you read the Bible, the word of God is being imparted to you. The Bible says that faith is not silly or irrational. It is not a feeling of closeness to God either. Instead, faith is being able to trust God for what He has promised in His Word.

How do we grow in faith? There are several different ways:

- Ask God to increase your faith. If you are struggling in your faith, ask Him for more of it. He will be glad to bestow it through the Holy Spirit.
- Focus on obeying God. No one is perfect and we all make mistakes, but if you focus on following God's word and commands, your faith will grow naturally.
- Spend time reading and hearing God's word. Spend time every day reading God's word and soak it into your heart and mind. If your lifestyle is busy, listen to a sermon or a Christian podcast. Putting His word into your heart and soul will fortify your faith in the rough times.
- Spend time with other believers. We are meant to worship together, pray together, and share our faith. Hearing about others' journeys in faith can be encouraging. Also study the Bible together, encouraging each other in godly disciplines.
- Spend time in fervent prayer. Scheduling a specific time each day to spend with God in prayer makes a huge difference. This is your time alone with Him to discuss anything that is on your heart and mind. Be still and listen carefully and your faith will grow in abundance.

Living in faith and not by sight means that you are willing to go into the unknown. It's trusting God even though you don't know where He's leading you or what the outcome will be. God is in control and that is where we find peace.

How to Keep the Faith in Times of Trouble

- Keep a positive attitude, reflecting on God's promises. We are to praise Jesus in all things and all circumstances.
- Surrender your circumstances to God. It can be so easy to get upset and shake our fists at Him when things aren't going right.

Instead, ask Him for help and to change your circumstances. Let Him take the wheel and trust what He is going to do.
- Be generous. The Bible says even in times of trouble, we are to give. It seems counterintuitive when you are struggling to keep your head above water. However, in giving and blessing someone else, you are blessing yourself too. God loves a cheerful giver.
- Spend more time in the Word. This will help keep you grounded and not go in another direction due to confusion or desperation.
- Reach out to friends and family. One of the best things to do in hard times is to draw close to those who love you most. Sit down and discuss your situation with a close friend or family member and let them give you some encouragement. Being connected to others is essential. Having faith means we are part of a covenant body of believers, a family of brothers and sisters united in Jesus Christ.

The truest act of faith, which is made possible by God's gift of grace to us, is complete trust in the Lord through every circumstance, even when we do not understand why something is happening or not happening. As a Christian, what is it you truly believe in? Christians should proclaim the absolute truth and authority of Scripture and provide a biblical role model to the global body of Christ, the community, and society at large. All Christians must evaluate their core beliefs.

CHAPTER 45

Heaven

Thankfully, God has secured our rescue from the just sentence of hell for our sins. For those who accept Jesus as their Lord and Savior, we can look forward to Heaven. Heaven is a very common term in the Bible. You will find it used for the sky; for the space beyond our atmosphere; and God's dwelling place. Jesus frequently talks about the Kingdom of Heaven as a present reality with a future final fulfillment. And Heaven is frequently associated with the home of believers when we leave this life. A home in Christ, in the presence of God.

That 'home in Heaven' that we look forward to is described in the pages of Scripture. But it can be beyond our ability to grasp. Heaven is a real place where the people of God will live one day. Jesus is in Heaven preparing a place for us to live. In Heaven, those saved by God will have new bodies without the curse of sin! There will be no one who is blind, deaf, or lame in Heaven. Although Jesus builds houses in Heaven, the Bible also says that those saved will also "build houses and inhabit them, they will also plant vineyards and eat their fruit" (Isaiah 65:21). Most importantly, God will be in Heaven and He wants to be your friend. He wants to dwell with you and wipe away all your tears. We will be in the presence of God in Heaven. Christianity.com, Jessica Miller, *What Is Heaven Like According to the Bible?* [1]

There are many popular myths about Heaven and where it is that create misunderstanding. According to the Bible, the universe is not only infinite but also filled with intelligent, friendly, benevolent beings.

The word Heaven (Hebrew: shamyim, Greek: Ouranos) can mean God's dwelling place. The Bible says: "The LORD has established His throne in Heaven, and His kingdom rules over all" (Psalm 103:19).

Heaven may also refer to the endless planets, stars, and galaxies of the universe. The Bible says: "When I consider Your heavens, the work of Your fingers, the moon, and the stars, which You have ordained" (Psalm 8:3).

The Bible also speaks of the atmosphere that surrounds the earth as Heaven or heavens. Please note: one must study the biblical context to understand which of the three meanings is implied.

The Bible is clear on the following: After Jesus was raised from the dead, He went to Heaven. The Bible says: "People of Galilee, why do you stand gazing up into Heaven? This same Jesus, who was taken up from you into Heaven, will so come in like manner as you saw Him go into Heaven" (Acts 1:11). Before this Jesus told His disciples: "In My Father's house are many mansions; if it were not so, I would have told you. I go to prepare a place for you. And if I go and prepare a place for you, I will come again and receive you to Myself; that where I am, there you may be also" (John 14:2–3). Bibleinfo, *What is Heaven like & where is Heaven?*[2] Gives us some information on what Heaven will be like.

What is Heaven Like?

- All things are new. "Now I saw a new Heaven and a new earth, for the first Heaven and the first earth had passed away. Also, there was no more sea. Then I, John, saw the holy city, New Jerusalem, coming down out of Heaven from God, prepared as a bride adorned for her husband" (Revelation 21:1–2).
- No tears or pain. "And God will wipe away every tear from their eyes; there shall be no more death, nor sorrow, nor crying. There shall be no more pain, for the former things have passed away" (Revelation 21:4).
- Perfect peace. "The wolf and the lamb will graze together, and the lion will eat straw like the ox; and dust will be the serpent's food. They will do no evil or harm on all My holy mountain, says the LORD." (Isaiah 65:25).
- Houses and vineyards. "They will build houses and inhabit them; they shall plant vineyards and eat their fruit "(Isaiah 65:21).

- Fruitful gardens. "The wilderness and the desert will rejoice, and the desert will shout for joy and blossom; like the crocus" (Isaiah 35:1).
- Perfect unselfish love governs all relationships in Heaven. The Bible says: "He who does not love does not know God, for God is love" (1 John 4:8).
- We will have physical bodies in Heaven. Our bodies will be free from disease, pain, and death in Heaven (1 Corinthians 15:40–49). "The Lord Jesus Christ, who will transform our lowly body so that it may be conformed to His glorious body" (Philippians 3:20–21). The body of Jesus after His resurrection was physical. Jesus said: "Behold My hands and My feet, that it is I. Handle Me and see, for a spirit does not have flesh and bones as you see I have" (Luke 24:39).
- We won't miss our old lives. The upgrade from Earth to Heaven will be vastly superior because we will experience all God intends for us. He fashions us to want precisely what He will give us so what He gives us will be exactly what we want.
- We won't become angels. Death is a relocation of the same person from one place to another. The place changes, but the person remains the same. "The same person who becomes absent from his or her body becomes present with the Lord" (2 Corinthians 5:8). We won't be angels but we'll be with them.
- We won't be tempted. We will never be tempted to turn our backs on Christ. What would tempt us? God will never withdraw His holiness from us; and in Heaven, we cannot sin.
- We will have work to do. The idea of working in Heaven is foreign to many people. Yet Scripture teaches it. When God created Adam, He took the man and put him in the Garden of Eden to work it and take care of it. Work was part of the original Eden. It was part of a perfect human life. God, Himself is a worker. He didn't create the world and then retire. Jesus said; "My Father is always at His work to this very day, and I, too, am working" (John 5:17). Jesus found great satisfaction in His work. Work will be satisfying and enriching, work that we can't wait to get back to, work that'll never be drudgery. We create, accomplish, set goals, and fulfill them—to God's glory.

- We will still experience emotions. In Scripture, God is said to enjoy, love, laugh, take delight, and rejoice, as well as be angry, happy, jealous, and glad. To be like God means to have and express emotions. Hence, we should expect that in Heaven emotions will exist for God's glory and our good. We know that people in Heaven have lots of feelings—all good ones. We're told of banquets, feasts, and singing. People will laugh there (Luke 6:21).
- We still won't know everything. God alone is omniscient. When we die, we'll see things far more clearly, and we'll know much more than we know now. But we'll never know everything. In Heaven, we'll be flawless, but not knowing everything isn't a flaw. Righteous angels don't know everything, and they long to know more. We should expect to long for greater knowledge, as angels do. And we'll spend eternity gaining the greater knowledge we'll seek.
- We will recognize one another. Scripture gives no indication of a memory wipe causing us not to recognize family and friends. Paul anticipated being with the Thessalonians in Heaven, and it never occurred to him he wouldn't know them.
- What will we do to avoid boredom? When there's fulfillment, when there's beauty, when we see God as He truly is—an endless reservoir of fascination—boredom becomes impossible. In Heaven we'll be filled—as (Psalm 16:11) describes it—"with joy and eternal pleasures."

If our loved ones are in hell, won't that spoil Heaven? In Heaven, we'll see clearly that God revealed Himself to each person and that He allowed each heart or conscience to seek and respond to Him. Everyone deserves hell; no one deserves Heaven. Jesus went to the cross to offer salvation to all. "The Lord is not slow about His promise, as some count slowness, but is patient toward you, not willing for any to perish, but for all to come to repentance." (2 Peter 3:9). In Heaven, we'll embrace God's holiness and justice. God will be our source of joy. Hell's small and distant shadow will not interfere with God's greatness or our joy in Him. All of this should motivate us to share the gospel of Christ with family, friends, neighbors, and the whole world.

Heaven is the New Earth for Believers. The current Heaven and earth will pass away. In their place are a new Heaven and earth. And then the New Jerusalem, later described as the bride of Christ descends from Heaven to earth. Finally, the announcement from the throne of God is that He will now dwell among us. This is similar in many ways to the description of Eden, the initial home of humanity. It seems like our end is a return to our beginnings, to what we were created to be in the first place. It would appear that our abode in Heaven is temporary. And that our permanent home is on a newly restored earth.

Heaven By Its Very Nature Is Perfect. God, is responsible for creating everything in the universe. This means that God created matter from non-matter and life from non-life. God has incredible, infinite, and unspeakable power. With muscle like that, God surely has the power to eliminate imperfection. This is why, as Christians, we believe that God is perfect; He can eliminate imperfection. The Christian God is not a good God after all. He is a perfect God. His standard is not good, it is perfection. We will live in a perfect place for all eternity.

SECTION 6
America and the Church

According to an ancient Chinese proverb, "A journey of a thousand miles begins with a single step." Very often, we focus not on those initial small steps but giant leaps, often undertaken by the government. But sometimes it's the small steps we take that change the country in profound ways. In 2008, 56% of Americans believed that gay marriages should not be recognized as valid. That same year, 52% of California voters voted to ban gay marriage, even as 61% backed Barack Obama for president.

Four years later, Vice President Joe Biden endorsed gay marriage during a memorable appearance on Meet the Press. A few days later, Obama declared his position had evolved. Today, 67% say gay marriages should be recognized — an all-time high. Millions of first steps led to profound change.

Today another series of small steps are altering how we live and act. For the first time, the Gallup Organization, Jeffrey M. Jones, *U.S. Church Membership Falls Below Majority for First Time*, reports that membership in a Christian church, synagogue, or mosque has fallen from 61% in 2010 to 47%. Meanwhile, those who profess no religious preference grew from 8% to 21% over the last decade. And among those who do express a religious preference, the number of congregants has declined from 73% to 60%. The value of the Church in America has greatly diminished in recent years and this will cause a major impact on our society. Will the Church survive? Where will the Church be in ten years, twenty years, or one-hundred years? This question can only be answered by digging deeper and looking into the history of America and the Church and looking closely at the Word of God.

CHAPTER 46

Is America Abandoning the Church?

Church attendance has been going down in America for many years now. Is this because people are falling away from God, are is it because in our modern world we just have so many things to choose from. It is clear that God is not at the top of most people's priority list.

Studies show that 66% of those aged sixty-five or older belong to a church. But only 36% of millennials attend church. Religion is fading more quickly in the United States than in any other nation. From 1981 to 2007, the United States ranked as one of the world's more religious countries, with religiosity levels changing very little. Since then, the United States has shown the largest move away from the religion of any country.

A profound cultural transformation is in progress – mostly happening quietly out of sight, little noticed in daily life. Old supernatural beliefs are vanishing among intelligent, educated, science-minded western people, especially the young. Religion is shriveling into the realm of myth and fantasy. Josh McDowell, A CRU Ministry, *Note from Josh: Are Youth Leaving the Church?*[1] discussing these issues of the state of the Church in America. Here are some of his frightening trends:

- Almost two-thirds of teens who grow up in a church drop out of religion in their twenties.

- The number of Americans who say they have no religion began to explode in the 1990s – from 10% then to 25%, and now in the 40% range.
- American church membership fell 20% in the past two decades.
- Southern Baptists dropped two million members since 2005.
- United Methodists fell from eleven million in 1969 to below 7 million today.
- Evangelical Lutherans dropped from 5.3 million in 1987 to 3.4 million.
- The Presbyterian Church USA had 3.2 million in 1982 but now is around 1.3 million.
- The Episcopal Church went from 3.4 million in the 1960s to 1.7 million.

All this has happened at the same time that America's population has almost doubled. As we talked about earlier, the more liberal Churches are declining in number far greater than their conservative counterparts, and these Protestant mainline denominations are at the top of the liberal list.

In truth, the decline of American religious practice can be traced not to the narrow-mindedness of America's religious institutions, but their desperate attempts to reach out to young people by forsaking key values. Values alienate. Behavioral requirements alienate. Talk about sin alienating. Talk about Heaven and hell alienates. And so religious institutions decided not to focus on such uncomfortable but eternal truths to fill pews. Major religious institutions across the United States decided that it would be more effective to draw constituents with honey rather than vinegar – forgetting, of course, that religion isn't either. Religion is fine wine: it may taste bitter when it first hits the tongue, but it is rich, sweet, and beautiful when you know what you're drinking. Religion without standards is kumbaya happy talk, requiring neither God nor Church.

Churches, to avoid losing government-guaranteed tax-exempt status, stopped speaking out about secular assaults on religious freedom. They stopped speaking against candidates who embraced the murder of the unborn or the corruption of the marital institution via the governmental embrace of alternative family structures. Instead, they suggested that church was for barbecues, get-togethers, date nights, and the occasional Psalm-reading session.

Americans quickly realized that the Churches had shifted focus from providing eternal truths to providing transient community-building exercises. And they realized that it's a lot more fun to go to the beach on a Sunday morning than to sit on uncomfortable wooden benches. They realized the entire family would prefer attending a baseball game to sitting through a Church service. When religious leaders decided to require less, rather than more, of their constituents, Americans decided religion was worthless. Religion is about upholding God's standards. Abandoning those standards means abandoning God. Religion cannot survive as an embodiment of the word without the values of the Living God.

This is why Islam is growing in the United States, as well as around the world. Islam requires more. It may require behavior many people believe to be wrong, but it requires behavior nonetheless. People are attracted to behavioral requirements, as secularists well know; that's why secularists require religious Americans to serve same-sex weddings, require acceptance of changing biological gender, and celebrate abortion like a sacrament. Even atheists and agnostics have a god that requires something of them.

School kids today are prevented from saying any kind of prayer at the beginning of the school day— and face drugs, threats of violence, perverted godless teaching, and sexual enablement throughout their school experience.

There are political and social campaigns to remove God's name from all public structures and observances. Some are still determined to remove Under God from our Pledge of Allegiance. Some in Congress want to make public preaching of God's Word hate speech if it confronts politically correct programs and policies. In addressing a huge women's conference, promoting abortion, Hillary Clinton said, deep-seated cultural codes, religious beliefs, and structural biases have to be changed.

There are countless examples, more every day, of attempts to remove virtually all consideration of God's will from our public life. Even the people of Israel demanded a king to lead them, such as all the other nations have and the prophet Samuel went to the Lord for guidance. Do everything they say to you the Lord replied, for they are rejecting me, not you. Look at what happened. God Almighty simply stepped back and let His people enact their plan, not His, and with a few notable exceptions, watched that plan led to the destruction of Jerusalem and the temple ... and the dispersion, captivity, and enslavement in Babylon of His people. For seventy years.

As we allow God to be shoved aside, as if to say we don't need you now, Lord. We appreciate your giving us this land, but we'll take it from here — He lifts His hand of protection and lets us make our own choices independently. He knows we're headed toward spiritual ruin, escalating internal violence, loss of world leadership, moral corruption, and eventual collapse of our government---unless we collectively call Him back into our national life!

He is fully able, even now, to restore, revitalize and raise us. But will only do that if we follow the instructions from 2 Chronicles 7:14 "and My people who are called by My name humble themselves, and pray and seek My face, and turn from their wicked ways, then I will hear from Heaven, and I will forgive their sin and will heal their land."

CHAPTER 47

Is America a Christian Nation?

Most people would say that America is a Christian nation. Some say that most Americans are Christians. This may still be true but many would mean that America is based on Christian values. Is this true? Is there anything in the Constitution or Bill of Rights that gives special treatment or preference to Christianity?

The answer to all of these questions is no. The U.S. Constitution is a wholly secular document. It contains no mention of Christianity or Jesus Christ. The Constitution refers to religion only twice. The First Amendment, bars laws respecting an establishment of religion or prohibiting the free exercise thereof, and Article VI prohibits religious tests for public office. Both of these provisions are evidence that the country was not founded as officially Christian.

The United States is not a Christian nation. The nation does not submit to God's word. America's people define their actions with unchecked lust, greed, violence, and distortion of the truth, and treat other people as subjects, not peers. America wages unjust immoral wars and has been a nation of war from the very beginning. We are not a Christian nation because we not only allow, we promote the slaughter of thousands of babies a day in our abortion clinics. We are an evil nation. Unfortunately, our evil nation is the way it is because too many good Christians stood by and watched as all this took place and decided not to do anything about it. Some work for good, but not enough.

America has been heavily influenced by the Bible, but it has never been a truly biblical nation or a truly godly nation. Since the 17th century,

America has always been a mixed multitude, and genuine born-again Christians have been a small minority.

What America has been above all else is a land of freedom: an unprecedented haven of personal liberty to pursue one's dream. Many came to America for religious freedom, but more came purely for personal freedom and economic opportunity. For this reason, it has rightly been said that the United States is both the most religious nation on earth and the most secular, the most devout and the most commercial. America is a free nation, and freedom of religion is still guaranteed in the constitution's first amendment. This is exactly why America is not a Christian nation. With freedom of religion, all religions are welcomed, not just Christianity. In the Old Testament that would be called idol worship. It is also a violation of both the first and the second commandment, as stated in Exodus 20:2–6, "I am the Lord your God, who brought you out of the land of Egypt, out of the house of slavery. You shall have no other gods before Me. You shall not make for yourself an idol, or any likeness of what is in Heaven above or on the earth beneath, or in the water under the earth. You shall not worship them nor serve them; for I, the Lord your God, am a jealous God, inflicting the punishment of the fathers on the children, on the third and the fourth generations of those who hate Me, but showing favor to thousands, to those who love Me and keep My commandments." If America were truly a Christian nation, there would only be Christian religious activities allowed and no other. So please realize here that I am not promoting whether America should or shouldn't be a Christian nation, I am just pointing out the obvious, that America is a nation that allows freedom of religion, which obviously violates the principle of having no other gods before me. Then the question we should be asking is, does America act as a godly nation? Unfortunately, the answer again is no. Today's society is very selfish and self-centered. We do not follow God's will; we follow our own will. We may go to Church on Sunday, but the rest of the week we give God very little thought.

Our society has become a magnet for every kind of evil spirit. Law and order collapsed; every human was a law unto themselves. The entire society was abandoned to the devil, and no moral force remained to hinder its headlong rush into hell. There was no honor, decency, or self-respect left among them, no reverence for life whatsoever. Justice and kindness faded away, and the people were overcome with lust and decadence. They sneered at virtue, their consciences seared and calloused. They scoffed at the fear of God and mocked righteousness. They became inhospitable, possessing the heart and indifference of a beast. They did not pity the poor. All spiritual desire was extinguished, and gross materialism and fleshly lusts became their gods. The people became shockproof so that the vilest, bloodiest crimes were accepted as normal behavior.

Homosexuals have come out of their closets and become activists, casting a demonic spell over a whole generation of people. They grew politically powerful, controlling everything. We have become a society so vile, wicked, and crazed with lust and violence that its sins thundered throughout the heavens, filling God's holy environment. Public schools are turning into disgraceful sex-abuse centers? Millions of children were victimized nationwide. One in five girls is abused before age sixteen, and one in seven boys has been abused by school personnel. Innocent children have been raped, forced into incest by their parents, and seduced by teachers, preachers, and priests.

Has America reached the flashpoint of God's judgment? Are we already like all past societies that permitted the rise of a dominant, defiant homosexual spirit? You can't tell me God is smiling on America! You can't say our holy, just Lord will sit by as millions more of our children are plundered, raped, and destroyed.

Will America soon be judged? Is our pandering to homosexuals, and calling it tolerance sitting well with God? People today do not see homosexual activity as a sin; rather, all sex is morally neutral. People advocate adolescent sex by teaching: Advocating just say no is not the answer. What we hope to teach young people is to make good choices — that when it's right to say no they will say no, and when it's right to say yes, they will say yes. I ask you: When in the world is it right for a child to say yes to sex?

In a newspaper article, the Rev. Rose Mary Denmore, a lesbian, says "she is angry that homosexual and lesbian ministers are kept from working with children." She says, "Keeping adult homosexuals separate from youngsters who may be homosexuals deprives them of adult confidantes they may need." World Challenge, David Wilkerson, *IS GOD OVERLOOKING THE SINS OF AMERICA?*[1]

This is a Christian, not following God's word, speaking here wanting access to our children to teach them what exactly? It's one thing for homosexuals to come out of the closet and demand equal and special rights to influence the media, to lobby for privileges as married couples and adoptive parents, to gain enough power to insist that the Empire State Building be bathed in lavender lights in celebration of Gay Pride Week, and to have New York's mayor lead their parade, dance with them half the night, call them a discriminated minority and equate them with civil rights leaders and Martin Luther King!

Are we trying to bring God's wrath down on us? America can read of its destiny by looking at the past historical accounts of God's dealings with other nations who continued in their sin.

Paul, in Romans 1:21–32, says; "For even though they knew God, they did not honor Him as God or give thanks, but they became futile in their reasonings, and their senseless hearts were darkened. Claiming to be wise, they became fools, and they exchanged the glory of the incorruptible God for an image in the form of corruptible humankind, of birds, four-footed animals, and crawling creatures. Therefore, God gave them up to vile impurity in the lusts of their hearts, so that their bodies would be dishonored among them. For they exchanged the truth of God for falsehood and worshiped and served the creature rather than the Creator, who is blessed forever. Amen. For this reason, God gave them over to degrading passions; for their women exchanged natural relations for that which is contrary to nature, and likewise the men, too, abandoned natural relations with women and burned in their desire toward one another, males with males committing shameful acts and receiving in their persons the due penalty of their error. And just as they did not see fit to acknowledge God, God gave them up to a depraved mind, to do those things that are not proper, *people* having been filled with all unrighteousness, wickedness, greed, *and* evil; full of envy, murder, strife, deceit, *and* malice; *they are* gossips, slanderers, haters of God, insolent, arrogant, boastful, inventors of evil, disobedient to parents, without understanding, untrustworthy, unfeeling, *and* unmerciful; and although they know the ordinance of God, that those who practice such things are worthy of death, they not only do the same but also approve of those who practice them."

This passage tells how homosexual lust tramples the truth, debauches society, and brings down God's wrath. The church has the same message for homosexuals it preaches to addicts, alcoholics, and all who are enslaved by sin: You must be set free — and only Christ can do it!

It's time to cry out to Almighty God. The church of Jesus Christ needs to pray and take authority against this evil!

America is not a Christian nation, but rather a sinful nation. We have chosen not to follow God, but to follow our desires. America and its people are guilty of many sins, the sins of carnality, impurity, greed, materialism, vanity, self-obsession, and far too many others to count, and the altars are covered with the blood of its innocent.

We have all been there, every single one of us is guilty. Look at Titus 3:3–7; "For we too were once foolish, disobedient, deceived, enslaved to various lusts and pleasures, spending our life in malice and envy, hateful, hating one another. But when the kindness of God our Savior and *His* love for humanity appeared, He saved us, not on the basis of deeds which we did in righteousness, but in accordance with His mercy, by the washing of regeneration and renewing by the Holy Spirit, whom He richly poured out upon us through Jesus Christ our Savior, so that being justified by His grace we would be made heirs according to *the* hope of eternal life."

We must realize that the true enemy is not flesh and blood. Paul clearly states in Ephesians 6:12; "For our struggle is not against flesh and blood, but against the rulers, against the powers, against the world forces of this darkness, against the spiritual *forces* of wickedness in the heavenly *places*."

The point is not about judging people, but just attempting to show truth. We have all sinned and all fall short of God's glory. All Christians need to look at the world through the eyes of Jesus Christ. We all need to focus on Godly values and God's truth.

Even though I would like to say that America is a Christian nation, the sad truth is, that it is not.

CHAPTER 48

Was America Founded as a Christian Nation?

I grew up with the idea that America was founded on Christian moral standards and therefore America was a strong Christian nation. America had done many things for not only its citizens but for many nations and individuals around the world. Our laws and policies were shaped by Christian moral and ethical values.

John Adams declared, "Our Constitution was made only for a moral and religious people. It is wholly inadequate to the government of any other." The Founders warned that when people increasingly ignore the Bible and its principles, our structure will crumble, be corrupted and perverted, and fall apart. Brainy Quote, John Adams, *Quotes*.[1]

We must ask, did the founders of our government create a government that gave special recognition to Christianity? As discussed in the previous section, America is no longer focused on God and His moral values. We are far away from God. The question is, did we get here by abandoning our formerly godly past and turning our back, as a nation, on God, or were we never a Christian nation to begin with? Perhaps we can find the answer by looking at our past. Sadly we see from our beginning that America was not founded on the Christian faith and we were not founded as a Christian nation? Here's why:

- <u>The American Revolution Was Sinful</u>: Although God oftentimes uses the sinful actions of people to accomplish His purposes, all political rebellions and revolutions are inherently sinful. Paul made this abundantly clear in (Romans 13:1–7) which says, "Every person is to be subject to the governing authorities. For there is no authority except God, and those which exist are established by God. Therefore, whoever resists authority has opposed the ordinance of God, and they who have opposed will receive condemnation upon themselves. Rulers are not a cause of fear for good behavior, but evil. Do you want to have no fear of authority? Do what is good and you will have praise from the same; for it is a servant of God to you for good. But if you do what is evil, be afraid; for it does not bear the sword for anything; for it is a servant of God, an avenger who brings wrath on the one who practices evil. Therefore, it is necessary to be in subjection, not only because of wrath but also for the sake of conscience. Because of this you also pay taxes, for *rulers* are servants of God, devoting themselves to this very thing. Pay to all what is due them: tax to whom tax *is due*; custom to whom custom; respect to whom respect; honor to whom honor." The text is absolutely clear, taking up arms against the government is a sin. The British colonial government may have been oppressive with its taxes, but they certainly were not asking anyone to do anything sinful. The Roman empire forced Christians to do evil acts or be put to death, far worse than what the British required, yet Paul is clear to not resist authority. Therefore, the actions of the American Revolution were clearly sinful, and the American Revolution was clearly not in line with the Word of God.

- <u>The Nation Tolerated the Sin of Slavery</u>: According to the 1860 census, there were 3.9 million slaves in the United States. There were many working at this time to end slavery, including the Church. But for the most part, slavery was viewed with cool indifference in the North as well as the South. Even the typical northern attitude toward black people was their belief that black people were inferior to whites. The sin of racism was commonplace and socially acceptable. And don't forget, then as now, The Supreme Court of the United States often ratified sinful attitudes. In the Dred Scott decision, the SCOTUS ruled that slaves were subhuman property, ineligible for citizenship, and had no rights of redress when they were subjected to criminal abuse.

- <u>The Constitution Codified Sin</u>: On May 25, 1787, a constitutional convention was convened in Philadelphia. And immediately one point of contention came to the fore; how to count slaves for taxation and representation. Slavery was commonplace in America, both in the north and in the south. This alone is itself enough to bunk the notion that early America was a Christian nation. For taxation and representation, slaves would be counted as $3/5^{th}$ of a person. Article one, section two paragraph three of the constitution reads: Representatives and direct taxes shall be apportioned among the several States which may be included within this Union, according to their respective numbers, which shall be determined by adding to the whole Number of free Persons, including those bound to Service for a Term of Years, and excluding Indians not taxed, three-fifths of all other Persons. It is positively un-Christian and sinful to say one human who is an image-bearer of God should have a lower value than another because of social status. As Paul wrote to the Galatians: There is neither Jew nor Greek, there is neither slave nor free, there is no male and female, for you are all one in Christ Jesus. A person's worth is not based on ethnicity, sex, or social status.
- <u>The Legacy of Injustice Against Native Americans</u>: We are mindful of deep national wounds in our relations with the First Peoples who inhabited America for thousands of years before the arrival of European settlers. Many treaties denied Native Americans the God-given human dignity, rights, and traditions, for their people. Forcing them off their lands and relocating them to reservations was purely evil. Many thousands died from disease, exposure, and starvation, on the Trail of Tears, and the Long Walk. The U.S. government failed to honor hundreds of peace treaties with Native Americans. Government policies supported the destruction of their basic economic survival and cultural identity, by killing off the buffalo, controlling all commodities, and removing children from families into boarding schools. The US government's treatment of the native peoples clearly shows little regard for Godly values, as the Bible clearly states that all people are created in the image of God, and all people have value in God's eyes.

- **The Post-Civil War Era Was Marked by Profound Immorality**: Prostitution was woven into the fabric of post-civil war America. It has been estimated that as many as 65,000 women were forced into prostitution against their will, and many more entered into prostitution out of desperation or ambition. That is hardly a sign of a God-fearing nation.
- **Americans Embrace Spiritualism**: Not only was the post-civil war period one where prostitution was commonplace, but also saw an explosion of interest in the occult. Séances were extremely popular in the waning decades of the 19th century and early 20th century. Séances were so common that the most famous American entertainer of the early 20th century, the magician Harry Houdini, dedicated himself to exposing the trickery of the mediums that were spreading across the nation and leading countless people astray. Consider the words of (Deuteronomy 18:10–12): "There shall not be found among you *anyone* who makes his son or his daughter pass through the fire, one who uses divination, a soothsayer, one who interprets omens, or a sorcerer, or one who casts a spell, or a medium, or a spiritist, or one who consults the dead. For whoever does these things is detestable to the LORD." Godly societies don't embrace or even tolerate what scripture identifies as an abomination to the Lord.
- **The Roaring 20's**: The 1920s were a time of great economic prosperity following the horrors of World War I. Despite prohibition, this was an era of unprecedented drunkenness. This was the era of Al Capone and the celebrity gangster. And this was also an era of sexual permissiveness. Mae West one of the biggest stars of the era, who famously said when forced to choose between two evils, she'll always pick the one she hasn't tried before, set Broadway alight in 1926 with her one-woman show "Sex". This show was a runaway commercial success and largely consisted of her saying sexually provocative things while wearing just enough clothing not to face criminal charges for public indecency. One of the biggest box office attractions of the 1920s, William Billy Haines was openly homosexual. Joan Crawford is quoted in Eve Golden's "41 Essays on Silent Film" as describing Haines and his lover as "the happiest married couple

in Hollywood." The 1920s were certainly not a golden age of godliness in America.
- <u>The Jim Crow South</u>: Up until the early 1960s racial segregation was the law of the land in much of the United States, and those laws were brutally enforced. And what's more, up until the mid-50s, no one in non-legally segregated states much cared. Racism was largely endemic and socially acceptable.
- <u>The 1960's</u>: In the early 1960's we see the removal of God from the public school system. No longer could God or the Bible be mentioned in our children's education. America's abandonment of God is for all sakes and purposes completed at this time. There is no way anyone could rightfully claim that America is a Christian nation after this. The 1960s also saw the beginnings of the sexual revolution, and by the end of the decade, free love had become a popular value. By the end of the decade, the counterculture of the sixties had turned dark. The anti-war movement had morphed into the violent terrorism of the weather underground.
- <u>Roe v Wade</u>: The '70s saw child murder legalized across all fifty states. And while that case is viewed now as a watershed, legal abortion was already widely available in the United States. Many states including the very populous states of New York, California, and Massachusetts essentially allowed for abortion on demand. Now babies are defined as sub-human just like the slaves were after the American revolution. Thankfully this horrible ruling has now been overturned. It will be up to each state to decide if abortion will be acceptable in their states. Even if it becomes legal in some states, it is still against the law of God and allows the murder of innocent children. The only way to permanently ban abortion is for law to be enacted that recognizes that life begins at conception and that life is defined as human. Science proves this with DNA. The DNA of a fetus is the same as DNA of a mature adult. Human DNA is human DNA no matter how old. As long as this is not established by the supreme court or federal law, there will always be room for some to justify and legalize abortion.

Add to all this that the '80s was the decade of greed, the 1990s are now regularly referred to as the noughties in popular culture, the aughts saw the rise of the hookup culture and the 2010's decade has seen unprecedented attacks on the family and the normalization of all manner of sin.

Are American values Christian values? No. Even though I believe the founding fathers had good intentions, and many if not all were Christians, they failed to establish any regard for Christian worship and values within the governing framework. Furthermore, failing to address many issues of the day is clear proof that America was never established as a nation dedicated to God or the pursuit of God.

Today many people have a glorified view of America, comparing America to ancient Israel. In ancient Israel, you have a nation established by God, with Biblical rules and values written right in their government. Israel was established as a Theistic nation, while the United States was established as a secular nation, allowing the freedom of any religion. A truly Christian nation would only follow the Christian faith, not all faiths. Nowhere in the Declaration of Independence or the U.S. Constitution does it state the purpose and call of the United States of America as being established to recognize and worship the Christian God. In the documents created by the founding fathers, there is no mention of following Jesus as a goal of the government for its people.

America was created as a secular nation throughout its entire existence. Freedom was the focus, not Christianity. Our nation is strictly governed by a phrase called "Separation of Church and state." Christian influence in our government is sadly strictly forbidden. With the abolishment of God from our public schools and the support by many for the evils of abortion, America lost its right to be considered a Christian nation. AlterNet, Bob Boston, *5 Reasons America Is Not - And Never Has Been - A Christian Nation.* [2]

We can appreciate and even respect the nation in which we reside, but we must not forget that our status is as foreigners and exiles in this world. Christians await the true King and His government. America was not founded as a Christian nation and has never been a Christian nation. The idea of America as a Christian nation isn't even a myth, it is a mirage.

CHAPTER 49

Does it Matter if America is a Christian Nation?

Even though some of us would prefer America to be grounded in Biblical and Godly values, and turn to God, does it matter for individual Christians? Again, as Christians, we look forward to Jesus' reign here on earth. We can still be ardent believers in Jesus, no matter what our government does, as long as we help to uphold the first amendment right of free speech, we are allowed to worship as we choose. We can still be a positive influence on our society and show that truth and love do matter, and we can still lead others to Christ. In the past, Christian growth has always flourished under extreme ungodly governments. The first Church was able to grow and reach the world under the harsh Roman government in the first century. Many Christians were killed and martyred, but they still stood for Jesus and were successful in leading much of the world to Christ. We must remember that Jesus lived during this time yet the gospel soon spread to the entire world. Israel fell under the weight of its corruption, and Rome fell under the weight of its debauchery. The Church rose from the ashes because of the intense discipleship and focused engagement of Christians.

We still can work to influence the direction of our government, and I believe many more Christians should get involved in politics and run for government positions. We still have the power to turn our society around, we just all need to pay attention to everything going on around us and get more involved.

We must still fight to eliminate abortion, we can change the hearts of our fellow citizens, even those who are not Christians. Christians should strive to follow God, and as God clearly states, we should follow the authority of the government, no matter how evil that government becomes. Christians can become more active in spreading our love to others in our society, this will help influence others to Christ. We must speak to unbelievers to offer hope and salvation.

We just need to vote with Godly values, and this could change our directions as a society. There is always hope. We can certainly be more involved in society and pray for revival and God's influence in this world and this country. We must remain focused on Christ, study the word, be involved in fellowship with like-minded believers, and stay true to our faith. The answer is to hold on tightly to the gospel, spread the gospel, and rely on God to meet our needs at all times, especially in difficult times. We must hold on to our Christian principles because they are worthy of our time, and, more importantly, are worthy of our action. Here then are the Christian principles we must adhere to:

- Our relationship with the creator is fundamentally personal. This means that what we do matters. The actions of each person matter. The actions of our neighbors do not matter more than our own, and certainly not to the creator.
- We carry free will. We are not slaves to fate, nor are we simply pre-programmed machines. We are free and individual moral agents. Our choices matter.
- We can improve. The Bible is the source of Christian development, it continually features people who had changes of heart, providing examples of positive change. That has taught millions to change in a more positive direction.
- Power and rulership are important to the creator and so is human progress. The Christian God cares not for the high, but the humble. He speaks not to the powerful but the powerless. This is seen in the Bible from one end to the other.
- Justice stands above the ruler. Over and over, the Christian God thunders against kings and leaders. He demands justice, especially for the downtrodden.
- The creator ... the ultimate ... is qualitatively good. The Creator is good, and this concept gave powerless people a way to prove

their rightness with God. The influence of their good God was visible in their goodness; it meant that they bore his image.
- We are obliged to our offspring, not them to us. Not only does God rage against children being made to pass through the fire to Molech, (this is certainly a representation of abortion today), but He frames his warnings in terms of what will happen to your children. Clearly, the needs of the child are shown as superior to the desires of the parents.
- A strong preference for production rather than plunder. From Abraham through the New Testament, Jewish and Christian writings assume they are addressing productive people. Jews and Christians never had anything like, as the Romans did, an Altar of Victory. Conquering resided in Judaism only in the sense of throwing off oppressors, not to become oppressors. And this is certainly a theme that continues in Christianity.
- Humanity is in a long-term, familial relationship with the creator. Regardless of the Bible's warnings, and even because of them, the fundamental connection between God and human is a familial relationship. This is sometimes shown in surprisingly intimate and touching tones.
- Love for the other, especially your enemies. The portrayal of the outsider, the other, as an entity to be despised has spawned hate and hundreds of millions of murders. The Christian principles, however, directly oppose it. Here's a very clear passage: The Lord our God executes justice for the fatherless and the widow, and loves the sojourner, giving them food and clothing. Love the sojourner therefore; for you were sojourners in the land of Egypt. You have heard that it was said, you shall love your neighbor and hate your enemy. "But I say to you, love your enemies and pray for those who persecute you, so that you may be sons of your Father who is in Heaven; for He makes his sun rise on the evil and the good, and sends rain on the just and the unjust" (Matthew 5:43–48).

These principles lie at the core of the Christian faith. They have been a tremendously important addition to the world. Their loss would be catastrophic. The Dispatch, David French, *"A Nation of Christians Is Not Necessarily a Christian Nation.*[1]

What are we as Christians to do? We should be in the world but not of it; love others as ourselves; see the lost not as our enemies but as the mission field. And most of all we must be steadfast, living quiet godly lives while longing for the return of Christ.

Is there hope for America? Yes! 2 Chronicles 7:14 says; "Then if my people who are called by my name will humble themselves and pray and seek my face and turn from their wicked ways, I will hear from Heaven and will forgive their sins and restore their land." If we repent from our apathy, complacency, compromises with darkness, serving of other gods, our sins committed in secret, withholding of life, and our failure to fulfill our call to be the light of the world, then God will hear us from Heaven and forgive our sins and heal our land. God's part is certain, it's up to us. It all rests on: *If My People!*

CHAPTER 50

What is a Real Christian?

Perhaps the best definition of what a real Christian is can be found in Romans 12:1–21 which states; "Present your bodies as a living and holy sacrifice, acceptable to God, which is your spiritual service of worship. And do not be conformed to this world, but be transformed by the renewing of your mind, so that you may prove what the will of God is, that which is good and acceptable and perfect. For through the grace given to me, I say to everyone among you not to think more highly of yourself than you ought to think; but to think to have sound judgment, as God has allotted to each a measure of faith. For just as we have many parts in one body and all the body's parts do not have the same function, so we, who are many, are one body in Christ, and individually parts of one another. However, since we have gifts that differ according to the grace given to us, *each of us is to use them properly*: if prophecy, in proportion to *one's* faith; if service, in the *act of* serving; or the one who teaches, in the *act of* teaching; or the one who exhorts, in the *work of* exhortation; the one who gives, with generosity; the one who is in leadership, with diligence; the one who shows mercy, with cheerfulness.

Love *must be* free of hypocrisy. Detest what is evil; cling to what is good. *Be* devoted to one another in brotherly love; give preference to one another in honor, not lagging in diligence, fervent in spirit, serving the Lord; rejoicing in hope, persevering in tribulation, devoted to prayer, contributing to the needs of the saints, practicing hospitality.

Bless those who persecute you; bless and do not curse. Rejoice with those who rejoice, and weep with those who weep. Be of the same mind toward one another; do not be haughty in mind, but associate with the lowly. Do not be wise in your estimation. Never repay evil for evil to anyone. Respect what is right in the sight of all people. If possible, so far as it depends on you, be at peace with all people. Never take your revenge, beloved, but leave room for the wrath *of God*, for it is written: Vengeance is Mine, I will repay, says the Lord. But if your enemy is hungry, feed them; if they are thirsty, give them a drink; for in so doing you will heap burning coals on their head. Do not be overcome by evil, but overcome evil with good."

A true Christian is a person who has been born again. Only those who have been regenerated by the Spirit of God are actual Christians. As mentioned previously, many people refer to themselves as Christian even though they are far from God. You must ask yourself, am I a friend of God, do I obey His Word and what the Bible teaches, or am I just a casual Christian that ignores God and the teachings of the Bible? Do you support abortion and same-sex marriage? If you do, you are not supporting God's teaching. To be a true Christian, you must believe in God's teaching over everyone else's teaching. This is what makes you a true Christian. This is certainly between you and the Lord, but if your beliefs are not pointing in God's direction, then can you honestly consider yourself to be a Christian? Are you more interested in worldly social justice, or God's values and teachings recorded in the Bible? Compelling Truth, *What does it mean to be a true Christian?*[1] The following four marks will be present in all those who have been born again. Not all four marks will be present to the same degree, but they will all be present in some measure in all true Christians.

- Everyone who believes that Jesus is the Christ (Messiah) has been born of God and is, therefore, a true Christian (1 John 5:1).
- Everyone who practices righteousness has been born of God (1 John 2:29).
- Everyone who has been born of God will love God and love the brothers (1 John 3:14).
- Everyone who has been born of God does not keep on sinning, but they who were born of God protects them, and the evil one does not touch them (1 John 5:18).

It is extremely important to obey God and His Word in order to be a true Christian. Romans 2:8 clearly states: "but to those who are self-serving and do not obey the truth, but obey unrighteousness, He will give wrath and indignation." Christians must obey God first, before the government, not culture, not their friends or family, and not societies beliefs. If you are obeying outside influences, rather than God, can you really call yourself a real Christian?

The world can be a competitive place and sometimes this can be good, and sometimes this can be bad. But one thing I have heard said about Christians is that "we are not to compete with one another, we are to complete one another."

CHAPTER 51

Turning to God

Most people change their belief system as they go through life. Doesn't matter if they start out believing in God or not believing in God. People just change their opinion over time because of the people and events that influence them. However, the percentage of people who do believe in God is rapidly declining. Millennials are less likely to believe in God than previous generations. Interesting enough, children of atheists are less likely to remain atheists than Christians.

For about half of these converts, strong friendships with Christians led to them investigating Christianity. There are many examples of atheists who researched the Christian faith objectively and became convinced that Christianity was true and came to believe in Jesus Christ.

University professors, attorneys, engineers, and other professionals, came to believe in Jesus because they were converted by evidence, ethical values or their worldview didn't measure up, or from challenges from their peers, and even from family disasters. People discovered God because they decided if there was even the slightest chance that God was real, it was important enough to check it out for themselves instead of just blindly believing what they have been taught all their lives. Looking at the two sources, Believers Portal, Bp-Pub-1, *List and Profile Of Famous Atheists Who Converted To Christianity,*[1] *a*nd Blog, Jay Wile,[2] *Category: Atheists Who Became Christians,* we see a list of former atheists who searched and through their efforts came to know the true God of the universe.

- <u>C. S. Lewis</u> – He fell away from his faith during adolescence and became an atheist at age fifteen. He eventually returned to Christianity, having been influenced by arguments with his Oxford colleague and friend J. R. R. Tolkien, whom he met in 1926. Lewis vigorously resisted conversion, but eventually gave in and was convinced of the truth in 1929 at the age of 32. Lewis admitted that God was God, and reluctantly became a convert. Lewis became an ordinary layperson of the Church of England, and his faith profoundly affected his work, and his wartime radio broadcasts on the subject of Christianity brought him wide acclaim.
- <u>Philip Vander Elst</u> - At the age of twenty-four, he met his future wife, who turned out to be a Christian. He determined to find out whether there was any good evidence for the existence of God and the truthfulness of Christianity. He read C.S. Lewis, whose Chronicles of Narnia he had enjoyed as a child. He was interested because C. S. Lewis had himself been an atheist, and also graduated from Oxford. He had two questions, is there a God? And, if there is, what is the connection between God and freedom? Growing up in a non-Christian family with intellectually gifted but unbelieving parents, he used to rely on science and didn't take religion seriously. As he read Lewis's three most important books, Mere Christianity, Miracles, and The Problem of Pain, he found himself not only following in the footsteps of a person who had wrestled with the same issues, he was discovering intelligence and convincing answers to all his doubts. Bethinking, Philip Vander Elst, *From Atheism to Christianity: A Personal Journey.* [3]
- <u>Frank Morison</u> - Doubted the life of Christ as reported in the New Testament and was particularly skeptical with regard to Jesus' reported resurrection. Over a ten-year period, Morison investigated the origins of the gospel accounts of Jesus' crucifixion and resurrection to sift some of the evidence at first hand, and eventually became convinced of the truth of Jesus' resurrection.
- <u>Gunther Scheizle</u> – Known for having a brilliant mind. As a nuclear physicist and professor of Physics, he kind of had to be. And for most of his life, he was a die-hard atheist. Things

like quantitative data, research studies, cold hard facts — these were the things that made sense. All of this faith in the unseen business that Christians believed in seemed like a joke to the man of science. That is, until God showed him the truth! God Updates, Mel Johnson, *Hardcore Atheist Converts After Jesus Visits Him In A Vision,* Gunther Scheizle. [4]

- Alister McGrath - An intellectual and specialist in Quantum theory and biology, McGrath had a rationalist worldview that rejects a blind trust in Divine existence. He viewed God as an infantile illusion, suitable for the elderly and intellectually feeble. His deep engagement in science is what led him to find faith and God as someone he could rely upon. Today he is articulate about his beliefs and a strong defender of Christianity. With respect to science, McGrath believes that religion and science complement each other. For McGrath, science and religion are not mutually exclusive. Religion is the motivation for humans that leads to unbelievable discoveries and miracles. Science can only provide you with partial accounts for the creation of the universe and the knowledge of humanity. He states, "If you believe that God made the world, you can get additional insights into God by studying nature." Science can't answer the big questions such as "Why are we here?" or "What's life all about?" Culture Watch, Alister McGrath, THE SPIRITUAL JOURNEY OF ALISTER MCGRATH. [5]
- Dr. Wayne Rossiter – Former atheist biologist who once described himself as a staunch and cantankerous atheist who sought every opportunity to destroy Christianity where it stood.
- Philosopher Edward Feser – The Associate Professor of Philosophy at Pasadena City College, previously a Visiting Assistant Professor at Loyola Marymount University, and a Visiting Scholar at the Social Philosophy and Policy Center. Feser speaks on how Studying Philosophy led him to God.
- Professor Sarah Irving-Stonebraker – Professor Sarah Irving-Stonebraker is a Senior Lecturer in Modern European History at Western Sydney University in Australia. In her article, *How Oxford and Peter Singer drove me from atheism to Jesus,* [6] Sarah shares the incredible story that led her to Jesus Christ. Dr. Peter Singer is a fervent atheist and a champion of the idea that some

human lives have little or no value. I am sure that if he learned he helped drive a fellow atheist to Jesus, he would be more than a little annoyed.

- Howard Storm – Atheist Professor whose Near-death Experience drew him to Jesus Christ.
- Rosaria Champagne Butterfield: Former Lesbian, Feminist, Atheist Professor of English, and Women's studies at Syracuse University. In what she describes as a train wreck, she shares the incredible story of her journey to Christ, laying aside her former beliefs.
- Michael McIntyre – Multi-Millionaire Atheist Who Hated God but Now, He Radically Accepts Jesus
- Jennifer Fulwiler, Leah Libresco and Holly Ordway – Three Powerful women whose intellectual journey led to their conversion from atheism to Christianity.
- Ronald Dabdoub – As an atheist, Ronald wanted to know the truth about God. For thirty days he asked God to prove his existence with more than words. Days later, he had a vision of Jesus Christ, and that was the start of a new life for him.
- Barak Lurie – Former Jewish atheist and profitable real estate/business lawyer who found Jesus as he searched for truth. Author of Atheism Kills.
- Caleb Kaltenbach: Former Atheist Raised by Gay Parents, but he embraced Jesus and today he's a preacher of Jesus Christ.
- Paul Ernest – Former Atheist Scholar, Paul Ernest has always been a deep thinker. Whether it was science or philosophy, he was the one constantly asking Why and How?
- Alexis Mason – A former Militant Atheist
- Steve Tillman – Former atheist leader who did everything to suppress the idea of God.
- Dezmond Boudreaux – "The whole time I was searching for peace and truth, but could never find it." "When I found Christ, that's when I truly found what I was looking for."
- Guillaume Bignon – A Staunch Atheist Who Hated God, Visited Church "As One Visits A Zoo To See Exotic Animals" but then God caught him.
- Jessica Jenkins – Was a devout atheist who believed in science and the theory of evolution.

- <u>Mark Edwards</u> – A rapper and former drug smuggler who was deaf in one ear.
- <u>Lee Strobel</u> – American Christian author and a former investigative journalist. Author of The Case for Christ.
- <u>Lauren Chen</u> – Canadian YouTube blogger and BlazeTV host who promotes right-wing talking points. Better known as Roaming Millennial.

And even more ...

Why these and many more came to believe in God and Jesus Christ?

The evidence for the historical truthfulness of the Gospel records in the New Testament, and closer scrutiny of the facts forced many to abandon their prejudices against Christianity. The internal evidence for the truthfulness of the Gospel accounts, far from being self-serving propaganda, the Gospels faithfully record the weaknesses and failings of Jesus' disciples, including their frequent inability to understand what He is talking about. Peter, to cite the most famous example, refuses to believe Jesus when He warns him of His impending arrest and execution and is firmly rebuked for it. At the Last Supper, Peter swears he will never abandon Jesus even if all the other disciples do, but then goes on to do precisely that, denying all connection with Him in the courtyard of the High Priest's house after Jesus' arrest in the Garden of Gethsemane. The other disciples are revealed in a similarly poor light. On one occasion they are shown quarreling about who amongst them will occupy the highest positions in Jesus' Messianic Kingdom. At other times they, like Peter, are shown to be either unwilling or unable to accept Jesus' teaching that He, the Messiah, must suffer and die as a ransom for many. Not surprisingly, they too abandon Jesus at the moment of supreme crisis in the Garden of Gethsemane.

Even more significantly, all the disciples are taken by surprise by the Resurrection, despite having been told in advance by Jesus, before His arrest, that He would come back from the dead. Indeed, this very fact, mirrored in their slowness to accept the testimony of their women and the evidence of their own eyes, offers powerful support both for the truthfulness and reliability of the Gospels as a whole and for the reality of the Resurrection. However, the two most compelling and convincing reasons for believing in the truth of the Christian message and the story on which it is based: the undeniable fact of the Empty Tomb, and the subsequent careers and martyrdoms of Jesus' closest followers. The fact of the Resurrection and the disciples' encounter with the Risen Jesus can adequately explain the change that took place in them and their path in life. Having been a frightened, broken-hearted, and demoralized group of people, they emerged from hiding and became a band of joyful and heroic missionaries, boldly and fearlessly proclaiming the Christian gospel, in the teeth of persecution and suffering.

None of Jesus' enemies and opponents of the newborn Christian Church could deny the disappearance of Jesus' body from the tomb in which He had been buried by Joseph of Arimathea. Despite having every religious and political incentive to do so, neither the Jewish religious authorities who condemned Him, nor the Romans who crucified Him, were able to produce Jesus' body. The disciples continued to preach the message of Jesus' death and resurrection, but if Jesus' body had been recovered, Christianity would have been snuffed out instantly. But they didn't because they couldn't.

What is more, all of them except John eventually suffered painful martyrdom for doing so. Three of them, including Peter, were crucified; two were stoned to death; another two were beheaded; Thomas was killed with arrows in India; Philip was hanged on a pillar in Phrygia; another disciple was beaten to death, and Bartholomew (Nathaniel) was skinned alive in Armenia. If the disciples had stolen Jesus' body (as their enemies alleged), it is unlikely they would have endured all this for something they knew to be a lie? Is it, in any case, psychologically credible to believe that these people, emotionally shattered by Jesus' arrest and crucifixion, would have had the will, motivation, strength, or courage to attempt to snatch away His dead body from under the noses of the soldiers guarding His tomb?

Paul had originally been the fiercest opponent and persecutor of the Early Church. Here was a man who had been passionately convinced that the Christian claims about Jesus were dangerous blasphemy and that those who believed them deserved imprisonment, beatings, and death. Then, suddenly, this same man changed a hundred and eighty degrees and became the greatest and most widely traveled evangelist of the fledgling Christian Church. What else, other than his encounter with the Risen Jesus on the road to Damascus, could explain Paul's dramatic conversion? This conclusion is further reinforced by the telling references in one of Paul's pastoral letters to the many different witnesses to whom Jesus appeared after His resurrection, most of whom, Paul declared, were still alive at the time he was writing. Would he have dared to say all this, implicitly challenging skeptics to interrogate these living witnesses, if Jesus had not risen from the dead? And would he, like the other apostles, have endured beatings, imprisonment, stoning by hostile crowds, and eventual beheading, for a message he knew to be false?

The evidence is just too overwhelming! Even more strikingly, when Jesus speaks of His divine status (He who has seen Me, has seen the Father), He doesn't convey any impression of madness or megalomania. Instead, His words seem to carry authority, and His enemies are never able to out-argue or outwit Him.

The final realization centers around the many external evidences for the authenticity and truthfulness of the Gospels. There are first of all significant corroborating references to Jesus' existence and execution in the writings of Roman historians like Tacitus and Suetonius, as well as in those of the first-century historian, Thallus. There is similarly corroborating evidence about some of the details of Jesus' life and death in other non-Christian sources like the Jewish Talmud. To quote one of these, the first-century Jewish historian, Josephus, writes in A.D. 93: "At this time [the time of Pilate] there was a wise man who was called Jesus. His conduct was good and (he) was known to be virtuous. And many people from among the Jews and the other nations became (his) disciples. Pilate condemned (him) to be crucified and to die. But those who had become (his) disciples did not abandon (his) discipleship. They reported that (he) had appeared to them three days after (his) crucifixion and that (he) was alive; accordingly, (he) was perhaps the Messiah, concerning whom the prophets have recounted wonders." *Antiquities of the Jews*, Josephus.[7]

The manuscript evidence for the authenticity and reliability of the Gospel texts is earlier and more plentiful than that for any other document of ancient times. In particular, the historical reliability of Luke's Gospel and its sequel, the Acts of the Apostles, which is full of explicit political, legal, medical, cultural, and topographical details, is confirmed by a lot of archaeological evidence as well as by plentiful documentary evidence from non-Christian sources.

In the book of Acts, eighty-four separate facts in the last sixteen chapters have been confirmed by archaeological and historical research. Confronted by all these facts and arguments, many former atheists, surrendered to God and asked Jesus into their lives.

If you are still unconvinced by all the evidence, please read *I Don't Have Enough Faith to Be an Atheist*, by Norman L. Geisler and Frank Turek, (Crossway, USA, 2004).[8] It is a very readable yet scholarly book that sets out, in massive and very interesting detail, the philosophical and scientific evidence for the existence of God, as well as the historical and archaeological evidence for the reliability and truthfulness of the New Testament.

CHAPTER 52

The Challenge

Many people view Christianity as a bloody religion that has caused many wars, and strife. We must remember that even though God is perfect, people are not. Christians are sinful and do not act according to the instructions, of God. More importantly, many who call themselves Christian are not. Don't blame God or Christianity for this, because it is imperfect people that make others think this. God did not teach us this, He taught us to love one another, even our enemies.

Wars have been started by so-called Christian nations or Christian people, but they are not acting in accord with Jesus' teachings?

After all, most murderers, tyrants, and rapists are not biblical Christians, and most have rejected the God of the Bible. Even if they claim to believe in the God of the Bible, they are not living like a true Christ-follower.

As an atheist, do you feel conflicted about the fact that atheism has no basis in morality? There is no absolute right and wrong; no good, no bad. If someone stabs you in the back, treats you like nothing, steals from you, or lies to you, it doesn't ultimately matter in an atheistic worldview, where everything and everyone was created by random chemical reactions doing what chemicals do. And further, knowing that you are essentially no different from a cockroach in an atheistic worldview because after all, people are just animals.

Are you tired of the fact that atheism, based on materialism, has no basis for logic and reasoning? Is it tough trying to get up every day thinking that truth, which is immaterial, really doesn't exist? Are you bothered by the fact that atheism cannot account for uniformity in nature because your worldview can't comprehend the supernatural? How could everything explode from nothing and, by pure chance, form beautiful laws like $E=MC2$ or $F=MA$?

Do you feel like you need a weekend to recoup, even though a weekend is meaningless in an atheistic worldview — since animals, like bees, don't take a day of rest or have a weekend? So why should atheists? Why borrow a workweek and weekend that comes from the pages of Scriptures, which are despised by atheists? Weeks and weekends come from God creating in six literal days and resting for a literal day, and then the Lord Jesus resurrected on the first day of the week (Sunday). And why look forward to time off for a holiday (i.e., holy day), when nothing is holy in an atheistic worldview?

For professing atheists, these questions can be overwhelming to make sense of within their worldview. And further, within an atheistic worldview, atheists must view themselves as God. Essentially, atheists are claiming to be God. Instead of saying there may not be a God, they say there is no God. To make such a statement, they must claim to be omniscient (which is an essential attribute of the God of the Bible) among other attributes of God as well. By saying there is no God, the atheist refutes their position by addressing the question as though they were God!

Do you feel conflicted about proselytizing the faith of atheism, since if atheism were true then who cares about proselytizing? Let's face it, life seems tough enough as an atheist without having to deal with other major concerns like not having a basis for wearing clothes, no basis for marriage, and no consistent reason to be clean (snails don't wake up in the morning and clean themselves or follow other cleanliness guidelines). There is no reason to believe in love. Your feelings are just random chemical reactions that have no meaning.

Are you weary of looking for evidence that contradicts the Bible's account of creation and finding none? Do the assumptions and inconsistencies of dating methods weigh on your conscience when they are misrepresented as fact? Where do you suppose those missing links have gone into hiding? Surely the atheist sees the folly and hopelessness of believing that everything came from nothing.

In fact, why would an atheist care to live one moment longer in a broken universe and all you have to look forward to is death, which can be around any corner? And in just a few years after your death, no one will care one iota about what you did or who you were, or how and when you died — because death is the ultimate hero in an atheistic, evolutionary worldview. What hope do you cling to with your atheists' beliefs? If you want hope, joy, peace, and value, you must search elsewhere. Answers in Genesis, Bodie Hodge, *Dear Atheist.* [1]

Conclusion

"Who do you say that I am?" Late in His life and ministry, Jesus wanted His disciples to define in His presence their beliefs about Him. So, He asked them the question: "Who do you say that I am?" (Matthew 16:15). The disciples were a bit stunned by the question, and only the apostle Peter attempted an answer. His answer needs to be your answer: "You are the Christ, the Son of the living God" (Matthew 16:16). Christian Answers.Net, *How do I witness to my peers when they seem to have knowledgeable answers against all of my beliefs?*[1]

As we reflect on who Jesus is, we find His uniqueness in His birth, conceived by the Holy Spirit, miraculously born of a virgin, His death upon the cross, and His resurrection from the grave.

Someday we will all face the last chapter of our life. Are we prepared for the end? About 6,000 years ago, a young couple by the name of Adam and Eve lived in a beautiful garden that their Creator had made especially for them. They were told by the Creator that they could enjoy this home fully with one exception: they were not to eat from the tree of the knowledge of good and evil, otherwise, they would die.

Sadly, they disobeyed God, and sin and death came into the world. As a result, everyone is born in sin, and we all are under a death sentence because we sin, too. But God is a God of grace and mercy and He did the unthinkable. He took that punishment upon himself due to His love for each one of us. Jesus Christ came to earth and paid the penalty for sin. He offers himself as a perfect and last sacrifice for us as our Savior.

The Bible is clear on the subject of salvation: Whoever believes in Jesus, has eternal life and salvation. As you consider the world's most important question, consider taking these action steps:

- Admit that you are a sinner (Romans 3:23).
- Repent of your sins before a Holy God and turn away from them (Mark 1:15).
- Receive Jesus Christ as Lord of your life (John 1:12).
- Realize that eternal life is a gift from God (Romans 6:23).
- Receive God's gift by faith—by taking God at His Word (Romans 10:8–11).
- Read and believe what the Bible says: "For by grace you have been saved through faith, and that not of yourselves; it is the gift of God, not of works, lest anyone should boast" (Ephesians 2:8–9).

Afterward, just talk to God. That is what prayer is all about. Speak to Him as you would to anyone else. If you want to become a Christian, simply say something like: Dear God, thank you for sending Your Son, the Lord Jesus Christ, to pay for my sins on the cross. Thank you that He died for me. I acknowledge that I am a sinner and that I cannot save myself. I repent of my sins and I receive Your gift of salvation by faith. Thank you for loving me enough to save me. In Jesus' name, amen. Then live your life daily with this attitude!

The Bible says "that if you confess with your mouth the Lord Jesus and believe in your heart that God has raised Him from the dead, you will be saved" (Romans 10:9). Then you will know that you are saved. The Bible says; "These things I have written to you who believe in the name of the Son of God, that you may know that you have eternal life" (1 John 5:13).

If you have trusted Jesus Christ as your personal Savior from sin, God has given you a new mandate. It is called the Great Commission: "Go therefore and make disciples of all the nations, baptizing them in the name of the Father and of the Son and the Holy Spirit, teaching them to observe all things that I have commanded you; and lo, I am with you always, even to the end of the age.' Amen" (Matthew 28:19–20). Our Lord wants us to reach all the ethnic groups in the world. He did not give us this assignment knowing it would be impossible for us to reach; rather, He gave us this assignment expecting us to fulfill it.

People need to hear about a loving Creator God who made them in His image and is the Creator of the universe. This God sent His Son, Jesus, to die on a cross in Jerusalem to pay the penalty of our sins. Evangelism answers modern humanities most searching questions and gives every reason for hope.

There are masses of unsaved people without hope. Some light incense, bow before statues, chant memorized prayers, beat themselves, and worship multitudes of gods. Jesus commands us to get the word out. Together we can dispel the hopelessness abroad with the hope of the glorious gospel of Jesus Christ.

Now Do You Believe?

Hopefully, some people reading this book are not believers in Christ. I say this not because I am happy that you are not a believer, I say this because you must be giving Christianity a serious look for getting this far in the book. Allow me to plead with you just a little longer. Lay down that rebellion. Lay it down. And simply embrace the gospel that Jesus Christ, the Son of God, the Righteous One, died for your sins. He loves you! He was raised on the third day, triumphant over all his enemies. He reigns until He puts all his enemies under his feet. Jesus forgives all sins and puts redeemed sinners in right standing with God.

Please reconsider what you believe about God. Only God can give you meaning, purpose, and value for your existence. Atheism cannot? Atheism is a lie. As a Christian, I understand that truth exists because God exists, and God is truth. We are made in His image. We are more than flesh and bone animals, we have a soul, a spirit, and a conscience, and deep down we all know this!

There is a God, and you are also made in His image (Genesis 1:26; 9:6). This means you have value. Whereas consistent atheists teach that you have no value, I see you differently. I see you as a relative (Acts 17:26) and one who — unlike animals, plants, and fallen angels — has the possibility of salvation from death, which is the result of sin (i.e., disobedience to God; Romans 6:23). We have all fallen short of God's holy standard of perfect obedience thanks to our mutual grandfather, Adam (Romans 5:12). And God sees you differently, too (John 3:16). While you were still a sinner, God stepped into history to become a man to die in your place (Romans 5:8) and offer the free gift of salvation (Ephesians 2:8–9).

Atheists have nothing to live for. When you die everything ends. All your hard work, accomplishments, and sacrifice are meaningless after you are gone from this world. However, Christians like me do have a reason to live, and that reason is to share the saving grace of Jesus Christ. We know that this life can be hard and painful, but we also know that it is temporary. We have a promise from God that we will live on after our physical death here on earth. We will live in a New Heaven and a New Earth where there is no more pain and no more tears. We know we are made in the image of an almighty perfect God and we can be friends with Him.

Christians can make sense of things around us because "in Christ are hidden all the treasures of wisdom and knowledge" (Colossians 2:3). Consider giving up atheism and receive Jesus Christ as Lord and Savior to rescue you from sin and death. Instead of death, God promises believers eternal life, and millions of years from now, you will still have value and worth in contrast to the secular view of nothingness.

Christians have a source of real love since God made us in His loving image. As Christians, we have a solid foundation for knowing there is right and wrong because God's laws are written in our hearts.

You can leave the false religion of atheism and its various forms and return to the one true God who came to rescue you. Jesus Christ, who is God the Son, loved you enough to come down and die in our place so we can experience God's goodness for all eternity.

The day is coming when we all will give an account before God for our actions and thoughts. Will you repent, change your mind, change your actions, and receive Christ as your Lord and Savior today so that you will join Christ in eternity?

I invite you to become an ex-atheist, like many other ex-atheists, join the ranks of the saved through faith in Jesus Christ, and become a new creation as we continue to advance with the gospel in peace that only God can provide. Answers in Genesis, Bodie Hodge, *Dear Atheist*. [2]

Our God is humble and loving. This is what God, in the form and person of Jesus did for us. Philippians 2:6-11 states, "Though He was God, He did not think of equality with God as something to cling to. Instead, He gave up his divine privileges; He took the humble position of a slave and was born as a human being. When He appeared in human form, He humbled himself in obedience to God and died a criminal's death on a cross. Therefore, God elevated Him to the place of highest honor and gave Him the name above all other names, that at the name of Jesus every knee should bow, in Heaven and on earth and under the earth, and every tongue declare that Jesus Christ is Lord, to the glory of God the Father."

If all the people of this world could only comprehend how much God truly loves them, they would all be eager to get to know Him. How about you? Would you like to get to know the true loving and Living God? The creator of the universe. He's waiting for you with all His love! What you can gain is unimaginable! What do you have to lose? So, I ask you ...

What are you waiting for?

Acknowledgments

I would like to thank my wife Michele for her valuable input and support, not only during this project but during our thirty-six years of marriage. She has stood by my side through thick and thin with positive affirmation and loving support. She is a true woman of God and has helped keep me grounded in the faith. Without her, I am sure I would be in a different place. No one can stand alone in this world, and God has given me the perfect companion to help me focus on Him, and fight the battles that come and go during this life here on earth. All I can say is Thank You, God!

Michele has also been instrumental during the review and editing of this project. But most importantly, she was able to convince me to share this project with others. I had set out to simply do a little fact-finding for my benefit, without any intention to share with the public. After many hours of research, Michele would ask what my intentions were? Was I spending all this time just accumulating all this information and keeping it to myself? After going through this cycle several times, she convinced me to take a stab at putting something together that could be useful to others. She was sure at least a few other Christians had the same questions I had and perhaps they would be interested in reading what I had found during my research.

Starting out I was very curious why Christians have so many extreme beliefs about God, the Bible, social issues, and politics, so I started browsing several websites to learn as much as I could on these, and other issues. I realize that Christians are deeply divided, that's why there are so many different Christian denominations, plus the differences between Catholic, Orthodox, and Protestant Churches. Even individual denominations are deeply divided and disagree on many points. It is for this reason this book has been written. There will always be minor issues of disagreement, but when God's Word is completely ignored and His commands are disobeyed or perceived as outdated by Christian organizations and individuals, that is completely wrong. There should be no disagreement on God's moral view on issues like abortion and homosexuality, which are clearly documented in the Bible. It saddens me that Christians are not better united with each other, in fact, we are our own worst enemy at times. If we could join together, we could make a much more significant impact for the Kingdom of God, and on our society at large.

The more I researched, and the more I discovered, the more questions I had. So I could refer back to what I had found, I began taking notes and searching more topics to get even more answers. I am thankful so many individuals and institutions take the time to post their research, viewpoints, commentaries, and teachings on the web for all to see. We certainly live in the information age, and there's much to discover. I found answers and valuable information on the questions and topics I was looking for. Sadly, I also found much division and anger out there as well. We must pray that we can all learn to love each other, realizing that none of us are perfect and that each individual is an image-bearer of God. We all have different backgrounds, viewpoints, and opinions, so we need to learn to live with this realization and not judge others because of these differences. Yes, we can stand for truth, but we must stand for truth by showing love and respect for those who disagree with us.

I relied on much information, and give much thanks to organizations like; Answers in Genesis, Creation Research Society, and The Institute of Creation Research for their valuable commentaries and scientific research. In addition, the following Christian websites were also very helpful in my search; https://www.gotquestions.org, https://www.cru.org, https://www.allaboutreligion.org, http://Christianity.com, http://christiananswers.net, http://biblestudytools.com, http://ligonier.org, http://bible.org, https://www.biblegateway.com, http://lifehopeandtruth.com, http://onlythebible.com, http://christianworldview.net, http://whatchristianswanttoknow.com, https://www.compellingtruth.org, http://thinkingonscripture.com, http://wellandgood.com, and http://pewresearch.org. There were also many secular websites that were extremely useful as well, such as https://wikipedia.org, http://

allaboutphilosophy.org, and http://differencebetween.com, just to name a few.

I also give many thanks to Dmytro Tolokonov, who lives in Kyiv, Ukraine, and whose artwork was used for the cover of this book. Thank you so much Dmytro! With this in mind, I would like to take this opportunity to ask for donations to be sent to one of the following charities: Boctok SOS at the link: https://vostok-sos.org/ or, Mercy Corps, using the following link: https://www.mercycorps.org/donate/war-ukraine-has-impacts-around-world-give-now, that provides support to those in need in Ukraine, Poland, and Romania, where many Ukrainians have fled to escape the attacks from the Russian government and military, or to Andriy Kalinichenko at Facebook link: https://www.facebook.com/andrey.kalinichenko.718. Andriy needs support the most. Because everything he bought - he bought with his own savings. Without the help of the government or charities.

Next, I would like to thank all the people I worked with at WestBow Press for making this publication possible. Thanks to Joe Anderson, Check-In Coordinator; Jeff Sloan, Editorial Assessment; Eric Schroeder, Senior Publishing Consultant; Leandra Drummy, Sales Account Specialist; Tim Fitch, Publishing Services Associate; and Kelly Wilson, Marketing and Editorial Consultant, and Deena C.

Finally, I give my highest thanks to my Lord and Savior Jesus Christ. Only through the works of Jesus, can we ever have hope of redemption, through His amazing and powerful grace. I am just so amazed that the ultimate being in existence would offer His sacrifice and unconditional love to a bunch of wayward people who are completely undeserving. His unconditional love is completely unexplainable ... but true!

I would like to conclude with the following scripture to offer additional hope to everyone reading this book. We all need hope. Without hope there is only gloom ... but,

"For the grace of God has appeared, bringing salvation to all people, instructing us to deny ungodliness and worldly desires and to live sensibly, righteously, and in a godly manner in the present age, looking for the blessed hope and the appearing of the glory of our great God and Savior, Christ Jesus, who gave Himself for us to redeem us from every lawless deed, and to purify for Himself a people for His own possession, eager for good deeds" (Titus 2:11–14).

For those interested in pursuing Christianity even further, I recommend the following books:

1. The Holy Bible: make it a priority to read the Bible every day. If you read only four chapters a day you can finish the Bible in a year. After doing this start over with a different translation of the Bible every year.
2. Seizing Your Devine Moment by Erwin McManus
3. Wild at Heart by John Eldredge
4. The Purpose Driven Life by Rick Warren
5. If You Want to Walk on Water, You've Got to Get Out of the Boat by John Ortberg
6. Mere Christianity by C. S. Lewis
7. The Cost of Discipleship by Dietrich Bonhoffer
8. Knowing God by J. I. Packer
9. More Than a Carpenter by Josh McDowell
10. Anxious for Nothing by Max Lucado

Bonus 1 – The Blessed Life by Robert Morris
Bonus 2 – The God I Never Knew by Robert Morris.

Reference Notes

Preface: N/A

Introduction
1   Cru, Evangeline Vergo, "How to Know God, What is a Christian?", https://www.cru.org/us/en/how-to-know-god/what-is-a-christian.html.
2   All About Religion, "What is a Christian?," https://www.allaboutreligion.org/what-is-christianity.htm.
3   Christianity.com, Jack Graham, "What is a Christian," https://www.christianity.com/jesus/following-jesus/evangelism-and-missions/what-is-a-christian.html.

Section 1 - The Bible, God, and Humanity: N/A.

Chapter 1 – The Bible
1   John Adams, alleged quote, no source of verification.
2   Barna, "What Do Americans Really Think About the Bible?" https://www.barna.com/research/what-do-americans-really-think-about-the-bible/.
3   Study and Obey, "What is the Bible," http://studyandobey.com/inductive-bible-study/bible/.

Chapter 2 – God
1   Merriam Webster dictionary, "The definition of God," http://webster.com.
2   God is Real, "Is God Real?" http://godisreal.com.
3   William Paley, "The Watch and the Watchmaker," From Natural Theology, or Evidences of the Existence and Attributes of the Deity Collected from the Appearances of Nature 1802, pp. 1-6.

4   Kwize, Isaac Asimov, "The Human Brain," https://kwize.com/Isaac-Asimov-quotes.
5   Evidence For Jesus, "Evidence for Jesus Outside of the Bible – 1" https://evidenceforjesus.home.blog/tag/phlegon/.
6   P. L. Maier, ed./trans., "Josephus –The Essential Works," (Grand Rapids: Kregel Publications, 1994).
7   Julius Africanus, "In Georgius Syncellus, Chron.," p. 322 or 256.
8   Cornelius Tacitus, "the Annals" (Ann., xv 44).
9   Mara-Serapion, "The Letter to his son," The letter is preserved in a 6th- or 7th-century manuscript (BL Add. 14658) held by the British Library.
10 Julius Africanus, "Africanus, Chronography," 18:1.
11 Cale Clarke, "Ancient Evidence for Jesus: Pliny the Younger," http://www.thefaithexplained.com/blog/ancient-evidence-for-jesus-pliny-the-younger/.
12 C. Suetonius Tranquillus, "Lives of the Twelve Caesars," The Heritage Press – 1965 Reprint.
13 Lucian of Samosata, "The Passing of Peregrinus," 11, 13.
14 James Bishop, "Greek Philosopher Celsus on the Historical Jesus," https://jamesbishopblog.com/2020/06/23/greek-philsopher-celsus-on-the-historical-jesus/.
15 Sefer Toledot Yeshu, "The Book of the Generations/History/Life of Jesus," 1874, when Sabine Baring-Gould published "The Lost and Hostile Gospels."

Chapter 3 – Humanity
1   EssayBasics, "Definition of Humanity," http://blog.essaybasics.com.
2   Wikipedia, "Humanity," http://wikipedia.com.
3   Patheos, Paul Bane, "The Nature of Our Humanity and Being," http://patheos.com.
4   Socianz, Atif Yaseen, "Humanity by Human being," http://socianz.com.
5   Life, Hope, and Truth, Ron Kelley, "What is Human Nature," http://lifehopeandtruth.com.

Section 2 – Worldviews and Beliefs: N/A

Chapter 4 – Worldviews
1   All About Worldview, "The Meaning of Life," http://allaboutworldview.org.
2   Ligonier, R.C. Sproul, "Christian Worldview," http://ligonier.org.

Chapter 5 – Humanism
1   American Humanist Association, Fred Edwords, "What Is Humanism?" https://americanhumanist.org/what-is-humanism/edwords-what-is-humanism.

2   Difference Between, Hasa, "Difference Between Humanism and Secularism," http://differencebetween.com.

Chapter 6 – Atheism
1   Difference Between, Admin, "Difference Between Humanism and Atheism," http://differencebetween.com.

Chapter 7 – Agnosticism
1   All About Philosophy, "Agnostic," http://allaboutphilosophy.org/agnostic.htm.

Chapter 8 – Moral Relativism
1   Stephen Law, "Relativism or Authoritarianism – you choose," https://stephenlaw.blogspot.com/2007/02/relativism-or-authoritarianism-you_22.html.
2   Moral Relativism, Bill O'Reilly, "Moral Relativism," https://www.moral-relativism.com.
3   George Washington, "Farewell Address to the nation," September 19, 1796.
4   William McGuffey, "McGuffey's Readers McGuffey's 5th Eclectic Reader," 1879.

Chapter 9 – Naturalism
1   Wikipedia, "Naturalism," http://Wikipedia.com.
2   The Spiritual Life, "Naturalism," http://slife.org.
3   David Papineau, "Naturalism: Ontological and Methodological philosophies," https://www.jstor.org/stable/2254801.
4   The Spiritual Life, "Naturalism in Philosophy," Paul Kurtz quote, https://slife.org/naturalism-in-philosophy.
5   RNS Religion News Service, Kimberly Winston, "Carl Sagan: The Cosmos is all that is or was or ever will be," https://religionnews.com/2014/03/05/carl-sagan-cosmos-will-ever.

Chapter 10 – Pantheism
1   Wikipedia, "Pantheism," http://Wikipedia.com.
2   World Pantheism, "Toland: father of modern pantheism," https://pantheism.net/toland/.
3   Baruch Spinoza, "Ethics," https://www.abigailadamsinstitute.org/baruch-spinoza-ethics.

Chapter 11 – Other Worldviews
1   Ligonier, R.C. Sproul, "Worldviews in Conflict," http://ligonier.org.
2   All About Worldview "Worldview," http://allaboutworldview.org.

Chapter 12 – The Christians Worldview
1. Compelling Truth, "Christian Worldview - What is it?" https://www.compellingtruth.org/Christian-worldview.html.
2. Christian World View, "What is a Christian Worldview?" http://christianworldview.net.
3. The Reb, Katelyn Brown "A Biblical Worldview: What It Is and Why it Matters," http://therebelution.com /?s=A+Biblical+Worldview%3A+.

Chapter 13 – The Meaning of Life
1. All About Worldview, "The Meaning of Life," http://allaboutworldview.org.

Chapter 14 – What is Truth
1. Got Questions, "What is truth?" http://gotquestion.org.

Section 3 – Morality and Values
1. Answers in Genesis, Dr. Elizabeth Mitchell, "Where Did Morality Come From?" http://answersingenesis.org.

Chapter 15 – Morality
1. Opinion Front, Lawrence Kohlberg, "The Heinz Dilemma and Kohlberg's 6 Stages of Moral Development," https://opinionfront.com/heinz-dilemma.
2. ABC News, Lee Dye, "Do we need God to be Moral?" https://abcnews.go.com/Technology/god-moral/story?id=18898993.

Chapter 16 – Christian Morality: N/A

Chapter 17 – Homosexuality
1. Law Teacher, "Laws Regarding Homosexuals," https://www.lawteacher.net/free-law-essays/family-law/laws-regarding-homosexuals-law-essay.php.
2. Pink News, Joe Williams, "Depression and low self-esteem rising among gay men," https://www.pinknews.co.uk/2015/08/06/depression-and-low-self-esteem-rising-among-gay-men.
3. JW.org, "Is Homosexuality Wrong?" https://www.jw.org/en/bible-teachings/teenagers/ask/is-homosexuality-wrong.

Chapter 18 – Marriage
1. Law Teacher, "Definition of Marriage," https://www.lawteacher.net/free-law-essays/family-law/marriage-should-be-confined-to-heterosexual-couples-family-law-essay.php.

Chapter 19 – Family Values
1. JW.org, "Values," https://www.jw.org/en/library/magazines/awake-no2-2018-jul-aug/successful-families-values.

Chapter 20 – Sexual Gender Identity
1. Reuters, Jonathan Allen, "New study estimates 1.6 million in U.S. identify as transgender," https://www.reuters.com/world/us/new-study-estimates-16-million-us-identify-transgender-2022-06-10.
2. Paul McHugh, Wall Street Journal article, "Transgender Surgery Isn't the Solution," updated May 13, 2016, https://www.wsj.com/articles/paul-mchugh-transgender-surgery-isnt-the-solution-1402615120.

Chapter 21 – Sanctity of Human Life
1. Compelling Truth, "What is the sanctity of life? Why do Christians believe in the sanctity of life?" https://www.compellingtruth.org/sanctity-of-life.html.

Chapter 22 – Values
1. PNAS, Francisco Ayala, "The difference of being human," http://pnas.org.

Chapter 23 – Ethics
1. Very Well Mind, Brittany Loggins, "Morality vs. Ethics: What's the Difference?" https://www.verywellmind.com/morality-vs-ethics-what-s-the-difference-5195271.

Chapter 24 – Liberalism
1. New American, Thomas Sowell "The High Cost of Liberalism," https://thenewamerican.com/the-high-cost-of-liberalism.
2. Townhall, John Hawkins, "The Left's War on Christianity," posted Mar 09, 2012, https://townhall.com/columnists/johnhawkins/2012/03/09/the-lefts-war-on-christianity-n930346.
3. TGS, Andrew Hoffecker "Liberal Theology," https://www.thegospelcoalition.org/essay/liberal-theology.
4. The Sun, Mollie Mansfield, "FURIOUS LADY Michelle Obama says white folks don't understand racism because black people don't exist to them," https://www.thesun.co.uk/news/12519913/michelle-obama-podcast-white-folk-dont-understand-racism.

Chapter 25 – Socialism
1. The Heritage Foundation, Samuel Gregg, Ph.D., "Young Americans Increasingly Prefer Socialism; Here's How to Change Their Minds,"

  https://www.heritage.org/progressivism/commentary/young-americans-increasingly-prefer-socialism-heres-how-change-their-minds.
2. Socialist Party of the United Kingdom, "OECD report: A system in crisis" (https://www.socialistparty.org.uk/articles/18439/09-04-2014/oecd-report-a-system-in-crisis)
3. Learn Religions, Austin Cline, "Religion as Opium of the People," https://www.learnreligions.com/religion-as-opium-of-the-people-250555.

Chapter 26 – Censorship and the Cancel Culture

1. Quote Investigator, "I Disapprove of What You Say, But I Will Defend to the Death Your Right to Say It," https://quoteinvestigator.com/2015/06/01/defend-say.
2. CARM, Matt Slick, "What is Cancel Culture," https://carm.org/social-justice/what-is-cancel-culture.
3. CATO Institute, Todd Zywicki, "Extending the Culture Wars," https://www.cato.org/regulation/fall-2021/extending-culture-wars.
4. Forbes, Evan Gerstmann, "What Is Cancel Culture?" https://www.forbes.com/sites/evangerstmann/2021/03/22/what-is-cancel-culture/?sh=285cfffbd559.

Chapter 27 – Liberalism in the Christian Church

1. LifeNews.com, Micaiah Bilger, "United Church of Christ Pastor Celebrates Her Abortion: I've Never Felt More Loved by God," https://www.lifenews.com/2022/02/07/united-church-of-christ-pastor-celebrates-her-abortion-ive-never-felt-more-loved-by-god/.
2. Whosoever, Rev. Candice Chellew, "Why Christianity Must Change or Die: A Bishop Speaks to Believers in Exile by John Shelby Spong | Interview," https://whosoever.org/battling-for-the-heart-of-christianity-an-interview-with-bishop-john-shelby-spong/.
3. Springer Link, David Millard Haskel, "Theology Matters: Comparing the Traits of Growing and Declining Mainline Protestant Church Attendees and Clergy," https://link.springer.com/article/10.1007/s13644-016-0255-4.
4. First Things, David T. Koyzis, "LIBERAL AND CONSERVATIVE CHRISTIANITY ... AND IN BETWEEN," https://www.firstthings.com/blogs/firstthoughts/2012/07/liberal-and-conservative-christianity-and-in-between.
5. Rachel Held Evans – "Post her beliefs," http://rachelheldevans.com.

Section 4: Science and Religion

1. Voddie Baucham, "Why I Choose to Believe the Bible," https://www.sermonaudio.com/sermoninfo.asp?SID=530914253.

Chapter 28 – Astronomy
1. Space.com, Jamie Carter, "What is astronomy? Definition & History," https://www.space.com/16014-astronomy.html.

Chapter 29 – Cosmology
1. Answers in Genesis, Dr, Danny R. Faulkner, "What About Cosmology?" https://answersingenesis.org/astronomy/cosmology/what-about-cosmology/.

Chapter 30 – Evolution
1. Religio-Political Talk (RPT), "Imagination and Plaster of Paris = Lucy," https://religiopoliticaltalk.com/tag/sir-solly-zuckerman/.
2. J. Assmuth and Ernest R. Hull, "Haeckel's Frauds and Forgeries," 1915, https://www.creationism.org/books/HaeckelsForgeries1915/index.htm.
3. The Guardian, David Adam, "History of Modern Man Unravels as German Scholar Is Exposed as a Fraud, Luke Harding," https://www.theguardian.com/science/2005/feb/19/science.sciencenews.
4. Conservapedia, "Essay: Is Richard Dawkins an intellectually fulfilled atheist?" https://www.conservapedia.com/Essay:_Is_Richard_Dawkins_an_intellectually_fulfilled_atheist%3Fhttp://safeguardyoursole.com.
5. Dr. Mike Sutton, *"Nullius In Verba: Darwin's Greatest secret, July 20, 2017."*
6. What is Merging.com, Josie Glausiusz, "SAVAGES AND CANNIBALS: REVISITING CHARLES DARWIN'S VOYAGE OF THE BEAGLE," https://www.whatisemerging.com/opinions/savages-and-cannibals.

Chapter 31 – DNA
1. CDC, "Frequently Asked Questions About Research Using NHANES DNA Samples," https://www.cdc.gov/nchs/nhanes/genetics/genetic_faqs.htm.
2. Hyper Physics, Werner Gitt, "In the Beginning Was Information," 1997, http://hyperphysics.phy-astr.gsu.edu/Nave-html/Faithpathh/Gitt.html.
3. Dr. Stephen Meyer, "THREE MAJOR SCIENTIFIC DISCOVERIES IN THE PAST CENTURY THAT POINT TO GOD," https://stephencmeyer.org/2021/04/02/three-major-scientific-discoveries/.
4. Rational Wiki, Patrick Glynn, "God: The Evidence," https://rationalwiki.org/wiki/God:_The_Evidence.
5. Academic Atheism, Patrick Glynn, "REVIEWING THE CASE FOR A CREATOR: CHAPTER 6," https://academicatheism.tumblr.com/post/89804411348/reviewing-the-case-for-a-creator.
6. Dr. Stephen Meyer, "SIGNATURE IN THE CELL," https://stephencmeyer.org/books/signature-in-the-cell/.

7   Stephen C. Meyer.com, Dr. Stephen Meyer, "RETURN OF THE GOD HYPOTHESIS," https://stephencmeyer.org/books/return-of-the-god-|hypothesis/.
8   Beyond Today, Mario Seiglie, "The Tiny Code That's Toppling Evolution," Professor Antony Flew, https://www.ucg.org/the-good-news/dna-the-tiny-code-thats-toppling-evolution.
9   Zion Christian Ministry, Shawn Stevens "Microbiology: Hard Evidence for Intelligent Design" Dean Kenyon, http://www.zionchristianministry.com/publications/books-by-shawn/microbiology-hard-evidence-for-intelligent-design/.
10 WWRN World-Wide Religious News, Richard N. Ostling, "Famous atheist now believes in God," AP, December 9, 2004, https://wwrn.org/articles/14608/.

Chapter 32 – Archeology
1   Wikipedia, "Archeology," http://wikipedia.org.
2   Crossway, John D. Currid, "10 Crucial Archaeological Discoveries Related to the Bible," https://www.crossway.org/articles/10-crucial-archaeological-discoveries-related-to-the-bible/.
3   Armstrong Institute of Biblical Archaeology, Christopher Eames *"Proof: Archaeology Proves the Bible Archaeology unearths historical fact—and proves the biblical record at the same time."* May 12, 2019.

Chapter 33 – Geology
1   Britannica, "Geology," http://britannica.com.
2   The Other Side, Derek Ager, "The Age of the Earth," http://www.thebibleistheotherside.org/currentarticlep11p2.htm.
3   Answers in Genesis, Bodie Hodge, "The 10 Best Evidences from Science That Confirm a Young Earth," https://answersingenesis.org/evidence-for-creation/10-best-evidences-young-earth.

Chapter 34 – Creationism
1   Wikipedia, "Creationism," http://wikipedia.org.
2   LIB Quotes, "Michael Denton Quotes," https://libquotes.com/michael-denton.

Section 5 – Salvation: N/A

Chapter 35 – The Narrow Path
1   Life, Hope and Truth, Florante Siopan and John Foster, "What is Salvation," http://lifehopeandtruth.com.

2   Got Questions, "Why did God make salvation such a narrow path?" https://www.gotquestions.org/narrow-path.html.
3   Beyond Today, Robert H. Berendt, "Narrow and Difficult," http://ucg.org/bible-study-tools.

Chapter 36 – Hell: N/A

Chapter 37 – The Plan of Salvation?
1   Ligonier, "One Way of Salvation," https://www.ligonier.org/learn/devotionals/one-way-of-salvation.
2   Learn Religions, Mary Fairchild, "The Plan of Salvation in the Bible," http://learnreligions.com.

Chapter 38 – How Did Jesus' Death Pay our Penalty?
1   Got Questions, "What does it mean that Jesus Christ conquered death?" https://www.gotquestions.org/Jesus-Christ-conquered-death.html

Chapter 39 – How to Receive Jesus Christ?
1   Got Questions, "What is the Christian doctrine of salvation?" https://www.gotquestions.org/Christian-doctrine-salvation.html.
2   Got Questions, "What Does it Mean to Receive Jesus?" https://www.gotquestions.org/receive-Jesus-Christ.html

Chapter 40 – Having a Relationship with Jesus Christ
1   Got Questions, "How can I have a relationship with Jesus?" https://www.gotquestions.org/relationship-with-Jesus.html

Chapter 41 – Being Born Again
1   Got Questions, "What does it mean to be a BORN-AGAIN Christian?" https://www.gotquestions.org/born-again.html
2   All About Religion, "Born Again Christianity," https://www.allaboutreligion.org/born-again-christianity-faq.htm.

Chapter 42 – Mercy and Grace
1   Got Questions, "What is the difference between mercy and grace?" https://www.gotquestions.org/mercy-grace.html.

Chapter 43 – Can a Christian Lose Salvation?
1   Learn Religions, Mary Fairchild, "The Plan of Salvation in the Bible" https://www.learnreligions.com/what-is-gods-plan-of-salvation-700502.

Chapter 44 – Faith
1. Wikipedia, "Faith," http://Wikipedia.com.
2. Paul E Chapman, "Examples of Faith (found in the Bible)" https://paulechapman.com/2020/05/16/examples-of-faith-found-in-the-bible/.

Chapter 45 – Heaven
1. Christianity.com, Jessica Miller, "What Is Heaven Like According to the Bible?" https://www.christianity.com/wiki/heaven-and-hell/what-is-heaven-like-according-to-the-bible.html
2. Bibleinfo, "What is Heaven like & where is Heaven?" https://www.bibleinfo.com/en/questions/where-is-heaven#what-heaven-like

Section 6 – America and the Church
1. Wikipedia, Chinese proverb, "A journey of a thousand miles begins with a single step." https://en.wikipedia.org/wiki/A_journey_of_a_thousand_miles_begins_with_a_single_step
2. Gallup, Jeffrey M. Jones, "U.S. Church Membership Falls Below Majority for First Time," https://news.gallup.com/poll/341963/church-membership-falls-below-majority-first-time.aspx

Chapter 46 – Is America Abandoning the Church?
1. Josh McDowell, A CRU Ministry, "Note from Josh: Are Youth Leaving the Church?" https://www.josh.org/note-from-josh-are-youth-leaving-the-church/.

Chapter 47 – Is America a Christian Nation?
1. World Challenge, David Wilkerson, "IS GOD OVERLOOKING THE SINS OF AMERICA?" https://www.worldchallenge.org/god-overlooking-sins-america. Quote from Rev. Rose Mary Denmore.

Chapter 48 – Was America Founded as a Christian Nation?
1. Brainy Quote, John Adams, "Our Constitution was made only for a moral and religious people. It is wholly inadequate to the government of any other." https://www.brainyquote.com/quotes/john_adams_391045
2. AlterNet, Bob Boston, "5 Reasons America Is Not - And Never Has Been - A Christian Nation," https://www.alternet.org/2014/10/5-reasons-america-not-and-never-has-been-christian-nation/

Chapter 49 – Does it Matter if America is a Christian Nation?
1   The Dispatch, David French, "A Nation of Christians Is Not Necessarily a Christian Nation," https://frenchpress.thedispatch.com/p/a-nation-of-christians-is-not-necessarily

Chapter 50 – What is a Real Christian?
1   Compelling Truth, "What does it mean to be a true Christian?" https://www.compellingtruth.org/true-Christian.html

Chapter 51 – Turning to God
1   Believers Portal, Bp-Pub-1, "List And Profile Of Famous Atheists Who Converted To Christianity" https://believersportal.com/list-and-profile-of-famous-atheists-who-converted-to-christianity/.
2   Blog, Jay Wile, "Category: Atheists Who Became Christians," https://blog.drwile.com/category/atheists-who-became-christians/
3   Bethinking, Philip Vander Elst, "From Atheism to Christianity: a Personal Journey" https://www.bethinking.org/is-christianity-true/from-atheism-to-christianity-a-personal-journey
4   God Updates, Mel Johnson, "Hardcore Atheist Converts After Jesus Visits Him In A Vision" Gunther Scheizle, https://www.godupdates.com/atheist-scientist-becomes-a-christian-after-a-visit-from-angels/.
5   Culture Watch, Alister McGrath, "THE SPIRITUAL JOURNEY OF ALISTER MCGRATH"
6   https://billmuehlenberg.com/2021/12/29/the-spiritual-journey-of-alister-mcgrath/
7   Professor Sarah Irving-Stonebraker, "How Oxford and Peter Singer drove me from atheism to Jesus," https://www.solas-cpc.org/how-oxford-and-peter-singer-drove-me-from-atheism-to-jesus/
8   Josephus, "Antiquities of the Jews"
9   Norman L. Geisler and Frank Turek "I Don't Have Enough Faith to Be an Atheist" USA, 2004).

Chapter 52 – The Challenge
1   Answers in Genesis, Bodie Hodge, "Dear Atheist," https://answersingenesis.org/world-religions/atheism/dear-atheists-are-you-tired/.

Conclusion
1   Christian Answers.Net, "How do I witness to my peers when they seem to have knowledgeable answers against all of my beliefs?" https://christiananswers.net/evangelism/responses/home.html
2   Answers in Genesis, Bodie Hodge, "Dear Atheist," https://answersingenesis.org/world-religions/atheism/dear-atheists-are-you-tired/.

Made in the USA
Coppell, TX
14 February 2023